A VOICE OF DISCONTENT

A Woman's Journey Through the Long Eighteenth Century

Best wishes,

Jerry Kelsey

17/4/12

A VOICE OF DISCONTENT

A Woman's Journey Through the Long Eighteenth Century

JENNIFER C. KELSEY

Matador
9 De Montfort Mews
Leicester LE1 7FW, UK
Tel: (+44) 116 255 9311 / 9312
Email: books@troubador.co.uk
Web: www.troubador.co.uk/matador

ISBN 978 1848760 363

A Cataloguing-in-Publication (CIP) catalogue record for this book is available from the British Library.

Typeset in 11pt Bembo by Troubador Publishing Ltd, Leicester, UK
Printed in the UK by TJ International, Padstow, Cornwall

Matador is an imprint of Troubador Publishing Ltd

Acknowledgments

For many years women have been communicating through the written word. Some were openly mocked, or ridiculed, for their outspoken opinions; others were forced to be more discreet. This book is dedicated to the female writers of the past who shared their thoughts and experiences and who, in so doing, were prepared to stand up as women.

I owe many thanks to family and friends for their enthusiastic support while I was writing this book, but particularly to Danuta, Doreen, Laure and Sheila who have done so much to help me on my way. I also wish to extend my thanks to the staff of the British Library for their assistance during the last four years.

Kind permission has been granted to use the following:

Cover Illustration, *Forbidden Fruit,*
Bibliothèque des Arts décoratifs, Paris, Collection Maciet.

Poem, *Poor Caged Lady*,
Regency House Party, Lucy Jago, published by Little, Brown Book Group

Contents

Chapter One
An Introduction

Imagine a room, a large unfurnished room, full of people. Famous personalities from the past; authors all waiting to tell you their story, all wanting to gain your attention. Focussing on, say, the nineteenth century, as that was my original intention, can you make out Charles Dickens, standing near a corner, head slightly bowed, grumbling to himself, impatient to start? And nearby Anthony Trollope, standing restlessly, tapping his foot, wanting to get back to his writing desk in order to complete his set word quota for the day. And standing at the back, a large, rowdy group of suffragettes, waving banners, jumping up and down and shouting, 'Votes for Women!'

When I originally started my research, I had wanted to study English literary classics of the nineteenth century in order to learn more about what life was like, particularly for women, and had this image of storytellers just waiting for me to open their works so they could speak directly to me. I did not want to read another textbook; I wanted to gain more of an emotional feel of the times, to focus on the people as they were portrayed by contemporary writers. Like John Sutherland, a well-respected expert on Victorian literature, I felt it was more important to read the works of many authors of the period, rather than focus on critical analysis of them. Of course I was familiar with Dickens, Trollope, the Brontes and Austen, but I had this feeling I was missing something. It took time to discover that there were many other voices waiting to be heard, their stories even more important than those of the accepted literary canon and those voices belonged to women. The more I studied, the more I discovered that there were many successful women authors in the nineteenth century that I had never heard of. When I was at school over thirty years ago I had been introduced to the delights of Jane Austen, and the skill of Charlotte and Emily Brontë, but no-one ever explained to me why these were the only famous women authors that were studied at school. Like many other women I had this feeling that maybe those authors *were* exceptional and no other women *could* write or *did* write- or at least not until the twentieth century. And I did not question the fact until much later, when I had time and leisure to investigate further.

It is now recognised that when studying any period of history, works of contemporary literature provide an extremely valuable resource. Certainly, when I began to look more closely at the works of women writers of the nineteenth century, it became obvious that their stories often revealed far more detail about the lives they had to lead than could be found in non fiction works, whether contemporary or modern. Although in academic circles such personal, emotional writing may be regarded with some disdain, as it may be 'subjective' rather than 'objective', much can be learned from careful reading of novels especially when they are supplemented by information from journals, letters and other works by the authors themselves. This is what I intended to do, but at a very early stage it became obvious that patterns and themes shown in the works of nineteenth century women's writing were not unique. Much of what was being said, about the restrictions, frustrations, anxieties and problems women faced, was common across history, and had been raised many times before. My research thus had to extend well back into the eighteenth century, and even into the late seventeenth century when women were beginning to air their voices of complaint in published written form.

I should add at this stage that for my source material I have relied on literature written by women, and that means that I cannot claim that the results apply to all social classes of the period. Although literacy was improving many if not most of the lower classes were not able to read or write, or at least not beyond the basics, and compulsory education for all was not introduced until well into the nineteenth century. Literate women did not tend to come from the lower classes, so these findings apply more to the middling and upper class women of the time, but all classes of women shared the same prejudice. I should also state that although my concern has been with English women, other cultures have faced the same problems, and this appears to have been reflected in their literature in a similar way, although obviously the details differ according to circumstance.

One of the 'other' female novels studied in schools is *To Kill A*

Mockingbird, written by Harper Lee, published in 1960. This contained one of the most important humanistic principles I ever learned, which I refer to as the Atticus Principle, and it helps to explain why reading women's literature is so important to us both historically and in the present day. Atticus was a lawyer, bringing up his children as a single parent in the American South – although greatly aided by his cook Calpurnia. He wanted his children to understand people and behave accordingly; his basic advice was, 'You never really understand a person until you consider things from his point of view...until you climb in his skin and walk round in it.'

The problem with women's history is that until fairly recently, that is perhaps the last forty or fifty years, it was by and large written by men, if written at all.

Even Jane Austen commented, 'Real solemn history I cannot be interested in ...The quarrels of popes and kings, with wars or pestilences, in every page; the men all so good for nothing and hardly any women at all.' *(Northanger Abbey*, 1818) Many 18th and 19th century works are now being republished, for example by OUP, Penguin Classics, and Broadview Press, and the rediscovery of women's literature enables us all to share knowledge that has been hidden away, or discretely put aside, and so gain a real understanding of what life was like for women in the past. By reading about their own experiences, or those of other women they knew, their aspirations, hopes, dreams, their problems, frustrations and even despair, we gain a much clearer picture of what life was really like through their emotional reactions and experiences; by climbing in their skin and walking round in it. I can almost hear the criticism at this point – surely emotional writing is less valuable, typically female, less academic and therefore has less importance than impersonal disassociated work. However, humans learn through experience, and emotional reaction is a key part of that experience. For females much of their understanding and learning is gained through the experience of emotion. When women started to put their own knowledge and experience into print and shared them with other females, they were able to do several things. They recorded their own histories, they helped to instruct, educate, warn and prepare each other for life, at a time when educational opportunities for women were very limited, and they have enabled us to share their experiences and learn from them.

Without such records it is very difficult to imagine what life could really have been like for a woman, or have any real understanding about her reactions to the difficulties she had to face. Were women happy with their lot? People may ask if it is actually possible for us to know how women really felt about conditions that seem so alien to us, or think that we are just using a modern interpretation of the facts and fictions. When reading Jane Austen, for example, with the benefit of modern media it is relatively easy to visualise the costumes, the settings and so on, but would a modern woman of today have coped with the restrictions and limitations on her behaviour then? There is a very clear way of illustrating this problem. Some years ago Channel 4 conducted an experiment called The Regency House Party. For several months some members of the public were transported figuratively back in time, into a stately home that had been partially commandeered for the occasion. One participant, Lady Devonport, had previously enjoyed the modern life style of an independent young woman and admitted to finding her style somewhat cramped under the restrictions and codes of Regency England. During the course of the experiment, she decided to write the following poem and dedicated it to the Regency woman whose portrait hung in her bedroom:

Poor caged lady, stroll or stride
Mask the clever mind that you must hide.
Poor caged lady, stroll and walk
To take you from the fatuous talk.
Poor caged lady, stroll and ride
To escape the rules you can't abide.
Poor caged lady, stroll and wince
In your clothes that bind and shoes that pinch.
Poor caged lady, stroll and play
Waste away another day.
Poor caged lady, stroll in defiance
With your head full of poetry, maths and science.
Poor caged lady, stroll and dance
As to the future you advance.
No more caged ladies will there be;
Your unborn sisters will set us free.
(Lucy Jago, The Regency House Party, 2004)

What is so interesting about this experiment is that, while it does show Lady Devonport's emotional reaction to the experience of life for women as lived nearly two hundred years ago, it also provides a very clear illustration of many of the issues that were raised by women *at the time* in the literature they produced. It is not *just* a modern interpretation that women must have felt second-class citizens with the rules and regulations that were applied to them. The lack of real education for women, the need to suppress what learning women did have, the strict rules of behaviour which often applied to women alone, the clothes that inhibited free movement, the lack of purposeful work and the desire by many for change – these were real issues for women of the time. Having found out just how cramped and limited life was like for women, particularly for those who felt unfulfilled by the options open to them, Lady Devonport felt the need to express her frustrations, to share her experiences, and to do so in a way that was typical of the women of the time – *she wrote.* And her writing very clearly portrayed the anger, the frustration, the boredom and the sheer waste of talent that many had felt, and that this book aims to reveal.

During the last forty or so years there seems to have been a realisation, at least in academic circles, that women did not remain passive about their allocated position in life. The noisy suffragettes mentioned at the beginning of the book did not suddenly appear out of nowhere. There are records dating back to the mid seventeenth century at least where protests, although written anonymously, have been made against the dominant male sex and their treatment of women. Take a look at these examples:

1688, *Sylvia's Revenge or a Satyr against Men*
1696, *An Essay in defence of the Female Sex- possibly Judith Drake*
1735, *The Hardships of the English Laws in relation to Wifes with an Explanation of the Original Curse of Subjection passed on Woman in an Humble Address to the Legislature.*

And these were at least fifty years before characters like Mary Wollstonecraft, Mary Hays and Mary Robinson were to draw attention to themselves with such publications as:

1792, A *Vindication of the Rights of Woman*
1798, *Appeal to the Men of Great Britain in Behalf of Women*
1799, *Letter to the Women of England on the Injustice of Mental Subordination*.

I discovered these questions, complaints and discussions were all included in the many novels, advice books, leaflets, articles, journals and letters that women wrote at the time. In fact it seemed highly amusing and appropriate that although I would not have agreed with many of Charlotte Yonge's personal comments, she stated in *Womenkind* (1876), 'A woman can hardly arrive at middle age without having thought over some of the duties and opportunities placed at the hands of her sex'. This is in effect what I have been doing – but it is a little disturbing to realise that individual women have been doing this before me for years and many times over. Looking back over the last century we seem to keep rediscovering our own history- I had not known the work that Virginia Woolf had contributed to feminism, or Dale Spender or Marilyn French to name but three. Many of my friends and contacts have shown great support for and interest in this project – I had a growing readership before I even put pen to paper. Women are interested in their history but, with the exception of female suffrage and the role of women during the world wars, they were not generally taught it at school, although the National Curriculum is slowly addressing this. Some do take it up in further education as Women's Studies or Gender Studies; this book is for everyone else – and that of course includes any men who wish to extend their own knowledge of the subject.

Apart from showing how women felt about their situation, I have also had to consider what outcome I would like. I have two daughters and a son, and have been grateful for the interest they have shown in my work, but a comment from one of my daughters particularly moved me. A young adult herself, she had been reading my quotes board and commented that she had known about the status of women, but she had not realised there was so much sadness. For women of today to know and understand more of their history, and for men to *accept* the achievements of women in the past, present and future, and *understand* more of the implications of the results of their earlier and sometimes current behaviour towards women, would in itself be a step forward. I have looked at my daughters and seen them grow into adults, and have considered their freedoms and privileges in the modern world. They have had a good education, one has graduated, the other about to start college shortly. They could have started work at 16, but chose to stay on to gain qualifications. They can choose their own friends, they choose their own partners, and they can marry if they want to. Many opportunities are open to them that would have been impossible in the past. It is important that they really understand this and appreciate what progress has been made. We should not take such changes for granted, but we should appreciate that much still needs to change.

What is undeniable is that women in the past have had a raw deal, from birth, through childhood, adolescence and throughout their adulthood to the grave. What is disturbing still is that, although many of the specific problems they faced have changed for the better as times have progressed, old prejudices and sexual biases have been replaced by modern instances of them. Even in this country many choices for women are recent achievements. Progress for women has been slow, often temporary, sometimes has gone backwards, and in some areas has been virtually non-existent. Knowing where to start was quite difficult – but I have decided to use the fundamental problem of prejudice that can still be heard at times today; a basic assumption that woman is inferior to man. But where did this prejudice begin? And how did it evolve? There are many theories and interpretations, but the underlying problem really is a question of what people thought the role and purpose of woman was, on what they based their authority and how they reinforced it.

With all the evidence I discovered I decided to shift my focus a little and concentrate on the eighteenth and early nineteenth centuries only. The Victorians would have to wait! I came across the term 'the long eighteenth century' during my research and, although the precise timing definitions have varied a little, in general the term has been used to apply to the last decade or so of the seventeenth century until the end of the Georgian era. This term neatly provided a clear definition of time for the period of women's writing that I wished to consider. Within the context of this work therefore I have taken the term to cover from 1690 until 1830, with the death of George IV, and will refer to it throughout the text.

The first thing I needed to think about was what were the major beliefs, and the systems that supported those beliefs, during the long eighteenth century. There were two major considerations here – Church and State. Both had significant implications for women and both were to be seriously challenged during the course of the period, but let us start by looking at the question of religion and how it had been, and continued to be, used as a highly effective control mechanism against women. Before I continue I should add a personal note – I am a Christian but for many years I have been aware of the difference between the formalised structure of organised religions and personal beliefs. And women, at least in the past, have been constrained in ways that may not have actually been intended at the outset of the early Christian church...

Much of the theoretical justification for the subjugation of women came from the Bible, specifically from Genesis – or at least from people who claimed that it did. It has always been possible to use the Bible, and similar key texts in other religions, as a means of controlling women by selective use of the contents – by emphasising the parts that downplayed the role of women, or forced them into a subservient position, and then conveniently ignoring others where their role was more significant. The eighteenth century was a highly devout period for many; going to church or being engaged in related reading or activities took up much of people's spare time and thought. Although in our day Bible reading may not be an activity carried out by the majority on a regular basis, there can be few people who have not come across the story of Adam and Eve, the temptation by the serpent and Eve giving Adam the forbidden fruit of the Tree of Knowledge. As a result of their disobedience Adam was condemned to work on the soil for the rest of his life, and Eve was to have pain in childbirth and submit to being ruled by Adam. Whether you now believe in the Old Testament as true or not is irrelevant – for those who followed the Christian faith in the past the command was real. Woman was to be subject to the rule of man, it was her punishment for her disobedience; God had ordained it. There could be no argument with that. With few exceptions, women who dared to question the *extent* that women should be subservient to men, or maltreated by them, still acknowledged the fundamental command in Genesis.

So where did this place woman? She was to be Adam's helpmate, his support, his companion, the bearer of his children but always under his rule and command. Whether she was a daughter, wife or mother the men in her life dominated her and this dominance was extended into making many value judgements about her own personal abilities, and therefore possible uses during her lifetime. Some saw her as characterless, until moulded by the men in her life, some as a child, or an imbecile, some as a slave to be used according to whim. In the nineteenth century the poet, Emily Dickinson, was to write:

I am nobody
Who are you?
Are you nobody too?

Many considered woman to be incapable of reason or intellectual thought. She only needed to know what men thought she should know. Frances Burney, a great female novelist – BEFORE Jane Austen – wrote about men's opinion of women, 'Women ought to be ashamed of talking much jargon: what can their little heads make out of such matters. What do they know? And what ought they to know? Except to sew a gown and make a pudding.' (*The Woman Hater*, 1800/2)

Some thought woman was naturally immoral and in need of constant moral guidance, indeed she was blamed for many of man's vices and weaknesses. Although woman was to support man in his 'more important role' in society she needed to be told how to do it. The church itself was a patriarchal system – it was there to protect and guide its female members, acting as a benevolent father, reading the word of God, interpreting it and enforcing it. There were many ways to reinforce female submission – in long hours of church attendance, through selected Biblical readings, prolonged sermons both given live and repeated in print – to be read at leisure or to be listened to while someone else read, as well as use of the many conduct books produced for women, popular during the eighteenth and nineteenth centuries. People took an active part in their religious devotions, and females were brought up and conditioned to accept their humble role within a male dominated religious establishment. Although women had played a greater role within the early Christian church, according to the New Testament, female preachers were actively discouraged in this period. They were kept out of church offices and subject to the dictates of male church members unless they preached independently or as Dissenters or Quakers. Men were to act as the interpreters of the Divine Word – women were subjected to the dictates of men and the situation was much the same with regard to the State.

Under a sovereign ruler, supported by a parliament of representatives of the nation, the legal system favoured the male nobility. They controlled the land; they provided the representatives for parliament and the interests they protected by laws and government tended to favour themselves. There was a heavy emphasis on property and inheritance. Suffrage was not for all men – and certainly was not for women. Women were seen as the weaker sex and were in need of 'protection'. Married women in fact had no legal status – put simply in the words of William Blackstone in his commentaries on the law (1769), 'The husband and the wife are one, and the husband is that one.' Females were seen as property, whether of a father or husband – and the phrase 'give away the bride' is still used today. Women had no say in the law, and many had no real knowledge or understanding of it. It is a little disturbing to find that even a judge commented in the 1730's that although where a woman was legally entitled to her jointure –a financial arrangement – 'he had hardly known an instance, where the wife had not been kissed or kicked out of any such previous settlement.' Similarly, when the Marriage Act of 1753 was to be read aloud in church after prayers at Kingston in Surrey, there was concern because almost all the congregation left. This Act was to impose a set of rules for marriage that we are still familiar with today – the reading of the banns, the signing of an official register in front of witnesses and so on. Many of those who left the church at Kingston would have been women, yet they could not have realised the serious consequences that one Act of Parliament could have for them later, if they had failed to comply with its new requirements – particularly if they had children. The legal scales were heavily weighted in favour of man.

So like the church, the state was a system of patriarchy and it was supported by a domestic patriarchal system within the home. The father ruled the household and as women had few economic resources or options they were often totally dependent upon him. Female obedience, subservience and complaisance were expected and frequently complied with. Feminine virtues of passivity, gentleness, meekness, were highly praised by the men who wished to encourage them – and in doing so reinforced their own position of superiority. In addition if woman's role was to please then beauty was an important asset. As a rule it was only males who received a 'proper education' that developed mental skills; it was far more important that girls should gain accomplishments – at least in the middling and higher levels of society- in order to gain a better place in the marriage market. Then at least they would be provided for. From an early age girls were prepared for marriage and taught to obey their future husbands in all things.

Let me give you a couple of examples I came across during my research. An early feminist, Mary Astell, wrote about how much a husband would get out of marriage, expecting a wife who would:

> *...manage his family, an housekeeper, one whose interest it will be not to wrong him, and in whom he can therefore put greater confidence than in any he can hire for money. One who may breed his children, taking all the care and trouble of their education, to preserve his name and family. One whose beauty, wit or good humour and agreeable conversation will entertain him at home when he has been contradicted or disappointed abroad, who will do him the justice the ill-natured world denies him; that is in anyone's language but his own, soothe his pride and flatter his vanity, by having always so much good sense as to be on his side, to conclude him in the right, when others are so ignorant or rude as to deny it...*
>
> *In a word, one whom he can entirely govern, and consequently may form her to his will and liking, who must be his for life, and therefore cannot quit his service, let him treat her how he will.*
> *(Some Reflections upon Marriage, 1700)*

Fifty or so years later Sarah Chapone wrote much the same thing in one of her letters, referring to a wife seeing herself as 'a puppet danced about by foreign impulses – a wooden thing upon wires.'

When we read such illustrations from over two hundred years ago, it is easy to empathise with the feelings of these two seemingly unusual women – even if these extracts may have been taken out of context. However it is not difficult to see how church and state did support each other and how societal customs developed that provided the cement to bind the whole together. Females were not important – except as property, income or service providers. With a basic lack of personal value it was not necessary to educate them in the sense we know today; lack of financial independence created a situation of complete dependency for many women. There were few opportunities to break out of the cycle of subservience for survival, unless you happened to be a rich widow or young heiress who refused to marry.

It wasn't just a question of believing that women were not important though; men did not want to think about how women felt and were very reluctant to let go of any of their powers or authority. Modern feminists have pointed out that supporters of the patriarchy would not have wanted to allow any criticisms of their systems to leak out, or gain popular support, as it could easily imply that there were faults in the system that needed closer examination, and may have ultimately required possible change. This was not something that could be acknowledged if the status quo was to remain and men were to continue to benefit from it: the threat of criticism had effectively to be reduced, if not removed. So it has been very interesting to find that some women did openly state their belief that they were hard done by, did feel that men's attitude should be corrected and were willing to stand up and be counted. I have already mentioned the comment one of my daughters made; my elder daughter too had her own contribution. She had *always* assumed that women *did* give voice to their grievances, even though she knew no evidence of it until the early twentieth century. She was right – these examples were written centuries before the suffragettes hit the headlines.

- From *Jane Anger Her Protection for Women* (1589), 'Was there ever any so abused, so slaundered, so railed upon, or so wickedly handeled undeservedly, as are we women?...they suppose there is not one amongst us who can, or dare reproove their slanders and false reproaches...and they think we will not write to reproove their lying lips.'

- A teenage girl called Sarah Fyge got so angry when a certain Robert Gould published a 'rude' attack on women's 'pride, lust and inconstancy' (1683) that she wrote a poem called *The Female Advocate* which she justified by saying, 'I think, that when a Man is so extravagant as to Damn all Womenkind for the Crimes of a few, he ought to be corrected'. Her challenge resulted in being estranged from her father and banished from her family home...

- 'Sophia' who translated some French works, adapting and adding substantial opinions of her own, stated in her *Woman's Superior Excellence over Man* (1740), 'I am resolved to show my adversary, and all his sex, that there is at least one Woman capable of preferring truth to flattery, sense to sound, and who dares assert her right in the face of usurpation, tho' hardened by custom into tyranny. And if one is so, why may not be all...?'

- And from an anonymous publication on *The Hardships of the English Laws in Relation to Wives* (1735) the searching question came, 'What shall restrain the strong from oppressing the weak if the laws of our country do not?'

What these early 'feminists' did was to challenge the notion that patriarchy was good for you – they showed that power can be abused, and prejudice really did exist. The whole issue of woman's personality, her intellect and abilities, even her sexuality was exposed and debated, and subject to control by those who had a vested interest in her, whether she liked it or not. Men assumed that women were incapable of logic and reasoning but these were the very tools that women used to question the laws, customs and beliefs of our society. They were also to analyse the reasons they felt were underlying patriarchy – fundamental fear and jealousy, issues that will be thoroughly considered later during the course of the book. Funnily enough, in spite of all the debates in the eighteenth century about freedom, equality and the Rights of Man, there were not many men who accepted that half of mankind were women – and so they were not included. The question raised by Mary Astell in 1700, 'If all men are born free, how is it that women are born slaves?' was to remain valid for many years.

It is known that the radical ideas of Mary Wollstonecraft so influenced Abigail Adams (whose husband John was later to become the second American President) that she wrote to him when he was involved in formulating new laws for the American Constitution. She requested that he, 'Remember the Ladies and be more generous and favourable to them than your ancestors. Do not put such unlimited power into the hands of Husbands. Remember all Men would be tyrants if they could.' She also warned that women would be likely to rebel if no attention was paid to their needs, and that women would not feel bound by laws in which they had no say or representation. It was a wonderful opportunity for positive change. Can you guess his reaction? In case you haven't heard it, his reply dated 14 April, 1776 was 'As to your extraordinary Code of Laws, I cannot but laugh.'

If men were not laughing at the 'silly' ideas of women they were equally likely to be telling them they talked too much – but for women who were powerless it may have been their only weapon. To quote from Mary Astell again, 'Men are possessed of all Places of Power, they make Laws and exercise the Magistracy, not only the sharpest Sword, but even all the Swords and Blunderbusses are theirs; which by the strongest Logick in the World, gives them the best Title to every Thing they please to claim as their Prerogative.' It is little wonder then that they could only talk or write -'The Tongue is the only Weapon Women have to defend themselves with, and they had need to use it dexterously.' (Bathsua Makin, *An Essay to revive the Antient Education of Gentlewomen*, 1673)

In novels, private letters, tracts, advice books, journals and articles, women have complained and justified their right to complain. Some grievances were direct and challenging; others cautiously worded, others carefully hidden. Through the medium of print, using a wide variety of genres, thoughts, ideas and opinions regarding the position and status of women were explored. Often in novels there were opportunities for different characters to have alternative viewpoints, so there was a chance to hear both sides of a situation, which in turn could make readers question their own views and encourage their own opinions. Readers could compare their own knowledge and experience with that offered by the female authors. Personal experiences could be passed on, and women could be educated and given warnings in a way that few if any men had done for them. One classic example of this is where the implications of Hardwicke's Marriage Act of 1753 were clearly shown in many subsequent novels and I will come back to this point later. Novels could be influenced by society but in their own way could influence it too.

The way I have chosen to present the results is through women's shared experience, because even now women share a common pattern to their lives. Of course the pattern is similar to men in terms of development, but the basic difference is that the systems worked against women then and this is obvious when you look at the detail of their lives; whether directly, or in fictional versions that were frequently semi autobiographical, women were aware of it. In each of the following sections you will find examples of women's discontent, alternative viewpoints regarding the issues and some of the suggestions or alternatives women made which they hoped would bring about permanent change. One unexpected finding was how some of the actions supported the move for progress and that some, however well intentioned, worked in completely the opposite direction. Women at times could be their own worst enemy.

Chapter Two
Women as Writers

I used to spend a lot of time browsing in the classical section of bookshops, in fact I was in one again today. It was actually quite a large section – considering the size of the bookshop – and I quickly located Jane Austen's key novels, and further on two of Charlotte Brontë's. It was not a surprise though to find that there were few other female writers squeezed between the many volumes of classic literature by the men folk, and I am gradually beginning to understand why.

As far as I am aware women have always been natural communicators; they like to talk! When they are unable to talk they communicate in other ways. For a twenty-first century woman the ways are endless – email, text, letter writing, magazines, newspapers, instant messaging via the Internet ... let alone writing a book. Three hundred years ago it was a different matter. Let us suppose a woman wanted to write – her memoirs, a novel, her opinions on the world, anything. What then could have stood in her way?

A fundamental problem was, of course, could she write anyway? Had she sufficient education not only to be able to put her own thoughts into words but then transcribe them onto paper? It was unlikely that she would have had the benefit of a classical education, with its reliance on Greek and Latin and the inherited wisdom of the great authorities of the time. She may have learned to read the basics and be able to read translations to have at least the benefit of example, but there again, she may not. Many women of the time accredited their education to their own efforts, for example like Mary Wollstonecraft teaching herself French solely with the use of a dictionary; others had occasional support from a persuadable or willing male relation or friend. Education was a major issue at the time and will be fully discussed in the next chapter. Until the eighteenth century, however, it is unlikely that a woman would have benefited from a wide heritage of female example, and even then there were widespread criticisms of females who wanted to write for commercial purposes. For to be a woman was to be a subservient, quiet, docile, complacent private individual whose sole purpose was to be the companion, the attendant, the servant of man – or so at least thought many of the dominant sex of the time! A woman who wanted to sell her wares, her work, her thoughts, could be comparable with a whore, a prostitute, selling her body and her talents for profit. There are plenty of examples of female authors who were criticised publicly and in print by males who could not damn them enough for their daring and brazen audacity. Small wonder then that some women were put off by such treatment and chose to keep their thoughts to themselves.

We do know that a considerable number of women did decide to write, regardless of whether they had had a formal education, but frequently they chose to write privately for themselves or others close to them. Keeping a diary or journal, writing memoirs, or an autobiography, or just writing letters – these were for personal perusal or for just the co respondent. Such writings were useful in that they enabled the author to voice her thoughts and opinions at a time when society paid little credence to them. The British Library, to name but one source, is full of them. Others like Jane Austen developed an early interest in writing for the entertainment of friends or family– but initially at least those works, like the private correspondence, were not intended for publication. It took a brave or very confident woman in the seventeenth or early eighteenth century openly to ascribe her work to herself. When Katherine Philips (1631-64) took part in a literary group she had not wanted her poetry made public and her translation of another work (Corneille- *Pompey*) was done anonymously. She wrote, 'Should I own it publicly, I think I should never be able to show my face again.' But some of her poems were published without her permission and she knew what the consequences would be. In time the printer did apologise and removed the book from sale – but it was enough to put a stop to her writing.

Slander is a difficult beast to combat. Not only do the targets get tainted, but also anyone related to, or associated with them. Fear of what the family would say or how it would affect them could be a major consideration. Jane Austen was lucky; she may well have written her pieces privately, hurriedly hiding them with a blotter when she heard the squeaky door open, but at least her family encouraged and supported her in her work and were much amused by it, in spite of her brother Henry's initial reservations. Some family comments and criticisms could be very offensive. For Elizabeth Avery in 1648, support had not been on the agenda, at least as far as her brother was concerned when he wrote, 'Sister, your printing of a Book, beyond the custom of your sex, doth rankly smell.'

For Frances Burney it was not so simple – her first work *Evelina*, (1778) written anonymously, was tremendously successful, but when she was willing to take a risk by writing plays she was dissuaded by her 'two daddies' – her father and a very close family friend – from doing so. The first reading of '*The Witlings*' had been successful, and a playwright of the time (Murphy) *had* felt it would succeed as a public venture. She was told however by the two daddies that it was similar to a French play, it might offend people, and it could fail. They did not wish to be associated with the work in case it failed and were prepared to use emotional blackmail to stop her, although previously her father at least had been very happy to ride on her public success. It is true that Frances had been very careful to avoid upsetting her father before her success was established – she had frequently acted as her father's amanuensis, so it had been necessary to completely change her own style of handwriting to prevent the printer recognising it. Increasing success had given her confidence, but still she withdrew the play. In contrast she was later to receive tremendous support from her husband, who not only admired and supported her writing, but he even acted as *her* amanuensis copying manuscripts for theatrical managers or printers. Similarly Lady Morgan's husband actually gave up practising medicine in order to go on tour with her when she was conducting research for her writing.

Maria Edgeworth had to work hard to get her family to support her writing. She did it at least in part in order to gain attention from her father who had four wives and more than twenty children – most of whom she helped to educate for him, once she herself was old enough! She assisted him in his work on educational books and incorporated his ideas into her stories for children, but he paid less attention to works generated on her own.

Women writers of the time seemed to have had to face an internal conflict – was it possible to still remain a woman, as understood by the term at the time, and be a writer, perhaps even a successful one? It was not unusual to have a first work published anonymously as Frances Burney or Amelia Opie (1790) did, or under a pseudonym like Susan Centilevre (1761). Some, like Eliza Haywood, chose to publish anonymously because the content of their books was decidedly political, knowing that women were not supposed to be involved in political thought or action. Similarly Mary Robinson had used the name Anne Randall when she published *Letter to the Women of Great Britain*. Others took the relatively safe option of having their book written 'by a lady' as indeed Jane Austen did herself. In the eighteenth century it was not just women who used a nom de plume. Indeed, odd though it sounds now, because of the success of women writers with their female readership, some men chose to write not only anonymously – as women frequently did – but even under a female pen name. So it was that the Gentlemans' Magazine in June 1770 was actually trying to find out the sex of the authors' work submitted to them.

During the course of the eighteenth century more women were becoming successful writers – and some of their works are being reprinted now for the first time in many years. Their recorded comments could show just how much attitudes towards women writers were to change over time. Clara Reeve had written a poem, published in 1769, acknowledging how hard it was to be a woman writer:

Those talents that were once my pride
I find it requisite to hide
For what in man is most respected
In woman's form shall be rejected.

Later she wrote, 'I formerly believed that I ought not to let myself be known for a scribbler, that my sex was an insuperable objection, that mankind in general were prejudiced against its pretensions to literary merit, but I am now convinced of the mistake, by daily examples to the contrary.' She too grew in confidence and was able to insist that the short pieces she submitted to journals for publication should be paid for – and not printed for free.

One way women combated the prejudice regarding their writing publicly was to react defensively, by making use of their prefaces and introductions to make apologies for their work. They referred to their lack of education, or stated "I am only a woman/poor female". Mary Chudleigh (1710) had written, 'Tis only to the Ladies I presume to present (my essays); I am not so vain as to believe anything of mine deserves the Notice of the *Men*; but perhaps some of my own Sex... to them they may prove beneficial... I hope they will pardon the incorrectness of my Stile.' A classic example was from the *Advertisement to the Reader* included in *The Adventures of David Simple* by Sarah Fielding (1744), 'The following...is The Work of a Woman, and her first Essay; which to the good natured and candid Reader will, it is hoped, be a sufficient apology for the many Inaccuracies he will find in the Style, and other faults of the Composition.' When *Evelina*, Frances Burney's first novel, had been published she cleverly addressed a note to the authors of the critical reviews at the front, 'Let not the anxious solicitude with which I recommend myself to your notice, expose me to your derision. Remember, Gentlemen, you were all young writers once...' Even Jane Austen in a private letter (1815) was to say, ' I think I may boast myself to be with all possible vanity, the most unlearned and uninformed female who ever dared to be an authoress.'

There was another factor that frequently worked against women writers, one just as difficult to combat as lack of family support or personal feelings of inadequacy, and that was the matter of time. A common complaint to be heard in many different forms was like Eliza Fenwick's, 'I cannot work perpetually surrounded by my family.' (*Secresy, or Ruin on the Rock,* 1798) In one of her letters to her sister Cassandra, Jane Austen wrote in 1816, 'How good Mrs (Jane) West could have written such books and collected so many hard words, with all her family cares, is still more a matter of astonishment!' Women could generally only write in their spare time, due to other family and domestic commitments. Those women who argued in support of the validity of female authorship were keen to justify their actions by saying it was perfectly possible to retain their femininity and be a writer, by making sure the domestic tasks were all completed first.

This problem was not confined to women centuries ago – it seems to be an ongoing difficulty. Twentieth century examples included Katherine Mansfield supporting her husband in his writings, but she had to stop her work whenever he wanted his tea. Lynne Spender, an Australian author, who was overloaded with writing commitments at one stage, had just worked out the solution – and that was the moment her child had an accident with his bike and had got the handlebars stuck up his nose! For women of all ages children are needful, no matter how old they are, and so one is constantly at risk of interruption in order to deal with their needs or, alternatively, having to try to find time when they are out of the way. Some of the women authors of my chosen period were childless – Elizabeth Inchbald for example, or Mary Wollstonecraft and Mary Brunton who died in or shortly after childbirth; and Sarah Fielding and Clara Reeve who did not even marry.

Many female writers, such as Jane Austen, had to look after sick parents or other family members, and some, like Charlotte Smith, even had to take on grandchildren if their own children were too sick – or had already died. For those who did want to write it was necessary to find time away from other demands. Mary Astell had a favourite technique – whenever she was in writing mode and wanted to avoid interruptions from various callers at her home, she used to call out from the window, 'Mrs Astell is not at home.' Returning again to the twentieth century for a moment Virginia Woolf was to put her own interpretation on the problem describing the need for 'a room of one's own', but one also needed the time and privacy to use it. It is not unknown for women writers to have to go away from home in order to fulfil these conditions – even Frances Burney wrote most of *Cecilia* (1782) away from home, but had commented, 'I know but too well the many interruptions from ill management, inconveniences, and ill nature I must meet with when I go (home), will retard me most cruelly and keep me back.'

With so many possible difficulties to overcome what then were the motives that were strong enough to make women take up the pen? Some had begun as children, writing for pleasure. Jane Austen is known to have had her sister Cassandra shrieking with laughter when she read some of her writings to her privately in their bedroom, and by her own admission, in later years, Jane's works were to become her children. Frances Burney had been an inveterate scribbler but went through a ritual burning of her early work when persuaded to by her stepmother. Others were to develop a need to write for a variety of reasons.

For women with little to do, increasingly from the middle band of society, boredom with the social round of polite conversations and regular visiting led to a desire to do something for themselves. Time and again female characters in their work discover their dissatisfaction with their lives and their need for a mission and purpose. If choices were limited, and the materials were available, writing was an increasingly acceptable option. Not necessarily for profit, but certainly to escape boredom and the monotony of daily routine – and this was a pattern that existed right through the nineteenth century. For Mary Hays her need to write developed out of an emotional crisis after her experience of unrequited love. Bitterly depressed she was advised by William Godwin, himself a writer and later husband of Mary Wollstonecraft, that she should write about her experiences. Her novel *Memoirs of Emma Courtenay* is thus based on them and even includes some of the letters she actually wrote to the man of her dreams. Therapeutic it may have been for her but others wrote to bury themselves in something different and forget their own problems in real life. This quote was from one of Frances Burney's characters:

> *When I work, I forget all my world; my projects for the future, my disappointments from the past. Mental fatigue is overpowered by personal; I toil until I require rest, and that rest which nature not luxury demands, leads not to idle temptation, but to sound, heavy, necessary sleep. (Cecilia, 1782)*

One of the major motivations for women writers throughout this period was their need for money. Ranging from the desperation after death, or desertion, by the male wage earner in their lives (father, brother, husband), to the need to maintain elderly or sick parents, or care for their own children or other relatives, women were forced to find appropriate work that would pay the bills. A constant plea throughout these years was, 'But what will become of us?' Rarely was provision made for women and children except where marriage settlements, more usually confined to the wealthier members of society, made arrangements for such circumstances. Eliza Haywood was one of many young women who received no provision after the death of her father. Lady Morgan even had to pay her father's debts.

As has already been stated working opportunities were considerably restricted for educated women and during the eighteenth century writing was increasingly popular as an option. Charlotte Lennox was one of many writers to realise that although conduct books may have commended the submissive role for young ladies, economic necessity might force them to enter the real world in order to survive; she like many other women had to work in order to live. Mary Wollstonecraft was to be another such woman, supporting both herself and other members of her family, including close male relatives who were happy to sponge off her success.

Mary Robinson, perhaps better known as Perdita, mistress of the Prince of Wales, son of George III, had a wastrel for a husband. She like several other women writers of the time went to prison with her husband when he was imprisoned for debt. She had to work in order to support him, and chose poetry – which was quicker to write and generally sold well – and even organised patronage from Georgiana the Duchess of Devonshire. Charlotte Smith had similar problems, resorting to writing poetry and novels, to support the family and avoid the creditors. Even after she had separated from her husband he was still a financial drain on her resources, as he refused to change his ways and regularly turned up when she was due to get paid in order to take money from her.

In spite of the difficulties they faced and in spite of, if not actually because of, the prejudice shown towards them by men, some women did feel they had a right to speak, and in their own way make an impression upon the world. Whether they wished to preach to their audience in the form of religious or conduct books, educate them in subjects and methods that they considered more useful or necessary than previously available, or whether they wished to raise their readers general awareness of situations that could affect their lives as females, increasingly throughout the eighteenth century women put pen to paper. In so doing they were gradually to challenge previous accepted notions of what it meant to be a woman, and how one should behave. Thus, rather than conforming to an idealistic image of the passive good woman, who listened attentively to the wisdom spoken by father, husband or significant male, and accepting or conforming to the opinions and beliefs they were expected to follow, women were more likely to begin to question what they heard. They would make their own observations, and come to their own conclusions – even if they were not always confident enough to state them in public. In her major political novel *Desmond* (1792), Charlotte Smith highlighted what had previously been the situation for many, 'I never inquired, as everybody ought to do, when such assertions are made – Is all this true?'

The problem was women were told they had no business with current affairs and politics, and yet women's lives were affected by political decisions in which they had played no part. Take for example foreign affairs and the long years of war with France – Charlotte Smith again, 'But women, it is said, have no business in politics – Why not? – Have they no interest in the scenes that are acting round them, in which they have brothers, husbands, sons or friends engaged?' The eighteenth century was a time of fierce debate. Discussions of philosophical issues and political events were commonplace, and just as the men were to engage in political debate of a wide range of issues from the French Revolution, the abolition of slavery, and the education of women, so too were these issues taken up by women of the day. There was a belief that, 'It is by reason only that abuses are gradually removed.' (Charlotte Smith, *Marchmont*, 1796) Open discussion could lead to attitude change, and that in turn could lead to progress. Another significant political writer Harriet Martineau was later to say, 'I want to be doing something with my pen since no other means of action in politics are in a woman's power.'

It would be misleading to give the impression that all women writers were radical in their thinking, for using print to spread your ideas to an audience worked equally well for any side in a debate. So, for example, women who disliked and feared the new radical ideas associated with the French Revolution and the Jacobin supporters, wrote tracts, treatises and novels that rejected the ideas of individual freedoms and rights, particularly of women, in favour of the established patriarchal system. Writers such as Hannah More and Jane West felt that leaving women uneducated and inferior in society actually made them targets for what they considered was the brainwashing of new philosophies that threatened the state. They were keen to promote education of women as a means of supporting the status quo, by making women better at fulfilling their allotted tasks. They were very aware of the fact that novels particularly were no longer just 'silly stories' but were actually being used to convey hidden messages and as such could be dangerous. Jane West argued in *A Tale of the Times* (1799),

'The novel is converted into an offensive weapon, directed against our religion, our morals, our government, as the humour of the writer may determine his particular warfare', and she wished to fight back. It was her intention to 'enforce opinions by argument and illustrate them by example.' She, like other late eighteenth century writers with anti Jacobin feelings, conformed to predictable patterns in plot development. Typically a good, hard working, law abiding family member would be misled by a character, frequently male, who followed the new philosophies of individualism and meritocracy, had some French connection, and then proceeded to destroy the stability of the family by seducing a daughter, ruining a son and so on. The obvious moral would therefore be that such philosophies were to be considered dangerous and should therefore be disregarded.

While these more conservative authors were taking part in the political debate, although justifying their actions by wishing to correct or act as an antidote to revolutionary ideas in other novels, they were still stepping outside the conventional boundaries of acceptable female behaviour by publishing their own ideas and opinions, and profiting by them. Other women writers were to be quite consciously more outspoken. Whether they were giving practical examples in popular novels, or expounding their theories and ideas in direct confrontational writing, they were to challenge some of the very foundations of society as they exposed weaknesses in a system that was supposed, at the very least, to protect its weakest members. The benevolent patriarch, the kindly but firm father figure who offered protection to his charges, whether in public or private level, was believed to be a sound basis for the structure of society. In practice women were to find it somewhat of a myth.

Men of the nobility, the ruling class, had not considered what life was like from a different point of view, and it was not uncommon for women to comment on the difficulty of appreciating the problems people faced in life if those in charge had no prior experience or knowledge of them. Thus Charlotte Smith was to ask, 'How few do we meet who can feel miseries they cannot imagine and are sure they can never experience?' (*Desmond*, 1792) Like many, she believed that you could educate through fiction and in time achieve change. Frances Burney too had felt that the novel was significant in that, 'It offers fairer opportunities for conveying useful precepts. It is, or ought to be, a picture of supposed but natural and probable human existence. It holds therefore in its hands our best affections, it exercises our imaginations; it points out the path of honour; and gives to juvenile credulity knowledge of the world, without ruin or repentance; and the lessons of experience without its tears.' (*The Wanderer*, 1814)

Many of the women writers mentioned so far used personal experience, or personal knowledge, in their work to convey their concerns about how women were treated in society. Charlotte Smith was actually upbraided by critics for making too much use of her own personal experiences in life in order to expose women's legal and sexual exploitation. Her novels contain fictional versions of many of the problems she faced when trying to sort out her family's legal affairs and the corruption of some of the members of the legal profession.

Other female authors were to show how some of the fundamental beliefs in the nature of women actually created dangers for them rather than creating opportunities for protecting them. Where women were denied education and had little experience of worldly matters, rather than remaining models of innocent virtue, their very naivety made them highly vulnerable, and as such they became targets for those lacking in moral virtue. Frances Burney's eponymous heroine Evelina had modelled herself on what she thought was an ideal model of a female, and she actually exposed herself as easy prey to unscrupulous male characters. What could be sport and entertainment for a man, in terms of conquest, could lead to the total downfall of a woman, and so knowing how to avoid such situations could prove to be a very useful lesson for an inexperienced girl. Similarly sheltering women from worldly experience and knowledge in order to 'protect' them meant they were ill prepared for coping with life's difficulties in times of family tragedy. Both concerns were thoroughly explored within the plots of many women's novels of the time.

Mary Robinson had some very negative experiences of men and wrote aggressively in *A Letter to the Women of England* (1799), 'Man is a despot by nature, he can bear no equal, he dreads the power of woman.' She believed that women were not 'mere appendages of domestic life, but the partners, the equal associates of man.' Certain of her male characters were portrayed in a very negative light, and she was not alone in this. Mrs Skinn and Rosina Bulwer Lytton are just two other examples of angry, frustrated women who wrote emotionally after personal experience. Just as other women were to justify their need to write by financial circumstances or personal convictions, so too Rosina justified the tone of her work in *Cheveley* (1834) when, 'Obliged to write in order to provide the common comforts she had been accustomed to...What wonder then that her pen is sometimes dipped in gall?' Mrs Skinn had written in verse on her title page of *The Old Maid* (1771):

> *If any here chance to behold himself*
> *Let him not dare to challenge me of wrong,*
> *For if he shame to have his follies known,*
> *First he should shame to act 'em.*

Mary Wollstonecraft had experienced unpleasant, violent and selfish behaviour in men from an early age, and the twentieth century writer Virginia Woolf pointed out that had Jane Austen had similar experiences to Mary, rather than her own positive experience of supportive males, her writings were likely to have been very different. Even so, Jane Austen (*Northanger Abbey*, 1818) was to comment that although there were laws against murdering a wife, there was little to help wives who were not loved, or women who did not even have the protection of marriage. Her novels like those of many other women writers contain detailed examples of husbands and fathers who were ineffective in their role, and whose behaviour caused many problems for the women of the family. She was known to have been a close observer of human behaviour and her characters, satirically though they may be presented, are likely to have been based on real knowledge.

Through their reading of works by female writers, women were to be encouraged to have their own opinions by looking at both sides of a situation taken on by different characters. Virtuous heroines and slightly more daring minor characters showed the benefits of taking responsibility for one's own actions, and of being prepared to challenge cruelty and neglect rather than merely accepting it, as conduct books had previously encouraged. Not all women were prepared to conform to the passive, humble, subordinate set image of a 'good and virtuous' woman that was used to reinforce the accepted orthodoxy of male dominance and superiority in society. Although many conduct books had in fact been written by women, which encouraged accepting submissive behaviour on the part of any female, characters in novels were to provide at least some interesting challenges to their ideas. Periodicals for women were also used for the discussion of female issues including the restrictions a patriarchal system placed on them, as for example in *The Female Spectator* (edited by Eliza Haywood 1744-46). Knowing how marriage was a key event in a woman's life, she gave guidance on how to avoid bad marriages, avoid marrying too young and understanding what elements were necessary for a more successful venture.

There were dangers though of writing too strongly, or emotionally. Not only could publishers be unwilling to print, but also the actual publication could fail commercially and the author be highly criticised. For any authoress wanting to make a success of her work for financial reasons this could be a major consideration. Authors also had to be sensitive to the political climate of the times. With the after effects of the French Revolution many in England who feared similar political unrest slated any ideas that seemed to be associated with the radical Jacobins. But there were other dangers too – many women were fearful of being associated with the radical ideas of Mary Wollstonecraft, not at the time of her writing, but after her husband exposed her less than orthodox sex life in *Memoirs*, published in 1798, after her death. Suddenly to have feminist ideas of any form linked you with a fallen woman and implied you could be one too... So women who wanted to make a direct complaint had to resort to anonymity – or accept the need to find a more indirect approach, even if it meant a complete change in style.

One particularly successful method of reaching the female audience was through humour. Women were avid readers – it was a safe and acceptable occupation for ladies with time on their hands. In one sense of course an amusing book that pleased its target audience was likely to be commercially successful, but it was also a particularly effective means of sharing dissatisfaction with established social practices and the ridiculous situations that women could find themselves in. Humour has been described as social glue, binding people together through their common understanding of a situation. It shines light into dark corners and is a great stress buster. Modern medical research acknowledges how it can improve your health. For women who lived under restrictive circumstances humour could help you cope. Where overt feminism could ruin your reputation comedy could be a hidden method of mutual support, by poking fun at patriarchy, challenging double standards and showing some form of defiance. Fanny Burney had Evelina refusing to dance with an ugly, undesirable partner at a ball, even laughing at the idea and having to face the consequences. Jane Austen had two of her heroines Elizabeth Bennett and Emma Woodhouse receiving ridiculous marriage proposals which seemed to benefit only the suitor, and even being told they were unlikely to get other offers. Jane Austen made it clear that though her stories were acceptable to all they may be understood only by those who read with intelligence- she did not write for 'dull elves'.

James Fordyce in his *Sermons to Young Women* (1767) had advised, 'Men who understand the science of domestic happiness know that its very first principle is ease... But we cannot be easy where we are not safe. We are never safe in the company of a critic, and almost every critic is a wit by profession.' Women had been instructed in conduct books that laughter, especially in public, was an inappropriate behaviour for a virtuous woman so one could interpret this as a control mechanism. Women were not to be critical of men. Novels however were frequently read in private, and at times furtively, so the humour could be savoured. In more private writings, in letters for example, the humour could be much more pointed – this was within a letter to Frances Burney from her stepsister Maria Allen in 1768, 'I like your Plan immensely of Extirpating that vile race of beings called man but I (whom you know am clever (VÈRÉE) clever) have thought of an improvement in the sistim suppose we were to Cut of their *prominent members* and by that means render them Harmless innofencive Little Creatures.' James Fordyce would have been horrified!

Women writers were only too aware of attitudes towards them; Mary Robinson had one of her male characters *(Walsingham*, 1797) expostulate, 'Men should assert their rights – women grow saucy- must be taken down- only invented to amuse the lords of creation- no business to write – arrogant hussys – well!'

So far I have discussed some of the difficulties women faced when wanting to write, and some of the strategies they developed in order to do so, but until now I have only briefly mentioned the process of publication. Other authors have chosen to focus on issues of publishing and readership during both the eighteenth and nineteenth centuries, so it is my intention only to raise a few relevant points here.

It is true, for the most part, that during this period printing and publishing were literally in the hands of, and controlled by, men and this too was to cause additional problems for women. As women frequently had little experience of business arrangements it was often necessary to gain some help from a male, albeit friend or family member to help with the negotiations, including finding a supportive printer/publisher like Samuel Richardson or Joseph Johnson willing to take on a woman's work. Henry Austen was to take on such a role for his sister, but not all his arrangements were satisfactory. Jane Austen had good reason to be frustrated when, after the purchase of one of her novels, *Susan* – later to become *Northanger Abbey*, no publication took place even though she had received the fee in advance. Later her brother was to buy back the manuscript but this novel was not actually published until after her death which was some *15 years* after Messrs Crosby had initially purchased it. It was not uncommon to find women changing their publisher if they felt they had been given a raw deal – financial rewards for women could be much lower than for men, and after one successful publication an authoress could at least hope for a higher settlement in her favour. Whether she was offered it by the original publisher was another matter...

All of these above considerations – the need for literacy, time and space, financial requirements, the desire to communicate, the need to cope with the pressures associated with prejudice, the need to handle the business side of the work, all laid constraints on women writers. But in considerable numbers they overcame them – these initial chapters have already named many who achieved success in their own time even if until fairly recently I had heard of few of them. Samuel Johnson once referred to women writers as 'Amazonians of the pen' and some were to use the pen as effectively as a weapon, even though, in the words of Mary Ann Radcliffe, 'All women possess not the Amazonian spirit of a Wollstonecraft.' (*The Female Advocate, or An Attempt to Recover the Rights of Women from Male Usurpation*, 1799) In the subsequent chapters my focus will be upon what these women writers had to say about the major phases of their lives as females, their perceived need for change and their hopes for the future.

Chapter Three
A Question of Education

From the time they were born girls were taught to respect, honour and obey the males in their lives. They would subsequently learn that their own needs and opinions were not important, and that they did not hold any significant place in society. Fierce debates in the eighteenth century, regarding philosophies and beliefs centuries old, continued in the attempt to fix woman's role in the world and establish what she should learn in order to fulfil it. The enlightenment philosopher Rousseau was popular with many; this is taken from a translation of *Emile*, originally published in Paris, in 1762:

> *... the education of women should always be relative to men. To please, to be useful to us, to make us love and esteem them, to educate us when young and take care of us when grown up, to advise, to console us, to render our lives easy and agreeable; these are the duties of woman at all times and what they should be taught in infancy.*

Reading this now it is not surprising if we think 'male chauvinist!'- for such a stereotype this must sound an ideal prescription. At the time Rousseau was by no means alone in his viewpoint. With the basic idea being commonly accepted that women were born to serve men, then it followed that there would be little point in educating a female for more than her place in the marriage market. After all she would only need to know how to provide the comfort, solace and domestic needs of her husband. These were to be her educational accomplishments. Mary Wollstonecraft also pointed out that daughters were married off for financial reasons – if you made them look good someone else would take over the responsibility for them. Women, certainly of the middle and upper levels of society, were not considered suited for, or capable of, earning their own living by using their brains. A young woman could easily be ousted from the marriage market by being too clever for it.

People did not like clever women. Less educated women could be jealous and men felt threatened. Comments like, 'I wonder which one of her books will teach her to be a housewife' (Sarah Fielding, *The Adventures of David Simple*, 1744), were not unknown. It was also far from uncommon to receive the advice – 'Hide your learning!' In novels women who were educated received open approval if they never showed their knowledge in public. Of course there was a basic fear – if women had received a proper education that developed their knowledge and reasoning, as the men had done, it was possible, indeed very likely, that they would become dissatisfied with their domestic and generally subservient role in society. According to Mary Robinson, men were only concerned about how this change would affect them, 'If we allow the softer sex to participate in the intellectual rights and privileges we enjoy, who will arrange our domestic drudgery?'(*A Letter to the Women of England on the Injustice of Mental Insubordination,* 1799) There had been others like her. As early as 1675 Hannah Woolley had stated that, 'Most in this depraved age think a woman learned and wise enough if she can distinguish her husbands bed from another.'

It was not just the fear of women being dissatisfied with domestic labour – there does seem to have been an acknowledged fear, even then, that women *could* outshine men. Put simply into verse anonymously in 1739:

Now all philosophers agree
That WOMEN should not LEARNED be;
For fear that as they wiser grow,
More than their husbands they should know.

Time and again women throughout the eighteenth century would pose the question 'Why?' but they already knew the answer:

Why are they so industrious to debar us that learning we have an equal right to with themselves, but for fear of our sharing with, and outshining them in those public offices they fill so miserably?
(Sophia, Woman not Inferior to Man, 1739)

and years later Frances Burney was still commenting that, 'Woman is left out in the scales of human merit, only because they dare not weigh her…'(*The Wanderer*, 1814) To be told that you have no need for learning – and to hear the justification that there was no place in society for learned women anyway, was rather a Catch 22 situation that educated women were not slow in working out. From Sophia again:

> *Why is learning useless to us? because we have no share in public offices. And why have we no share in public offices? because we have no learning.*

So what was it like to be born a girl? How did her early experiences differ from her male siblings? There are many examples that illustrate the lowly status of a female birth – from reactions to recorded events in real life, as well as those narrated in literature. It was hardly a cause for celebration in some households and was in direct contrast to the active delight, congratulations and even public celebrations that accompanied the news of a male heir, whether to a mere estate or the throne itself. This was written by Mrs Parsons in 1796, 'I was ushered into the world to the dissatisfaction of all parties as a boy was most devoutly wished for.'(*Women as They Are*) At least we were not as bad as those in Japan who used to leave their daughters outside for the first three days and only care for the survivors. In a similar vein the pregnant daughter of one eighteenth century authoress, Eliza Fenwick, wrote to her mother jokingly, 'Well then, I am determined to have a boy, for certainly a girl cannot be worth all this trouble…if mine is a girl I shall sell it.' A joke maybe, but she had a point.

It was not uncommon for young children of middle and upper levels of society to be raised together for the early years. Then when the boys were old enough to be educated properly, away from mother or governess, they were sent off to school or taught by masters. Classical education was thought to prepare boys for life, teaching them to reason, to think, to use their brains. The girls on the other hand were left behind in more ways than one.

One can imagine how they might have felt having to learn how to perform domestic chores, or being stuck with their embroidery, or left playing inside with a doll, while the boys were outside playing, or going off into the outside world. A girl or woman looking out of a window was a frequently used image in eighteenth and nineteenth century literature. Even as late as 1883 there were examples of girls feeling they were missing out:

> *We sit with our little feet drawn up under us at the window, and look out at the boys in their happy play. We want to go. Then a loving hand is laid on us, 'little one, you cannot go,' they say, 'your little face will burn and your nice white dress will be spoilt.'*
> *(Olive Schreiner, The Story of an African Farm)*

And before we consider too quickly that such days are long gone it is worth remembering that Ladybird books for children were full of such images as late as the 1960's and about a decade later had to be republished with active girls in trousers– and no more clean white dresses!

Boys in the long eighteenth century were encouraged to question, to learn, to challenge, but for the girls it was another matter. Put simply, daughters could be told by their fathers, 'Your duties in life are easily performed. I have chosen a path for you; and nothing is required for you but obedience.' (Eliza Fenwick, *Secresy*, 1795). Girls were expected to be quietly submissive in their behaviour, and accept a life of servitude towards their male relatives or, in later life, their husbands – without question. Similarly another young female character was told:

> *Don't be curious child. I never encourage curiosity. It always leads to disagreeable questions. You may tell me anything you please, but ask nothing. That's my manner of dealing with little girls.*
> *(Frances Burney, Camilla, 1796)*

There are many other examples. Women remembered the preferential treatment their brothers received as children and wove their experiences into the texts of their novels, as well as in treatises they wrote on education itself. These experiences were widespread and varied, occurring throughout the incidences of childhood from gentle activities to more physical pursuits. Take for example the occupation of reading – a quiet, passive pastime; particularly commended if the subject matter was considered 'improving'. Not all girls were content to read such conduct literature – they had active brains and wanted to make use of them. Sarah Fielding illustrated this point well:

I loved reading and had a great Desire of attaining Knowledge; but whenever I asked any questions of any kind whatsoever, I was always told such Things were not proper for Girls of my Age to know. If I got any book that gave me pleasure, and it was any thing beyond the most silly Story, it was taken from me. For Miss must not enquire too far into things- it would turn her Brain... She had better mind her Needlework – and such Things as were useful for Women- Reading and pouring on Books would never get me a Husband. (The Adventures of David Simple, 1744)

Mary Wollstonecraft had some interesting comments for those who said girls naturally played with dolls in preference to other activities. Having had far more practical experience with young children than many of the so-called experts, she asserted:

... that a girl, whose spirits have not been damped by inactivity, ...will always be a romp, and the doll will never excite attention unless confinement allows her no alternative. (A Vindication of the Rights of Woman, 1792)

Like Mary Wollstonecraft, other early 'feminists' were to comment on the more physical side of education too. They had noticed that whenever boys were freed from periods of study they were given the freedom to enjoy that time, running, playing at will, but girls were generally treated rather differently:

... if little miss is inclined to show her locomotive tricks in a manner not entirely agreeable to the trammels of custom, she is reproved with a sharpness which gives her the consciousness of having highly transgressed the laws of decorum. (Catherine Macaulay, Letters on Education, 1787)

It was not just the unfairness of watching the boys doing activities girls were not allowed to do, for those who were intelligent it must have been very frustrating watching some brothers struggle with things they could have easily achieved, or watch them being forced to learn things the girls were dying to know. Sarah Fielding had obviously had some knowledge or experience of this too:

And yet what aggravated my Misfortunes was, my having a Brother who hated reading to such a degree, he had a perfect Aversion to the very Sight of a Book; and he must be cajoled or whipp'd into Learning, while it was denied me, who had the most Eagerness for it. Young and unexperienced as I was in the World, I could not help observing the Error of this Conduct, and the Impossibility of ever making him get any Learning, that could be of Use to him, or of preventing my loving it. (The Adventures of David Simple, 1744)

Frances Burney highlighted another side of the problem:

I and all my sisters have been the sufferers the whole time: and while we were kept backward, that he might be brought forward, while we were denied comforts, that he might have luxuries, how could we help seeing the evil of so much vanity and wishing that we had all been brought up according to our proper station.
(Cecilia, or Memoirs of an Heiress, 1782)

This was an additional factor – education cost money and in order to make sure the boys' education was financed adequately, in some families the girls and women had to do without the luxuries and sometimes even the basics so that the boys' schooling could be completed. While it is true that in the above example the speaker was only a character, the sentiments she expressed are undeniably real. Girls experienced this and women writers reflected this experience through the female characters of their novels.

The whole idea of only males having a proper education, in addition to being in charge of knowledge and controlling its distribution, was definitely galling to those who questioned the justification of the basic principle and they were also to comment on the use men and boys made of it. Semi autobiographical novels record the frustration, in spite of the overall family loyalty, of seeing such financial deprivation wasted on a boy who did not value his schooling or appreciate just how much his family had had to contribute to his privileged status. The subject of young boys has already been mentioned but the difficulties continued through college and into later life. Some, though by no means all, student males wasted their education neither appreciating what opportunities they were missing nor how those opportunities could have been used by others less fortunate. Frances Burney demonstrated this when a Mr Lovel was being asked about his classical studies at university:

> *At the university! He repeated with an embarrassed look; why as to that, Ma'am, – no I can't say I did; but then what with riding,- and- and- and so forth,- really, one has not much time, even at the university, for mere reading. (Cecilia, 1782)*

Similarly another authoress, Charlotte Lennox, made such men appear dull and stupid, in spite of their apparent education, in direct contrast to her intelligent female characters that had received little or no formal education.

These criticisms and comments may sound petty to a modern reader, especially regarding the aspirations for further education, as student life nowadays is accepted for having a social as well as an academic function – but you have to remember that during this period women were denied university education, denied access to the professions and their lack of knowledge was then held against them. Fictional these examples may be, but these stories create windows through which it is possible to see and feel the sadness, and sometimes the resentment, that accompanied the lack of opportunities experienced by women of the time. For what did their actual 'education' consist of? What were these accomplishments that girls acquired in order to later gain status and prestige within the marriage market? Did they have any real value or significance beyond surface decoration?

I have already mentioned that girls needed to look good. Being well dressed, preferably fashionable to some degree, with hair in an up to date style, being able to take part in a polite conversation, and knowing how to act with decorum – all of these skills counted and would be used to increase their value on the marriage market. Other accomplishments that were sought were an ability to play music, to sing, to draw, to be able to entertain, to converse in French and, of course, to dance. These 'subjects' provided the main curriculum content of most ladies educational establishments in the long eighteenth century. If we look a little closer though it is not difficult to see their limitations. The focus of these curriculum subjects, beyond personal presentation, seems to have been on the creative/performance arts –

but not everyone had real talents in this area. Elizabeth Hamilton had this to say about one girl's musical abilities:

> *On a piano forte she was said to possess wonderful execution; and certain it was that both on that and the harp she made a very loud noise, and rattled away with the most perfect conviction that her auditors were amazed at her facility. (Memoirs of Modern Philosophers, 1800)*

Mary Robinson too was to make broad criticisms of boarding schools:

> *She had passed the daily routine of boarding school tuition with a sort of mechanical precision, which neither expands the heart nor enlightens the understanding. She had read authors she did not comprehend, prattled a foreign language without knowing the meaning of the words she uttered, finished needlework which within half a century would adorn the lumber room of her granddaughter… (Walsingham, 1797)*

Others were not only to be critical of the curriculum itself, but made a direct connection with the future consequences that may be in store for a woman so educated. This was from Mary Ann Hanway:

> *Let us examine what are their real accomplishments; they are to totter a minuet, rattle the keys of a piano forte, twang the strings of a harp, scream an Italian song, daub a work basket, or make a fillagree tea caddy; they are just able to decipher a letter of intrigue, and scrawl an answer, have enough French to enable them to read… by the help of a dictionary, … of the authors of their own country, of its history… of its laws or policy they know little. When men marry such women, where is the wonder that, after their persons grow familiar, precluded by ignorance from being rational companions of men of sense, they treat them with cold neglect, which at last terminates in cold disgust? (Ellinor, or the World as It Is, 1798)*

For a well-known illustration of such cold disgust, one only has to think of the contempt with which Mrs Bennett was regarded by her husband in *Pride and Prejudice* – it was his way of coping with the mistake that he had made by marrying a woman for her external attributes alone!

Few educational establishments were to encourage academic achievement for girls at this stage – girls who did learn classics for example tended to learn them either through the kindness of a sympathetic brother, father, uncle or even husband, unless they were able to gain some support and encouragement from a tutor employed for their male siblings. This was taken up by Mary Lamb (poetess and sister of poet Charles Lamb), who even wrote poems entitled '*The Sister's Expostulation on the Brother's Learning Latin*' and '*The Brother's Reply*' In this case the girl was fortunate for, having first complained that her brother had grown conceited with his learning and had abandoned her, the brother then promised she could learn Latin with him *if* the parents agreed. In real life girls were not always so successful in their pleas – Frances Burney's father forbade her from learning Latin because it was 'too Masculine for Misses'. Such decisions were not always treated with respect apparently, for her friend Mrs Thrale reacted by privately calling him 'a narrow Souled Goose cap!' And there was Sarah, the sister of Henry Fielding, the novelist, who had been encouraged by her brother in her learning of the classics – until she outshone him, but then it was another matter entirely and he taunted her about it. We have already had several other examples of her thoughts on the unfairness of girl's education.

While it is true that many girls were sent off to schools, at the time anyone could set one up, charging fees at will without having any training, qualifications or experience, and curriculum offerings tended to favour the popular accomplishments. Some of the experiences endured in these establishments sound rather scary. Maria Edgeworth, for example, was at a boarding school where ' all the usual tortures of backboards, iron collars and dumb-bells' were used; she had to endure additional torture though because she was short, and so was subjected to being swung by her neck in order to draw out the muscles and increase the growth. It was not her most pleasant memory of school. For those who were educated at home governesses were frequently employed, who could be basic childminders to keep the children completely out of their parents' way, or who could make a more positive contribution to their educational and moral development. There is much to say about governesses later- their role, their status and their working conditions – but for now it is sufficient to say that the problem of lack of knowledge or experience was just as relevant for governesses as within named educational establishments. Of course, there were other girls who received no formal education at all.

During this period women in real life, as well as in fiction, were to consider the weaknesses of their own earlier education, and to ensure that for them at least education would be an on going process throughout the rest of their lives. It was not just a question of feeling that their treatment in childhood could have been unfair. They were well aware of the importance of education in many respects: skill development, the ability to reason and think, the ability to act independently, to be able to fulfil roles as a mother/ wife more successfully, to assist a husband in business affairs, to be capable of using time purposefully when alone – to name but a few concerns. Education was a major issue in the development of feminist ideas and would be supported, in different ways, by radical and conservative thinkers alike. There seems to have been general agreement by many women by the end of the eighteenth century that education for females was inadequate for the roles women had to play in life, and that in many ways it did little to prepare them for future trials and tribulations during it. Whether they argued from a conservative standpoint which accepted male dominance in society, saying they would serve man's needs better if more educated in real skills, or whether they argued in favour of the equality of the sexes and therefore felt there was a fundamental need for a broader curriculum for girls, the subject was a political issue, fiercely debated.

Every facet of education was subjected to scrutiny, and a wide variety of publications were produced, debating the issues and making recommendations according to the views of the women concerned. Some were direct, like '*Thoughts on Education*' by Mary Wollstonecraft; others were embedded in fictional texts which still were able to expose the limitations of education for girls as well as making some direct challenges to the myth of male supremacy based on their educational achievement. There were also criticisms of those women who supported limited education for girls. Mary Ann Hanway had this to say:

> *Did we make greater exertions and call into action those powers entrusted to us by the creator of the universe, we should find that he had distributed his gifts nearly equal between the sexes. There are very*

few arts or sciences that women are not capable of acquiring were they educated with the same advantages as men.
(Ellinor, or The World as It Is, 1798)

Many of the myths regarding women were based on their ability (or lack of it) to learn – women were naturally stupid, education would make them mad, women were the inferior species – but they were then denied the one resource that would combat such prejudiced thoughts against them. As one writer Eliza Haywood wrote, 'Why do men call us silly women and not endeavour to make us otherwise?' (*The Female Spectator*, 1775, vol. 3) Kept in an ignorant state women had been, and would continue to be, inferior – but with learning they gained weapons, they became armed with that most dangerous of tools – reasoned argument. If women were capable of arguing with them, men would lose their authority. It did not take much effort to work out that men liked being considered superior, and having control in all established areas of society, and that they would be reluctant to relinquish that power.

The passport to this world of power was seen by some as the knowledge of classical languages and literature, an area considered as sacred to the male province – and hence the resentment shown if women attempted to learn Latin or Greek. In satirical novels there was the suggestion that knowledge of the classics was rather like being a member of a club or having a secret code, which could be flaunted in public or used to remind women of their inferior status yet again. It was only when some females were able not only to access classical languages, but also spread that knowledge – for example by publishing their own translations of major works- that they were able to break the code, although they could be frowned upon for so doing. As later feminists were to realise though, it was not just a question of learning the classic languages that gave males such a head start in life, as Julia Kavanagh – a Victorian writer – noted in relation to Maria Edgeworth:

It is not the Latin or Greek of boys that gives them a future advantage over their more ignorant sisters. It is that they are trained to act a part in life, and a part worth acting, whilst girls are either taught to look on life, or worse still, told how to practise its light and unworthy arts. (English Women of Letters: Biographical Sketches, 1863).

Women were very aware of the fact that if females receive a poor education and then later became responsible for at least the early years of childhood as mothers, teachers or carers of children, there would be increasing problems for generations ahead:

> *And, who, alas! can tell where the mischief may end. This unfortunate herself will become a mother...she will bring into the world creatures to whom she can only transmit her errors and weaknesses.*
> *(Susan Ferrier, Marriage, 1818).*

It was a common complaint that lack of stimulation led to a wasted life of idleness, which in turn could lead to the seeking of other less reputable diversions like frivolous chattering, reading less than desirable books-such as novels- or even engaging in scandalous behaviour. Such limited education as that outlined above certainly did not prepare girls for facing the problems that occurred when events such as bereavement or family disaster removed their financial security, and they were left to fend for themselves. What good would it be to know how to dress, or play a few party pieces, if one was unable to earn a living? Of what use then would be conduct book guidance if young women were left to their own devices to find employment or accommodation?

Conduct books themselves were not without critical review. When I was beginning my research I must admit to finding some of the fashionable conduct books for women rather nauseating. Patronising many of them certainly were, and time and again women were told to suppress their feelings, please their menfolk, and accept their subordinate status in society. Some were even written by women and were just as popular. What is not clear is to what extent these were written as part of an ongoing tradition of teaching female submission or whether they were, at least in part, a reaction to more active moves for change by a growing number of individual women themselves. Was it possible that these books were always taken seriously? Surely some women must have taken a step back and thought about the role they played in educating young women – or suppressing them. It was quite a surprise to find that Jane Austen, who is so often held up as a more conservative writer, had actually done so. On my first reading of *Pride and Prejudice* I had not really taken on the significance of a tiny incident – Mr Collins was reading from Fordyce's *Sermons* to the Bennett girls.

Lydia interrupted to pass on some local gossip. So where was the significance in that? Only that Fordyce was one of the major conduct writers, whose works were to be regularly republished throughout the eighteenth and well into the nineteenth century, and aimed to keep all females well under control. Lydia interrupting was shocking indeed and yet again Jane Austen was getting away with it!

There is an even better example of the point I am making here regarding women not happily, passively, accepting being lectured about their conduct. In an early manuscript of *Camilla*, Frances Burney showed a young man trying to 'educate' his intended spouse. He was enraptured with the prospect, 'If she were unformed, might he not form her? If she were uninstructed, what bliss to instruct her! What rapture to watch the growth of improvement in so beautiful a disciple...' After he had read a sermon and two essays Cleora sighed and said belittlingly, 'I'm sure I've counted thirty carriages...while you have been reading that last thing.' (pre-1796)

For centuries women refuted the claim that being educated desexed or defeminised them. They were to assert it was perfectly possible to complete domestic tasks and be properly educated without becoming more masculine. But as George Savile was to acknowledge in his *Advice to a Daughter* (1688) – another conduct book that was very popular – it may have been unfair but it would not change. 'You are therefore to make the best of what is settled by law and custom and not vainly imagine that it will be changed for your sake.' In one sense he was right – the key point was isolation in ignorance, as it would help to maintain the status quo. If they shared their knowledge, or at least experience, more would come to question common practices and ultimately want to make changes – and that leads me to another vital point concerning women and education.

Women took pride in claiming they were self-educated combining private reading, developing supportive friendships, learning languages and, where possible, travelling abroad themselves or at least sharing the experiences of others who did. Those who were educated often spread the word, whether teaching other children, setting up their own actual schools, writing educational books for adults to use, or even texts for children themselves – like Anna Letitia Barbauld's *Lessons for Children*, and Maria Edgeworth's *Moral Tales*. Although I have not chosen to study children's books of the period in detail, it is not difficult to see that the writing of such books could easily provide an ideal vehicle for passing on one's own particular beliefs regarding the upbringing and education of both boys and girls, and preparing them for a society that the writers considered desirable. I am indebted to Margaret Kirkham, a writer in the 1980's, for the idea that women reading and writing in the eighteenth century was the equivalent of our Open University. So it seems. Some women writers like Clara Reeve actually included recommended book lists within their texts- hers specifically included history, grammar, French texts, books by Samuel Johnson, religious works, poetry as well as the more traditional conduct books. (*School for Widows*, 1791)

I was amazed to find how many authors that I recognised as writers of novels had written serious works on education: Maria Edgeworth, Elizabeth Hamilton, Hannah More, Mary Wollstonecraft, Clara Reeve to name but a few. Education was being debated by both sexes and it is worth noting that women took notice of some of the key features of the male debate, analysed them from a female point of view, took relevant recommendations that had been made for boys education but then added many of their own.

At the beginning of this chapter I gave an example of Rousseau's views on women's education and mentioned the popularity of his ideas at the time. Some of his ideas were undoubtedly valuable – the importance of experience for example – but his main concern was with the education of boys. In essence he was a misogynist – his idea of a woman was purely to serve the interests of man. Single women, unattractive girls and old women just did not fit into his plans. In his fictional work *Emile*, Sophie was a girl raised and educated by a man solely for the purpose of pleasing Emile as a husband. Women writers used the plots of their novels to take apart this element of Rousseau's plan by raising issues that seemed obvious to them. Surely a man could quite easily change his mind and leave a young girl stranded, with no thoughts for her future livelihood at all. A girl so raised was not likely to be completely empty headed – she was likely to have at least some of her own thoughts, ideas, wants and needs regardless of what he deemed correct for her. And with all the concern for virtue, morality, and decorum prevalent at the time, it was hardly likely to develop in a very virtuous fashion if a girl was taught that she only had to please a man...

Maria Edgeworth had seen the results of Rousseau's ideas applied in practice. Her own brother was raised without restraint and turned out to be a major family disappointment – conceited, selfish and uncontrollable at home so they packed him off to school. Her father's friend Mr Day tried to educate a girl to be his future wife – and that was a predictable failure too. Like many other women Maria was concerned with far more practical systems of education, that would enable females to develop physically, mentally and morally in order to become far more useful members of society whether as wives, mothers or independent women. Many of these women writers were to realise the importance of early childhood experiences and the particular significance of the mother, and it was generally accepted too that if a mother herself lacked education then it was imperative she took remedial action in order to prepare herself adequately for the task. Amelia Opie pointed out:

> *A child's education begins almost from the hour of its birth; and the mother who understands her task knows the circumstances which every moment calls forth, are the tools with which she is to work in order to fashion her child's mind and character. (Adeline Mowbray, 1805)*

One book of fiction, *Adelaide and Theodore*, translated from the French work of Madame Genlis, (1783) gave the example of members of the nobility taking their role as primary educators so seriously that they abandoned their frivolous life in the high society of Paris. They retired to the country for some years in order to devote themselves to the task of educating their young son and daughter while developing an entire system of education appropriate for them – including writing their own text books, stories and preparing suitable educational materials. Realising that this was perhaps a little extreme, the English writer Clara Reeve commented that it was not necessary to give up everything and retire to a castle in Wales in order to do the job properly- but it was worth selecting the ideas that were most in accord with your own views and personal situation. (*Plans of Education*, 1792)

Authors like Catherine Macaulay, Hannah More and Mary Wollstonecraft were all to realise how important it was for the future of society that women should receive a good education. Elizabeth Hamilton put it in these terms:

> *If women were so educated as to qualify them for the proper performance of this momentous duty, it would do more towards the progressive improvement of the species than all the discoveries of science and researches of philosophy. (Letters on Education, 1801)*

There certainly was a call by these pioneers of girl's education that women in general should be prepared to acknowledge and accept their responsibilities for educating the females of the future. Where, for example, a single mother was unable to take on the responsibility, she could at least leave instructions for another responsible adult to do so. Take this example from Mary Hays:

> *Shelter her infant purity from contagion, guard her helpless youth from a pitiless world, cultivate her reason, make her feel her nature's worth, strengthen her faculties, inure her to suffer hardship, rouse her to independence, inspire her with fortitude, with energy, with self respect, and teach her to contemn the tyranny that would impose fetters of sex upon her mind. (The Victim of Prejudice, 1799)*

While it is true to say that not all women writers made an overt connection between the prejudice towards women in society and the way the children of the two sexes were reared, some of them undoubtedly did. Elizabeth Hamilton even referred to the

> *... foolish partiality that some mothers have to sons (which) might make a spectator think they have embraced the religion of Mahommed and taught to believe only men have souls and that female children, whom God has sent them, have been brought into the world for no other purpose than to contribute to the pleasure and submit to the authority of the Lords of Creation.*
> *(Letters on Education 1801)*

While boys received a different type of education, and a different range of experiences, they would grow up accepting a false sense of superiority and would continue to be affected by, and to accept, prejudicial practices towards the female sex which they could easily pass on in turn to future generations. Catherine Macaulay and others supported the idea of educating the children together:

> *Confine not the education of your daughters to what is regarded as the ornamental parts of it, nor deny the graces to your sons. Suffer no prejudices to prevail on you to weaken nature...let your children be brought up together; let their sports and studies be the same.*
> *(Letters on Education 1790)*

There was awareness that boys' education needed modification too. Even from early childhood boys could be subjected to a different set of moral standards, or be subjected to a different type or level of discipline than those of their female siblings. Boys could get away with things for which girls would be severely rebuked. Realising that this was another way boys could be encouraged to view girls differently, writers like Elizabeth Hamilton, Maria Edgeworth and Catherine Macaulay advised that boys should be subjected to the same moral education as the girls, rather than being taught a double standard which was to have serious consequences for women in later life. There was a need for both sexes to learn the benefits of self-control and self-restraint. Hannah More pointed out that:

> *It is a singular injustice which is often exercised towards women, firstly to give them a very defective education, and then to expect from them the most undeviating purity of conduct...to train them in such a manner as shall lay them open to the most dangerous faults...*
> *(Strictures on the Modern System of Female Education, 1799)*

I will be devoting a whole chapter to the subject of the double standard and 'fallen women' later in the book.

In addition to the need for boys to receive an improved moral education, it was similarly proposed that girls, in turn, should be encouraged to develop their powers of reasoning and understanding, to learn a wide variety of subjects and not to rely on rote memory learning. Maria Edgeworth and her father, Richard, wrote '*Practical Education*' in 1798 for children of both sexes. This covered a wide variety of topics including the use of 'rational' toys, spelling, rewards and punishments, useful arithmetic and had much to say on the need to make learning enjoyable, with short periods of intensive work and a balance of activity, as well as students learning at their own natural pace. They, too, were concerned with moral development, although religion did not play a significant part in their work. In contrast Hannah More particularly was to lay great emphasis on religion and moral development within her educational plans, for she saw women of the future being responsible for the moral regeneration of society. Although differing in the extent of their commitment to equality of curriculum studies, or belief in the actual function and ultimate purpose of education, women writers knew it was to be a significant development for the future. There was a real call for women to raise their expectations:

> *O! my unenlightened country-women, ...*
> *Shake off the trifling glittering shackles which debase you ... let your daughters be liberally, classically, philosophically and usefully educated; let them speak and write their opinions freely, let them read and think like rational creatures; adapt their studies to the strength of their intellect; expand their minds and purify their hearts, by teaching them to feel their mental equality with their imperious rulers.*
> *(Mary Robinson, A Letter to the Women of England, 1799)*

By the end of the eighteenth century girls' education was changing – what people were not prepared for was just how much change it would bring in over time. Education was just the start.

Chapter Four
A Marriagable Commodity

I wonder what can make the generality of women so fond of marrying? It looks to me like an infatuation – just as if it were not a greater pleasure to be courted, complimented, admired and dressed by a number, than be confined to one, who from a slave becomes master.
(Eliza Haywood, The History of Betsy Thoughtless, 1751)

The reality of the situation was that it was generally understood and accepted that a girl *would* marry, indeed *should* marry and was therefore not merely unfortunate, but likely to be somewhat of a social outcast if she did not. Through their relationships with men females gained definition in life – a daughter, a wife, a mother – even an old maid. Females were thought to need protection by males although, if the novels are anything to go by, most protection needed to be *from* males. As few women were wealthy enough to have real financial independence, and the opportunities for working women in the middle or higher levels of society were limited (an area I will need to consider in more detail in a later chapter), most of these females remained in a state of economic dependency throughout their lives. When a girl married she transferred from the protection and support of her father to her husband; with both she was in a position of relative powerlessness, but as a wife she could expect to be given a home, security, food, clothing and other basic needs in exchange for her domestic service, her obedience and her person. This was the marriage contract and in many ways marriage could be seen partly, if not primarily, as a business transaction between the parties. For most women marriage was essential. In *Pride and Prejudice* for example, although Charlotte Lucas did not think much of men or matrimony, she still considered marriage, 'the honourable provision for well-educated young women of small fortune, their pleasantest preservation from want.' (Jane Austen, 1813)

A girl may have dreamed of love, especially if she was fond of reading romances or what were called 'silly' novels. Some notable men however, including Dr Johnson, feared that reading too many such works would have a bad influence on young minds and make them have unrealistic notions about married life. Mutual love was not necessarily part of the contract, but increasingly though it was to become a desirable consideration, particularly where the women were concerned, for 'what lady in romance ever married the man that was chosen for her?'(Charlotte Lennox, *The Female Quixote*, 1752) Perhaps Dr Johnson was right!

So young women would look towards marriage, but life after marriage took on an entirely different perspective. One grew up, one settled down. The process of change could even be noted when comparing a single girl with one who was engaged, 'Why my little rose of beauty you have all your thorns about you tonight... there's my little sister Kitty (who was engaged)... she begins to look tame and demure already. (Eliza Haywood, *The History of Betsy Thoughtless*, 1751) It was not unknown for a previously lively heroine, contemplating her imminent marriage, to make similar comments to this:

> *The icy bonds of matrimony are upon me already: I feel myself turning into a fond, faithful, rational, humble, meek spirited wife! Alas I must now turn my head into a museum, and hang up all my smart sayings inside my brain, there to petrify, as warnings to all pert misses.*
> *(Susan Ferrier, Marriage, 1818)*

Early 'feminist' authors like Lady Mary Chudleigh and Mary Astell had recognised the parallel between wives and slaves. They pointed out that although in courtship a man may be a woman's slave for a few days, it was only in order to make her his slave – for the rest of his life. But that was all in the future – to a young girl, just old enough to be entered into the marriage market, the immediate future could look very rosy. Dresses and finery, bonnets and ribbons, a flurry of balls and social activities, possibly even visits with relatives to London or Bath – such opportunities to get out in the world, to meet new people, to see new sights – such an opportunity to have a life. Women writing found it easy to convey the pleasure of anticipation, excitement, and the glamour that they themselves had experienced or observed. Details about hair dressing, fashion styles, fabric choices and matching trinkets, or the urgent need for a dress repair when a hem got torn during a ball, may hold little interest for male readers but they hold far more relevance for females who understand the complexities involved. When someone once said 'Girls just want to have fun', they knew what they were talking about.

Giving advice to daughters was a favourite theme in conduct literature, and girls may well have openly listened to, or read for themselves, advice about the need to modify their behaviour, the need to behave with decorum. I have been amused to find little comments though, that indicate that young women did actually have private opinions about such matters. Just as Lydia in *Pride and Prejudice* interrupted the reading of a sermon, another young female character even said:

> *I am so teased and so lectured that I sit mimpetty mimp before them for peace sake...I am very honest my dear Caroline, though I am forced to be a hypocrite now and then to save myself from being lectured to death; but there is no reason why, when you and I are alone, that I should not say as I think.*
> *(Charlotte Smith, The Young Philosopher, 1798)*

Some girls inevitably got a reputation, especially if they lacked any real education, for being very, very silly. This was from Susan Ferrier:

> *Then there are the daughters of these ladies – Misses, who are mere misses and nothing more. Ah! The insipidity of a mere Miss! A soft simpering thing with pink cheeks, and pretty hair, and fashionable clothes;* ***sans*** *eyes for anything but lovers,* ***sans*** *ears for anything but flattery,* ***sans*** *taste for anything but balls-* ***sans*** *brains for anything at all.*
> *(Marriage, 1818)*

If you bear in mind the lack of useful education for many girls, it is not really surprising that their attentions were diverted into more frivolous activities while they had the chance and were not having to attend to the more serious occupations of being a wife or mother. While also remembering the importance of gaining accomplishments in order to attract attention from males who were surveying the market, it is not difficult to imagine that there were probably a fair number of such girls as these. Frances Burney, through her own observations and knowledge of her father's experiences as a music teacher, used the example of a harp teacher discovering that her pupil wanted to be seen and admired by others as she learned to play a popular instrument. Thus it was more important that she learned how to pose around the instrument, or hold it, rather than learning to play a single note correctly. (*The Wanderer*, 1814) In spite of all the attention paid to music during their education it was not at all unknown for those girls with little real musical talent, or appreciation, to abandon their pretensions after marriage.

Some girls took the risk of being real coquettes and chose to face the danger of being labelled as such; it was obviously part of the fun – however you had to know when to stop as it could damage your reputation, and ultimately affect your value on the marriage market. Frequently in literature a girl's reputation was compared to the most delicate of flowers:

> *The honour of a young maid like you, is a flower of so tender and delicate a nature, that the least breath of scandal withers and destroys it – In fine...it is not enough to be good, without behaving in such a manner as shall make others acknowledge us to be so.*
> *(Eliza Haywood, The History of Betsy Thoughtless, 1751).*

What they were referring to, of course, was her chastity, that most prized of commodities, particularly in an unmarried woman. A young girl was considered as property and had value – so if the goods were tainted, whether by falsely tarnished reputation or actual fact, her marketable value went down and she was treated accordingly, indeed harshly, by society.

I will need to come back to the idea of a girl being a marketable commodity later in this chapter, but for now let us return to the young girls practising their skills in attracting the attention of a suitable male – innocent perhaps, but cunning nevertheless. 'I not only knew the full value of a smile, a sigh, or a blush but could practice them all upon occasion.' (Charlotte Lennox, *The History of Harriet Stuart, Written By Herself*, 1751). There was also a rather delightful example of scheming in *A Tale of the Times*, (Jane West, 1799) where one female character, called Arabella, was trying to gain the attention of a particularly desirable male. She had limited cards to play so needed something a little more dramatic than dropping a handkerchief or using her fan, and considered that throwing a fainting fit would be more effective. So, 'She performed it in the greatest perfection, but on opening her eyes was mortified to find, that neither he nor the countess (someone else she wished to impress) appeared in the circle that had gathered round her.' All that effort for nothing!

Some women remained unmarried in spite of all their exertions, for example one character called Miss Bellenden who:

> *... had not any idea of higher excellence than beauty, greedy of admiration and would be a coquet, if she had wit enough to secure her conquests, but although nature directs her to throw the bait, and the gaudy fry often catch at it, she has not yet skill enough to bring her prey to land and they always escape her.*
> *(Charlotte Lennox, Euphemia, 1790)*

Such women could end up as old maids, a situation that seems to have been a dreaded state for many, one open to derision and mockery from both sexes. So you had to keep trying, no matter how long it took.

Rather than just flirting with different men for fun, as a coquette, for some there was a genuine desire to see who was available, and desirable, within the group of marriageable males on hand. Authors like Eliza Haywood had lively heroines, such as Betsy Thoughtless, who argued that it was only reasonable she should be allowed to hear all the proposals likely to be made to her, before she made her choice – if indeed she chose to marry at all:

> *Marriage is a thing of too serious a nature to hurry into, without first having made trial of the constancy of the man who would be a husband, and also of being well assured of one's own heart.*
> *(The History of Betsy Thoughtless, 1751)*

During the mid eighteenth century such ideas were rather too radical to allow a heroine, a possible role model for her readers, to be allowed to maintain throughout her life. Betsy ultimately had to learn her lesson and settle to the accepted normal submissive role of a wife before the last page was turned.

Serious thinkers, like Mary Wollstonecraft, had been concerned that girls who lacked a decent education would find it hard to make a good choice regarding future husbands, as they lacked worldly experience and were not practiced in the art of decision-making. The decisions they made could therefore be ill judged, made too quickly and then regretted for the rest of their married lives as they discovered the real meaning of unhappiness. The problem was considered from a variety of angles. One young female character received an early proposal of marriage but:

> *I had never thought of anything so serious as matrimony; and indeed was just but out of the nursery, where I had never been told it was necessary to think at all. (Charlotte Smith, Emmeline, 1788)*

The problem of education, or lack of it, had many repercussions.

Girls were advised to show no preference towards males until their intentions had been made clear, and preferably marriage proposed; they were not supposed to have, or at least acknowledge, sexual feelings, To be told to deny such feelings, or to hide them, must have put considerable emotional strain upon young women, especially those of a more passionate nature. Examples such as Mary Hay's *Memoirs of Emma Courtney*, however over the top or irritating a modern reader may find them, provide powerful testimonies of girls who did experience love, passion and desire. In earlier times women were considered licentious, always on the prowl, and men were fearful of such sexual predators; during the long eighteenth century the ideal woman was to keep such feelings under strict control, if she had them at all.

I was quite impressed too with the highly unusual idea that the two central characters had in one novel where they had been promised to each other, in matrimony, for some years by their fathers. When the time came for them to marry they decided to engage in some action research, to find under what conditions marriages were actually happy and therefore successful. They observed what happened when marriage was solely for financial considerations, or where the partnership had been forced, or alternatively was made between partners who had similar dispositions and respected each other. Their conclusions were predictable. (Eliza Haywood, *The History of Jemmy and Jenny Jessamy*, 1753)

Some girls were to question why it was necessary to find a husband so quickly just when they were starting to have fun. Eliza Haywood continued the theme in several of her novels, 'They want to deprive us of all the pleasures of life, just when one begins to have a relish for them…'(*The History of Betsy Thoughtless*, 1751) and, 'I wonder how people can resolve to cut themselves off from all the pleasures of life, just as they are beginning to have a relish for them – how should I regret being confin'd at home by my domestic affairs, while others of my sex and age were flaunting in the mall, or making one at the rout of a woman of quality.'(*The History of Jemmy and Jenny Jessamy*, 1753) One of my most favourite quotes occurred when a family of young females had just finished getting ready for a night on the town, having been supervised in all their preparations by their mamma. She warned, 'Well heaven help the men tonight, girls.'(Regina Maria Roche, *Children of the Abbey*, 1796)

To counterbalance the pleasures of such activities, it is time to introduce some of the less pleasant aspects of the process. Once put out on the marriage market, the general aim was to find a husband for the daughters as quickly as possible, if there was a suitable opportunity. Not everyone felt comfortable about the principle of a 'market' and there are many references and comparisons to animal markets and their sale to the highest bidder. Mrs Bennett in *Pride and Prejudice* was notorious for changing her opinion of her daughters' suitors every time their circumstances changed or their characters became better known. There is a definite image of the mothers involved bustling about, trying to show off their daughters to the best advantage – Mrs Bennett was by no means the only mother to do so. Mrs Fairfax, in *Desmond*, (Charlotte Smith); Mrs Kilcorban in *Children of the Abbey*, (Regina Maria Roche); Lady Mellasin, *The Adventures of Betsy Thoughtless,* (Eliza Haywood); all did the same. Jane Austen in her unfinished work, *The Watsons* (1805), referred to a particular type of spinster, and wrote, 'There is nothing she would not do to get married.' Becoming a frustrated old maid, forced to earn a meagre living or remain in a state of dependence was not a desirable alternative for most young women.

Those families with some money to spare used to make the seasonal excursions to Bath and London, where a gala of activities and festivities could show off unmarried women to their best advantage:

> *She was constantly exhibited at all the elegant amusements in London, produced for admiration in Bath seasons, dragged from one fashionable watering place to another, evidently to be disposed of to the highest bidder. (Mary Ann Hanway, Ellinor, or the World as It Is, 1798)*

Some authors were to show that not everyone approved of the system. Elizabeth Hamilton wrote of a Doctor Orwell, who had daughters of his own and was horrified by the degradation involved in the process. He heard that, 'Had he come to Bath, he might have held a perpetual fair, where every ballroom might be considered as a booth for the display of beauty to be disposed of to the highest matrimonial bidder.' He reacted strongly, 'I had rather see my daughters reduced to the necessity of earning their bread, than behold them raised to the highest pinnacle of fortune by such methods as you have described.' (*Memoirs of Modern Philosophers*, 1800) But in the same book it was noted girls were, '… hawked about in such quantities at every place of public resort that if the poor things did not lay themselves out to court attention, that they would have no chance of being taken notice of.' Charlotte Smith had her own way of describing the events from the perspective of an unwilling victim:

> *Dragged to a scene, where she considered herself exposed as an animal in a market to the remarks and purchase of the best bidder, it was with extreme reluctance that Rosalie entered the ballroom.*
> *(Montalbert, 1795)*

The problem was mentioned regularly for years to come; even Charlotte Brontë, writing much later in the nineteenth century, had her own comments on the idea of girls being exhibited in order to get a husband:

> *The great wish – the sole aim of everyone of them is to be married, but the majority will never marry: they will die as they live now. They scheme, they plot, they dress to ensnare husbands. The gentlemen turn them into ridicule, they don't want them, they hold them very cheap: they say – I have heard them say it with sneering laughs many a time – ' the matrimonial market is overstocked.'*
> *(Shirley, 1848)*

In addition to these problems, another point that was frequently raised was the negative behaviour of some of the girls themselves. While girls were out, either having fun or being on the prowl, there was one aspect of behaviour that had rather more potentially serious consequences in its later forms as far as general progress for women was concerned. Jealousy of other pretty girls, or witnessing preferred males ignoring their own personal charms, could lead some young women into rude behaviour, idle gossip and the spread of damaging slander. Jealousy and rivalry may have promoted and protected self-interest, but would work against the formation of any ideas of 'sisterhood' or shared female identity.

To find one girl whispering gossip about another was not unusual in novels, even to the extent of casting doubt on her reputation, but occasionally it got more serious. Anonymous letters and even setting up a clandestine meeting for an unsuspecting girl with a known immoral gentleman, complete with an audience in tow ready for public humiliation, were all extensions of the basic principle of self-assertion, and the necessary removal of rivals for male attention and conquest. In the summerhouse incident, for example, in *Ellinor*, the eponymous heroine was rescued from such a situation – not by a male, but surprisingly by a very strong independently minded woman, Lady John. She commented:

> *I could not see a young woman hurled at once from all her proud prospects; driven with ignominy from the bosom of her protectors, exposed to the jealous fury of an enraged wife, the taunting insults of insignificant girls and the outrageous virtue of mouldy spinsters: for to have seen her without reputation, friends or fortune, thrown upon an unfeeling world would have been acting against the principles I possess. (Mary Ann Hanway, 1798)*

There was also a later comment about the whole incident that put such behaviour firmly in its broader context:

> *How estimable does (Lady John's) conduct appear, when opposed to these female harpies, whose highest happiness arises from the destruction of their own sex. The most ferocious beasts of prey, the lion, the tyger, and the wolf, destroy not their own species, it is the reasoning brute of the creation, – it is man who alone lives and feels his gratification in the destruction of his fellow man.*

One of the most surprising elements revealed in this study of woman's literature was the frequent exposure of just how unpleasant women could be both towards each other and towards the opposite sex. Jealous rivalry in a ballroom, with sneers and sniggers, whispers behind fans and pointedly ignoring or blocking other women was just the start. Those women who had gained an element of power, over lovers and rivals and later husbands and servants, were unlikely to want to risk yielding it. When some women began to develop a greater awareness of their real status in society and their ultimate powerlessness, and wished to challenge the status quo, they met with surprisingly fierce opposition from women themselves. The ultimate extension and consequences of this behaviour would in turn have a significant effect on the progress of women's developing freedoms and rights. Women at times could be their own worst enemy.

So while some begrudged the attentions paid to other women by males, those who benefited were able to thrive on it. It was not unusual for a girl during the socialising and courtship process to receive excessive flattery – and find the whole experience thoroughly enjoyable. It was known to be a female weakness then and, to some extent at least, we are, if we are honest, still susceptible to it. One period when flattering words seemed particularly well used was during rituals of courtship and more frequently during an actual marriage proposal. However it seems clear that some proposals at least left a lot to be desired. In his book, *Advice to Daughters*, George Savile was not really being facetious when he said that girls have power in looks and tears, although he was only too aware of how limited their power really was in most facets of their lives and how unfair that could be. Take for example the right of a young woman to refuse the offer of her lover to take her hand in marriage – in theory it was simple. A man could propose marriage and either be accepted as lover and future husband or he could be rejected. Jane Austen, in her novels, showed only too clearly how such refusals could become worthless, at least initially. Frequently she and other female writers were to show how men expected an automatic acceptance of their marriage offer, regardless of their own personal attributes, financial situation, age or health. A girl who refused must either be flirting with them, in which case she would accept with a little extra wooing and repetition, or she must be mad. Knowing the need for her future financial security, according to such notions, a girl must be foolish indeed to put aside the offer of a home for life.

In novels at least, one suspects that women may have used the opportunity to have said exactly what they would like to have said in such a situation – even if in real life it would have been unrealistic, impractical, or highly improper to do so. In the eighteenth century they did not award Oscars for acting, but it would have been a considerable put down if the following response to a proposal actually had taken place:

> *I burst out a laughing and told him, fate had been unkind to the stage, in making a lord of one who seemed so every way calculated for a buskin (a tragedy actor) thought he was quite a hero, thanked him for the diversion he had afforded me, and whenever I found myself inclined to the vapours, would send for him by way of an antidote.*
> *(Mrs Skinn, The Old Maid, 1771)*

Proposals of marriage were not laughing matters; indeed conduct books thought laughter in public highly inappropriate behaviour for young ladies. In *Evelina* (Frances Burney, 1778) for example, the inexperienced heroine laughed when an ugly man asked her to dance and she wished to refuse him. She did not know, however, that it was not behaving according to the rules when she chose to dance with other men later, having refused the earlier offer. In theory it was a girl's right to refuse to dance with a man she did not take a liking to – surely she should not be criticised or deprived of her evening's further enjoyment for exercising her right? Proposals of marriage should be taken more seriously though and the suitors treated with great respect, but it was Jane Austen who showed in many ways how such proposals could actually be quite insulting to the women concerned. Take two of the proposals in *Pride and Prejudice* – firstly where Mr Collins told Elizabeth Bennett what pleasure and convenience she would bring him, and had the audacity to tell her that it is by no means certain she would get any other offers – so ought to take this one. Then cool, classy Mr Darcy emphasised how everything affected him, and said it was against his will, reason and character to love Lizzie, how his relatives would not approve and he thought some of her family were awful. In *Emma* too Mr Elton explained he had been told to marry by his patroness and Emma would do.

Like Frances Burney, Jane Austen was a notable observer of the intricate details of people's behaviours – you get the feeling that she had known of such proposals to women and how they felt about them. It is worth remembering as well that although Jane Austen did accept a proposal of marriage in her youth, she changed her mind within twenty-four hours and apparently never reconsidered marriage seriously for herself again.

Considering also how women were less likely to travel than men, and therefore were more restricted in the number of males they were acquainted with, they were sometimes vulnerable to the flattery of males who pretended to be virtuous and loving, when in fact they had a less than desirable background or personal history. It was unusual to find women rejecting males with such bluntness as in *Millenium Hall* (Sarah Scott, 1762) when immoral Lord Robert was told his behaviour was undesirable and his conduct was too bad for Miss Selvyn to even consider him as a possible future husband:

> *She was obliged to confess that had she been better inclined to enter into the matrimonial state, his lordship was not the man she should have chosen, not from any dislike to his person or understanding, but from disapprobation of his principles; that, in regard to her sex he had a lightness in his way of thinking, and had been so criminal in his conduct, that of all men she knew, she thought him most improper for an husband.*

I mentioned earlier that young women were not unaware of the parallels between wife and servant; this too was highlighted in some refusals contained in novels. I would be very surprised if there were many women who dared to respond so strongly as in this next example, but I suspect that not a few would like to have done so if their own feelings were similarly neglected. The suitor concerned summarised his proposal:

> *'In short madam I have seen you two or three times, although you did not know it, I like your person (ie appearance) hear you have had a sober education, think it time to have an heir to my estate and am willing, if you consent to it, to make you my wife...I shall expect nothing of you, but that you will retire into the country with me and take care of my family. I must inform you that I desire to have everything in order, for I love good eating and drinking, and have been*

used to have my own humour (i.e. own way) from my youth, which if you will observe and comply with, I shall be very kind to you, and take care of the main chance for you and your children'. I made him a low curtsey and thanked him for the honour he intended me; but told him I had no ambition to be his upper servant.
(Sarah Fielding, The Adventures of David Simple, 1744)

It does seem as though young women had the opportunity to wield some power over males – some not only thoroughly enjoying the experience of doing so, but also being quite capable of exploiting it too. 'It is a rule, you know, to deny nothing to a bride elect; probably, poor wretch, because everyone knows what a fair way she is in to be soon denied everything!' (Frances Burney, *The Wanderer*, 1814) Certainly for girls reared on romantic stories, or even those who just desired a little romance the prospect of courtship was a rosy one. In essence it was a time when a young lady did have some powers, or at least thought and acted as though she did. Even Jane West, who tended to have some quite conservative views in her writings noted, 'Since it was at least doubtful whether she could be queen for life she was desirous to protract the period which acknowledged her right of government.' (*A Tale of the Times*, 1799) It was not just a question of being given gifts and trinkets, being able to choose activities and refreshments; women could be far more manipulative. This is but one example:

'I neither love him, nor hate him; but I cannot help owning I feel a strange kind of pleasure in exercising a little tyranny over him'
'What do you mean child?'
'Why madam, I think Mr Campbell just cut out for a lover. He seems to possess a thousand old fashioned amiable qualities, which would give a mistress such a charming advantage over him! How I could like to sport with the honest sincerity of his heart. Make him feel fear and hope, joy and grief in such a swift vicissitude...'
(Charlotte Lennox – The Life of Harriet Stuart, Written By Herself, 1751)

Similar sentiments are also expressed in *The History of Betsy Thoughtless*, 'That young lady, in the meantime, was far from having any commiseration for the anxieties of those who loved her; – on the contrary, she triumphed in the pains she gave...'(Eliza Haywood, 1751) I do not think other instances would be hard to find.

It would be misleading to give the impression that this stage of a girl's life was all plain sailing. Certainly marriage was necessary for most women in order to have financial security during their lives, although the two did not necessarily always go together. Increasingly girls did wish to have their opinions and wishes taken on board, but there were various factors that provided real restraints upon their choices of marriage partner. Such basic considerations as marrying for love or money, marrying freely or feeling obliged to accept their filial duty when a parent had strong or forceful views, or less frequently, having an unusual desire for independence (i.e. wishing to remain a single woman), were powerful influences which could make the difference between a 'happy' life or one of complete misery. Freedom of choice of partner, as we know and appreciate in the modern world, had not yet become a general right for women. Not everyone was to be like Elizabeth Bennett (Jane Austen, *Pride and Prejudice*, 1813) who said, 'I am only resolved to act in that manner, which will, in my opinion, constitute my happiness', and have a father who supported her in doing so.

One key cause for concern was money. There are numerous instances in fiction of young girls being left without provision after the death of a beloved father and the problems they subsequently faced. We cannot help being left with the impression that women authors knew that it was a real problem for many. We know that working opportunities were limited for girls in the middling classes until well into the nineteenth century – marriage was a necessary career. Fathers were to repeatedly tell their daughters to accept the proposal of a man with money, whether the girl liked him or not, 'for your own happiness'. (Charlotte Lennox, *The Female Quixote*, 1752) But happiness was not an emotional consideration here; it was purely a financial one. Although I have rarely quoted from works by male authors, I was quite impressed with one by Robert Bage, who was unusually supportive over women's issues, where his heroine was being pressurised into such a marriage. She replied:

> *I should say venerable sir, it is I who am to be married not you, it is I who am to bear his follies and humours by day and by night, not you; it is altogether my own affair and ought to be regulated by my own*

> *feelings. I allow you to have a right to advise, and I give you leave to advise provided you do it quietly. But I tell you beforehand I will not take it, if it be to throw myself away. (Hermsprong, 1796)*

This may have been taking things a little too far for those faced with similar situations, but there is plenty of evidence of such imagined, if not realised, responses in women's writings too. This was from Mrs Skinn, 'I will never be controlled in my choice of husband. Lord the matrimonial pill is hard enough to swallow at any rate. What in the name of liberty must it be when we are obliged to take it by constraint.' (*The Old Maid*, 1771) More directly from Charlotte Smith came, ' I will tell you plainly once and for all that I will not be controlled in the most important concern of my life, I will not be wheedled or threatened into marrying' (*The Young Philosopher*, 1798)

In spite of such outbursts as these it was not at all uncommon to find unpleasant, tyrannical, patriarchal fathers who did impose their will on reluctant daughters, 'I may with reason expect you will conform to my will in the choice of husband I have made for you.' In her reply this particular daughter acknowledged, ' I am not allowed any will of my own.' (Charlotte Lennox, *The Female Quixote*, 1752) Similarly in another novel one daughter was told, 'I will have no answer unless it be an answer of compliance.' (Charlotte Smith, *Montalbert*, 1795) The problem of course was that frequently, as young women had little economic independence, they were financially dependent upon their fathers and the ties of filial loyalty were tightly bound. Loyalty and duty were taken very seriously by females from a very early age, and unfortunately could be abused by unfeeling fathers and husbands.

Women who had experience or knowledge of forced marriages, or unhappy ones, include detail in the course of their novels that shows their understanding of the situations faced by young women of the time, and what the emotional reactions to them may have been – even if they were unable to actually express them in reality at the time. Eliza Haywood had one such young girl refuse a richer man's marriage proposal and justify the decision in detail by saying:

> *It will doubtless seem strange to you... that I should mention as a misfortune what you might expect a girl in my precarious situation would have rejoiced at, and been elated with as the greatest good that*

> *could have befallen her; – the world I know condemns me for my folly, – I condemn myself – yet it was as impossible for me to act other wise, as it is to repent to what I have done. You will perhaps imagine that he is some deformed and loathsome creature, but I assure you he is not... making an allowance for his age, which by his own account is near fifty, few men can boast of having a more agreeable person....but all this was insufficient to engage my affection, and I have a certain delicacy in my nature...which will not permit me, on any consideration whatever, to give my hand where my heart will not go.*
> *(The History of Jemmy and Jenny Jessamy, 1753)*

Frances Burney had included a highly emotive reaction to such an unwanted marriage in one of her drafts for *Camilla*:

> *I knew not til this moment the excess of my antipathy. By and by I thought I might endure him; but I feel now a fixed rooted abhorrence. Good heaven! To be his! Irrevocably his! To inhabit the same mansion- to bear the same name- to belong to him of right- impossible! Impossible!*

Ideal women did not acknowledge any sexual feeling. Some learned men even asserted that women did not possess any, but I always wondered how young women forced into marriage with partners not of their choosing may have considered the physical side of the relationships to come. Hidden amongst the texts are tiny revelations of their concerns, like references to marrying 'a grey bearded cupid' (Sarah Scott, *Millennium Hall,* 1762) or with a more explicit physical reference, 'The thought of being sacrificed to a man for whom it was impossible for her to have either love, or esteem; – or to be obliged to yield that through duty, which inclination shuddered at ...' (Eliza Haywood, *The History of Betsy Thoughtess*, 1751). There will be more to say on this when I look into marriage itself in detail in the next chapter.

Look closely at novels from the mid eighteenth century onwards, and more and more female characters declare their unwillingness to be forced into marriages, against their choice. Faced with a situation where they were told, 'when your father and I think proper to dispose of you, take care to obey us without murmuring' (Charlotte Lennox, *The Life of Harriet Stuart Written by Herself*, 1752), young women frequently complained, argued and defended their opposition regarding lack of freedom of choice in a marriage partner. They knew that being forced to marry someone without mutual love or respect could be a recipe for disaster. Hardwicke's Marriage Act of 1753 had been introduced with one of its primary aims being to prevent forced marriages, particularly where money, as in the case of a rich heiress, was concerned. It was this Act that brought in the marriage banns, marriages in churches and official recordings of the event. It is rather ironic that one of the heiresses protected by the Act was actually kidnapped by the grandson of the early feminist Priscilla Wakefield, and the marriage took place, but in 1827 the case went to trial and her grandson was sent to prison; the marriage over. Although in this case the marriage did not last, long term forced and arranged marriages did happen, for a variety of reasons, and within some cultures represented in this country, they still do today.

Charlotte Smith was one of the young women in the eighteenth century who was forced to marry someone of their parents' choice, in her case to get her out of the way when her father remarried; relations between her and the stepmother were not successful. As a female writer she was known to give some of her own opinions and details of her own experiences quite openly in her novels, much to the annoyance of the literary critics of the day. One of her female characters, a daughter being forced into marriage by her unfeeling father, was in despair:

> *The words I had heard, the dreadful command I had received, still vibrated in my ears and the horrors of my fate so forcibly presented to my mind, that the few distinct thoughts that passed through it pointed to suicide as the only way to escape a destiny I was utterly unable to support.*

Over the top perhaps, but it is not difficult to understand her point, especially when the father followed it up with a physical threat –'He declared in a voice that made me tremble like a leaf, that if I did not obey without remonstrance or hesitation, he knew how to punish and would punish me as I deserved.' (*Montalbert*, 1795)

I have previously mentioned that females were generally regarded as property of the male who was responsible for them – albeit their father, guardian or husband. This lack of individual status had serious consequences for women as they could potentially be 'disposed' of in anyway that was pleasing to that man, rather than themselves.The word 'disposed' is used remarkably frequently, even allowing for the alteration in actual meaning of words over time. Uncomfortable though it is for me personally considering females as property, I suppose it is understandable why chastity was so important in an unmarried girl; unspoiled goods had more value. Marriage could be a straightforward business contract between father and suitor unless the girl concerned was allowed her say. An innocent and unsuspecting girl could find herself disposed of without being involved in the process at all. Sarah Fielding noted this possibility in one novel, where the young girl was busy playing a game with the man who was to be her husband, without knowing anything about her father's arrangement:

> *He supposed my father had informed me that they two had agreed on a bargain. I replied, I did not know my father was of any trade or had any goods to dispose of; but if he had, and they could agree on their terms, he should have my consent, for I never interfered in any business of my fathers. (The Adventures of David Simple, 1744)*

Taking this idea of a female as property, it is not surprising that some women were aware of their lack of individual importance, and considered that they were nobodies. Frances Burney, in her own journal, addressed her writings to 'Nobody' and posed the basic question 'but, why, permit me to ask, must a female be made Nobody?'(*Early Diary of Frances Burney,* 1768-78, vol. 1) In one of her novels, the eponymous heroine Cecilia had run away and, when found, was actually advertised in a newspaper – as lost property:

> *Whereas a crazed young lady…ran into The Three Blue Balls (an inn)… on Thursday night, and has been kept there since out of charity…Whoever she belongs to is desired to send after her immediately. (Cecilia, 1782)*

If a female actually had money or property of her own, or was likely to inherit, she could easily be wooed into believing that a prospective suitor loved her for her own attributes, whereas the fundamental concern could easily be gaining the total rights over her wealth once the marriage had occurred. If a girl was susceptible to flattery, or had particular interests that could be pandered to, she could be in a vulnerable position indeed. Mrs Skinn was well aware of this aspect of eighteenth century marriage when she cynically had a male suitor state, 'I wish it was over, for I am weary of playing the lover and long to be handling the cash. – Ah, the dear chink of £20,000'! (*The Old Maid*, 1771) Similarly Jane West showed that the feelings of a future wife had no bearing on such considerations:

> *He on the other hand is too busy balancing the chances of the lady's fortune against her father's demands of settlement, and the possibility of privately clearing off his most pressing incumbrances, to consider his destined wife in any other light than as a necessary appendage, which entitles him to take possession. (A Tale of the Times, 1799)*

Undoubtedly some marriages were arranged for financial and social gain. But it was not just the suitors who hoped to improve their own personal affairs. Aspiring or tyrannical fathers who wished to be linked to higher social status or hoped for direct financial gain from the marriage could easily put pressure on their daughters to accept the appropriate male suitor, rather than them being able to freely choose for themselves. It cost money to feed, clothe, educate and entertain a daughter – with marriage she became the responsibility of another man. Emotional blackmail often featured in novels, with the ultimate threat of parental illness and death being a highly persuasive argument for a thoughtful and dutiful daughter to consider. I do not doubt that for some, it happened.

The whole point with examples like these is that they highlight how easy it was to pressurise females into submission – whether by using the financial argument, or abusing patriarchal privileges, or exploiting filial loyalty. The powerless female could be vulnerable in the matter of choice. After all:

> *Where was the female...who had not been persecuted by a cruel hard-hearted father, in favour of some one of the detested wretches by whom she was beset? Why then should she complain? Her sufferings were only such as, in the present depraved state of society, were the inevitable lot of her unhappy sex.*
> *(Elizabeth Hamilton, Memoirs of Modern Philosophers, 1800)*

Custom and law supported men at the expense of women, and that was not to change for many years.

There is of course a danger that I am painting a false picture here, writing with the benefit of modern hindsight and interpretation, for it would be unfair to say that all women despised the idea of marrying for money. Some undoubtedly chose to do so, for example those who wished to escape from parental authority, or were left without a father, home or income of their own, and those who were resigned to being married to a rich man not of their choosing. There was after all some compensation to be considered which women writers were aware of, even if they did not necessarily agree with or approve of them. Material possessions, family and household, finery and fashions, carriages and social life, trips perhaps for some to Bath, London and even abroad – all could provide entertaining distractions from a relationship that lacked love and affection. Some were to choose this route for themselves:

> *Always surrounded by admiring multitudes; or practising those accomplishments by which that admiration is acquired, they seem to be in danger of forgetting they have hearts – appearing to feel no preference for any person, but those who have the sanction of fashion, or the recommendation of great property; and affluent as they are themselves, to consider only among the men that surround them, who are likeliest to raise them to higher affluence or superior rank.*
> *(Charlotte Smith, Desmond, 1792)*

Others were to find that such compensations were not enough once the initial novelty factor had worn off. Sarah Fielding gave the example where one husband had swiftly grown old, ill and bad tempered so, 'She (the wife) had not lived long with him, before the only comfort she had was in the hopes of outliving him.' (*The Adventures of David Simple*, 1744) One had so many considerations to bear in mind before a decision was made.

Although many girls were prepared to accept their marriage partners, whether through free choice or persuasion, the idea of not marrying at all was being considered through the medium of the novels and the direct experience of the writers themselves. Some girls were to challenge the fundamental principle that marriage was good for you:

> *It could not be advisable for her to marry; for enjoying perfect content, she had no benefit to expect from change; and happiness was so scarce a commodity in this life, that whoever let it once slip, had little reason to catch it again. For what reason should she then alter her state? (Sarah Scott, Millenium Hall, 1762)*

This was not just a consideration of marrying for love; it went further than that. Would it be possible for a woman to choose not to marry, to live as a single woman accepted by society around her, fulfilling some useful purpose other than that of wife or mother? These were issues for the future.

Chapter Five
Marriage, For Better, For Worse...

And after many unimaginable hardships, trials and tribulations, the happy couple, the Lord and his Lady, the Prince and his Princess, finally reached their wedding day, and after due ceremony and glorious celebration, they said their fond farewells to the supporting cast of family and friends and drove off in their carriage to live happily ever after...

So runs the plot summary, with predictable ending, for many romances and fairy stories but the contents of this chapter will not be like that. When Frances Burney was sixteen she saw a wedding and recorded in her diary, 'How short a time does it take to put an eternal end to woman's liberty?' Marriage did not necessarily guarantee happiness in real life and it was to be a constant theme or subplot in many novels of the period, raising issues and grievances that would not in the main be resolved, even in part, until Victorian times or later. Marriage and the difficulties surrounding it have continued to be a constant theme in women's writing ever since. The trouble was that there were many assumptions made about marriage, by both men and women, which were to lead to serious difficulties when reality set in after the event. Problems for women were not always taken seriously, or were considered so trivial as to be unimportant, as William Hazlitt showed in his review of Frances Burney's last work, *The Wanderer – or Female Difficulties*. In the Edinburgh Review of February 1815 he stated, 'They are difficulties created out of nothing.' Apart from interventions on an individual basis, there were to be no general moves for change for many years.

Women writers were, as individuals, to take on a vital role here; they became spokeswomen 'wielding their pens', hoping to reform men and their behaviour towards women by highlighting the problems, guiding women towards alternatives and at least in theory showing men how they should behave. So many books of the period have cruel or tyrannical fathers, brothers, husbands – even lovers, before they underwent some reformation process during the plot. Laws and legal systems that allowed such behaviour to happen, however exaggerated by gothic horror settings, were to be questioned. Jane Austen was very sharp in *Northanger Abbey* when Henry Tilney was reprimanding Catherine Morland, saying it was impossible for such horrors to take place in society without people doing something about it:

> *Dear Miss Morland. Consider the dreadful nature of the suspicions you have entertained. What have you been judging from? Remember the country and the age in which we live. Remember that we are English, that we are Christians. Consult your own understanding, your own sense of the probable, your own observation... (1818)*

Jane Austen relied on her own observations and she knew better. During the course of the long eighteenth century, while many economic changes were taking place, women of the middling and upper classes of society were to have more leisure to reflect on their own situations and make comparisons. They were to become more aware of the inequalities and more able to express their own wishes. Not all marriages were bad, not all men were tyrants, but the whole institution of marriage was open to corruption and left women in a very vulnerable position.

I have already explained the necessity of marriage for most women in the previous chapter but there were other factors that influenced the attitude of women towards marriage and their behaviour during it. There was some questioning of the need to marry but few individual women apart from Mary Wollstonecraft were to openly challenge the institution per se. Marriage was a sacred institution, ordained by God and, as such, was:

> *... too sacred to be treated with Disrespect, too venerable to be the subject of Raillery and Buffoonery. It is the Institution of Heaven, the only honourable way of continuing Mankind, and far be it from us to think there could have been a better than infinite Wisdom has found for us. (Mary Astell, Some Reflections upon Marriage, 1700)*

Even though before Hardwicke's Marriage Act of 1753 it was not requisite to be married in a church, people frequently had chosen to do so – one of the reasons being that, 'Obligation would make a greater impression, and have more weight with those who enter'd in it, if celebrated in a place which was consecrated to divine worship.' (Eliza Haywood, *The History of Jemmy and Jenny Jessamy*, 1753) If you undertook your marriage vows seriously, you should always keep them and in so doing you helped contribute to 'the mass of happiness and virtue in the world'. (Amelia Opie, *Adeline Mowbray*, 1805)

Referring to the Bible again, many women also accepted that Eve deserved her punishment after her temptation in the Garden of Eden, and so Adam was rightly placed in charge of her. As Sarah Chapone affirmed in her correspondence during the mid eighteenth century, a husband 'may dispose of (his wife) when he sees fit, and then he may tell her what he thinks fit she should know, and order what he thinks fit she should do, and be a complete regulator of her conscience and actions also.' Similarly it had been noted some twenty years earlier that a wife:

> *… shall depend upon her Husband in all Matters of Pleasure, Diversion and Delight; her Desires should be circumscribed by his, whom she should reverence in Acquiescence to divine Authority: He should have the Supreme Command in his family and she should act in Subordination to him.*
> *(The Hardships of the English Laws in Relation to Wives with an Explanation of the Original Curse of Subjection passed on Women in an Humble Address to the Legislature. 1735)*

It was also said that marriage suited woman's nature perfectly; she was docile, created only to serve others. She was altruistic and was happy in her role, having no concerns for her own pleasures or satisfaction beyond it. The perfect woman indeed would say, 'All my happiness is centred within the limits of my own walls; and I grudge every moment that calls me from the pleasing scenes of domestic life.' (Hannah Foster, *The Coquette*, 1797) Some men even felt that a woman was not complete without a man in her life…

Marriage was also seen as 'the very Basis, Foundation and Cement of society ' (*Hardships of the English Laws,* 1735). It was seen as the way to increase the wealth of the nation, as well as its strength. Any real challenge to the institution of marriage by women could be interpreted as a danger to society, to the status quo – let alone the power of men within it. Making use of the Biblical subjugation of women in the Old Testament, and conveniently ignoring any more positive view of them, put men in a very strong position. Through marriage man and woman became one flesh; similarly in law the husband and wife were seen as one person. She was to be covered by him; his was the one flesh, the one person – through marriage she had lost her status as an individual. No longer would she, as a rule, hold property in her own right, even her children were considered as her husband's property. She had no legal rights over them. She needed his permission to leave his house and if she left without it, she could be forcibly returned and even locked up. There were to be many consequences for married women because of this 'coverage' and the subsequent loss of individual rights, which I will illustrate in some detail shortly. It is not surprising that one clergyman was to comment that religion had been a good friend to *man*kind, 'You may from this doctrine ... learn how great a friend religion is to the comfort and happiness of man in this life.' (John Sprint, *The Bridewoman Counsellor*, 1699)

As Mary Astell pointed out as early as 1700 there was a fundamental lack of respect for the female sex as a whole and, while it was accepted by many that woman was created for man, that did not give him the automatic right to abuse her. Man may have been given authority over her, but he did not have a carte blanche. A comment like the following was by no means unknown:

> Tis granted the woman was created for the man, but we deny that this is any pretence to use the limited power which Heaven has given him to the unhappiness and ruin of a creature that was made for him.
> (*Eugenia, The Female Advocate; or a Plea for the just Liberty of the Tender Sex and more particularly of Married Women*, 1770)

However it was not enough to just voice an opinion; merely naming the problem would never be sufficient to bring change. It was such a complex issue. Woman was dependent upon man, who was the very being causing the problems for her ... so would it even be in man's own interest to make changes? Mary Hays in her *Appeal to the Men of Great Britain in behalf of Women* (1798) optimistically thought that if men were only made to really understand the difficulties, they would certainly be prepared to make changes, or was she just being ironic? It is undoubtedly true that how a woman fared in marriage was dependent upon many factors – her own assumptions and beliefs obviously playing their own part – but much was to depend upon the beliefs and expectations of marriage held by the man she married; he was the one with status and power. While it is undeniable that both sexes had received years of conditioning prior to their wedding, the reality of the married state would depend to a large extent on the attitude of her husband; and she may not have been prepared for it by a brief courtship.

Let us look first at man's expectations – what could he look forward to once married? Putting aside for the moment any considerations of companionship, a man could anticipate an improvement in his personal domestic circumstances as, 'When a lady falls violently in love, the favoured gentleman has a right to expect that she will make an obliging attentive wife, rather more studious of his own humour, than devoted to the indulgence of her own.' (Jane West, *A Tale of the Times*, 1799) James Fordyce in his *Sermons to Young Women* (1766) stated that 'Men who understand the science of domestic happiness know its first principle is ease...' It was commonly accepted that 'The welfare and happiness of most families depend in a great measure on women.' (Sarah Fielding, *The Adventures of David Simple*, 1744) Indeed widowers left with children to look after often remarried quickly because of their domestic needs. A wife was to make the home agreeable for a husband, dealing with all domestic issues as well as bearing and rearing his children when the time came.

It was believed that women were so adaptable, so flexible, that they could be relied on to modify themselves to the needs of any man. They could be trained or 'educated' to suit his individual personal circumstances or needs. Advice from conduct books, such as that from Wetenhall Wilkes, emphasised the point:

> *If the love of a wife be tempered with a tolerable share of good sense, she will be sure never to have any private views of her own; nor do*

> *anything of consequence, which her husband may possibly dislike, without consulting him.*
> *(A Letter of Genteel and Moral Advice to a Young Lady, 1740)*

You may remember the quotation from Rousseau used in an earlier chapter; he felt that 'The first and most important qualification in a woman is good nature or sweetness of temper.' Maria Edgeworth described one such paragon, Sophia:

> *She had those habits of independent occupation, which are necessary to the wife of a professional man, who must have many hours to spend alone... She also had that cheerfulness of temper, readiness to converse or be silent, which are necessary to a man, whose mind is alternately engrossed with serious business, and in want of relaxation after tiresome exertion,- on his return home every evening, he was sure to find a smiling wife, a sympathising friend, a cheerful fireside, as delightful to the intellectual as to the corporeal labourer. (Patronage, 1814)*

Taken to extremes it is not difficult to see how it was possible to go from domestic harmony to a domestic nightmare if the husband expected to be very much the dominant partner. Eliza Haywood, who contributed much to the subject of matrimony in the eighteenth century, warned of characters like Mr Munden whose:

> *... notions of marriage had always been extremely unfavourable to the ladies;- he considered a wife no more than an upper servant, bound to study and obey, in all things, the will of him to whom she had given her hand;- and how obsequious and submissive he appeared when a lover, had fixed his resolution to render himself absolute master when he became a husband. (The History of Miss Betsy Thoughtless, 1751)*

Another key form of control a man could look forward to on his marriage was regarding money. Although it is fair to say that both men and women married for money, the resultant situation was hardly the same. A woman may have married a rich man, but it was *his* money. Unless a bride's family had undertaken a carefully detailed marriage settlement to protect her interests, once a marriage had taken place any wealth, property or other assets that belonged to her became the husband's property and therefore under his usage and control. Although negotiating a marriage settlement did seem like apparent mistrust of the future husband, to some wealthy families it may have seemed a wise precaution. Many women writers told of fortunes that had accompanied heiresses on their marriage and were subsequently squandered and lost by their husbands.

There are several important points here. Regarding the marriage settlement, I mentioned earlier that a judge had openly commented, 'He had hardly known an Instance, where the wife had not been kissed or kicked out of any such previous settlement.' (*The Hardships of the English Laws*, 1735) Mary Astell had also been aware of this some thirty years earlier when she wrote:

> *There have been too many instances of Husbands that by wheedling or threatening their wives, by seeming kindness or cruel usage, have persuaded or forced them out of what has been settled on them. So that the Woman has in truth no security but the Man's Honour and Good Nature, a security which in this present Age, no wise Person would venture much on. (Some Reflections upon Marriage, 1700)*

Certainly I am aware of at least two authors who were not afraid to be outspoken in their fictional works, who warned their readers of such possible events. Clara Reeve had Mrs Darnford advised to refuse her husband, who persisted in wanting her to give up her jointure, because it would ruin her. When she did refuse, her husband was displeased and she actually replied, 'You cannot be so base as to ask it.' (*School for Widows*, 1791) Charlotte Smith had Mrs Verney recalled by her husband from her retreat in the country in order to persuade her to give up her settlement so he could continue with his wild career. (*Desmond*, 1792)

Some supporters of English law proclaimed that laws existed in England to protect women, but if women were uneducated or unaware of these protections they were unable to have recourse to them, and a man with knowledge of the world would be only too aware of how to set circumstances to his advantage. *The Hardships of English Laws in Relation to Wives* had highlighted the problem:

> *If we reflect how extremely ignorant all young Women are as to points in the Law, and how their Education and way of Life, shuts them out*

> *from Knowledge of their true Interest in almost all things, we shall find that their Trust and Confidence in the Man they love and inability to make use of the Falsehood, leave few in a Condition to make use of that Precaution. (1735)*

It had been of major concern to some members of the aristocracy that a rich heiress could be forced into marriage, and thus out of her inheritance. This resulted in moves being made towards changing the laws regarding marriage in the mid eighteenth century. There was also concern that a family's estate could in effect be diluted by it being transferred to an unsuitable partner if the marriage was unannounced (e.g. with an elopement) and therefore uncontested. Hardwicke's law of 1753 was supposed to change all that, introducing marriage banns, full registration of marriage with witnesses and the service being performed in church. At least with Hardwicke control of her fortune would go to an approved man, but it was to have other consequences for women which we will come to later.

Even for women who expected financial support from their husbands problems could arise. Women writers like Charlotte Smith and Mary Robinson were misled about their husbands' financial situation or future prospects, which meant them living in unexpected poverty, even prison, and always having to struggle to maintain themselves and their families. It was not a criminal offence to mislead a future wife – yet the situation has an interesting parallel. Some men were undoubtedly influenced by the beauty of their wives to be, after all much time and attention was, as we know, paid to the all-important task of catching a husband. Yet I wonder how many people know that in 1770 Parliament passed a statute saying if women seduced men into matrimony:

> *... by means of scents, paints, cosmetics, washes, artificial teeth(!), false hair, Spanish wool, iron stays, hoops, high heeled shoes (!) or bolstered hips(!), (they) shall incur the penalty of the law now in force against witchcraft and like demeanours and the marriage shall become null and void.*

So much for marrying under false pretences...

As Mary Hays (in her *Appeal*, 1798) pointed out, man's expectation of marriage was very much linked to his image of the ideal woman. That in itself may not sound unreasonable: a woman may have held a romantic view of man in the same way, however if beauty alone had been a key element in matrimonial choice, problems would arise later when beauty faded. Women who were less than beautiful or ageing could face neglect, contempt and derision. To marry for looks, even to marry for money, did not provide an ideal basis for a long-term relationship and women were increasingly aware of that. In exchange for the domestic and familial duties expected of her if love and affection faded quickly a wife could feel somewhat taken for granted if she kept her vows faithfully. In addition to which a married woman was very much tied to her home, while her husband at least could venture into the world and spend much of his time away from it, on business interests, socialising with his friends or even entertaining other women. Mary Wollstonecraft referred to such a neglected wife as, 'the patient drudge, who fulfils her task, like a blind horse in a mill, (and then) is defrauded of her just reward.' (*A Vindication of the Rights of Woman*, 1792)

There could be other problems in store for women who frequently were left at home while their husbands pursued business interests or pleasure activities elsewhere. They could suffer from feelings of loneliness and isolation, particularly if the wife concerned was not an educated woman and had few pursuits of her own. Women needed tasks to keep them busy while the menfolk were away. Many references were made to needlework as a pastime – i.e. a way to pass the time. For those who had unhappy marriages in store an absentee husband would not necessarily be a bad thing, but for a bored and lonely housewife there could be dangers too. If she were to receive inadequate attention from her husband and was seen to be unhappy, it would not be impossible that she would receive the attentions of any male with particular pleasure. If the male was a rake and not averse to misleading or deceiving women it would be very easy to flatter an unhappy wife and in time lead her astray. Many novels touch on the possible consequences of neglecting a sensitive wife – but the actual issue of women having affairs will be dealt with in the next chapter.

So when the honeymoon period was over the dawn of realisation could set in. Either partner may have received a severe shock when it was discovered that the other half did not match their expectations or hopes. Mary Astell had warned that a glittering bride 'will find a terrible disappointment when the hurry is over, and when she comes calmly to consider her condition, and views it no more under a false Appearance, but as it truly is.' (*Reflections upon Marriage*, 1700) Nearly a century later Frances Burney used the character of Mrs Lissen to illustrate how a young girl, with aims of becoming her own mistress, and gaining a freedom she had not experienced at home under her father, discovered that the reality of marriage was very different to what she had expected:

> *She found* ***her own house*** *the house of which she must take charge; being* ***her own mistress***, *having the burthen of superintending a whole family, and being* ***married***, *becoming the property of another, to whom she made over a legal right to treat her just as he pleased. And as she had chosen neither for character, nor for disposition, neither for sympathy nor respect, she found it hard to submit where she meant to become independent, and difficult to take the cares where she had made no provision for the solaces of domestic life. (Camilla, 1796)*

Mary Wollstonecraft similarly stressed that if a woman had been treated like a goddess before marriage she would be most unlikely to be content with the position thereafter of an upper servant. (*A Vindication of the Rights of Woman*, 1792) A period of adjustment may have been necessary on both sides.

There were many books to advise women on appropriate behaviour, written by both men and women. Several have already been referred to during the course of this book. Even characters within novels were to give young women advice on how to make marriage successful. Back to Eliza Haywood again, Lady Trusty was to advise Betsy Thoughtless (who had become Mrs Munden) that her happiness would depend on how she acted, and although she should have respect for herself, she should yield to her husband to oblige him in matters of dispute, and she should not notice any of his errors or attempt to correct him. She also warned Betsy that she should be very careful of her behaviour as a married woman in general although, 'There is no necessity that because you are a wife, you should become a mope.' (*The History of Betsy Thoughtless*, 1751) Taken to extreme one of Mary Hay's characters, Mrs Neville, was to be one such mope:

> *I sought in his eyes to read and to prevent his wishes; I modelled to his temper, my character, my words, my actions, even the expression of my feelings. I had no individual existence; my very being was absorbed into that of my husband. I was the slave...*
> *(A Victim of Prejudice, 1799)*

Once married, women were expected to behave in an appropriate way, 'In fact, a woman should never expose herself to any hazard.'(Maria Edgeworth, *Patronage*, 1814) The rather unorthodox Emma Courtney, when married, found herself told off by her husband's assistant for inappropriate behaviour after she attempted to care for an injured man:

> *'Mrs Montague', said he in an emphatic tone- 'in your sympathy for a stranger do not forget other relations' 'I do not need, sir, to be reminded by you of my duties...' (Mary Hays, Memoirs of Emma Courtney, 1796)*

Married women also assumed a more dignified status in society. They were generally treated with respect; after all they had become someone's special property and were legally covered by him and should take their responsibilities seriously. Any misdemeanour could reflect badly on her husband for, 'The honour of a husband is sometimes in the custody of a wife,' (Charlotte Smith, *The Young Philosopher*, 1798) *and* she was now dependent upon him. Little marks of respect were given to married women in open society, for example newly married Lydia in *Pride and Prejudice* (1813) took great delight in rubbing in the fact that she had married before her elder sisters Jane and Elizabeth, and could thus lead in to dinner in precedence over them.

A wife was bound by law and by duty to her husband, and religion has already been shown to be a key element in this too. Some women were to argue that by taking a high moral stance, women could take on the reform of a licentious society that was much in need of improvement. The philandering ways of the Prince of Wales, later George IV, and the leading *ton* – the self-indulgent members of the aristocracy – led to much moral criticism from many lesser members of society. Women like Hannah More, Jane West and others wrote to educate women particularly in order to raise moral standards and behaviour. A married woman could provide an exemplary role model for society around her; she could influence her servants, raise her children appropriately and, many believed, her behaviour could even lead to the reform of selfish, unruly and even unfaithful men. Novels based on conduct book advice were very reassuring, 'The practice of virtue is not so difficult as we imagine... Habit will soon make it easy for us.'(Elizabeth Griffith, *The Delicate Distress*, 1769) They also gave detailed examples within the plot so an ideal wife would know how to handle situations that may have confronted her.

Conduct books gave some advice that may seem rather strange to modern readers. Whereas it is not unknown nowadays to hear such statements as 'Once a cheat always a cheat', dutiful wives in the long eighteenth century were being advised to ignore any devious or unwelcome behaviour in their husbands. One character, Lady Straffon, wrote, 'If we wish to be happy, we must make it a constant rule, to turn away our eyes.' (*Ibid*) The alternative was to suffer – and many women did. Comments like the following appeared frequently during the period, 'Inured to disappointments and sorrows, she bore what was related to herself with the calmest resignation... and was never heard to complain.' (Charlotte Smith, *Marchmont,* 1796) If a woman took no notice of her husband's extra marital affairs, avoided any critical comment and preferably showed no signs of distress, according to conduct book theory the man would be so shamed by the contrasting behaviour of his virtuous wife, that he would turn over a new leaf and become, in time, a perfect husband, and it would be all thanks to her. Perhaps I am being rather cynical here, but to me it sounded rather more like wishful thinking when one Lady heard about her husband's behaviour in such a situation. He, Sir William, had informed his friend that her behaviour, '...had not only made him esteem, and admire, but love (her) also, a thousand degrees more, than he had ever done before. He declared, that he felt the impatience of a lover, to throw himself at (her) feet, and felt he never should forgive himself, for having rendered (her) unhappy, by his infamous conduct.' (Elizabeth Griffith, *The Delicate Distress*, 1769)

Jane West, who has a reputation for being a more conservative writer of the period, took great care to show too that although a woman may choose to ignore her husband's misbehaviour, it did not by any means remove the pain or distress when he was unfaithful, and how it must have been hard not to react when you cared so much:

> *I am the mother of his children, the faithful repository of his secrets, the partner of his sorrows. I have soothed his anxieties, composed his ruffled temper and watched him in sickness…words cannot express how much this agonised heart preferred his interest and happiness to my own. (A Tale of the Times, 1799)*

Even spinsters like Martha Taylor were to give advice to unhappy wives, warning that if a wife complained things would undoubtedly get worse, and they should actually look for blame within their own behaviour. A letter written by her in 1736 explained that the art of being a good wife consisted simply of her studying the likes and dislikes of her husband, in order to make herself and his house more agreeable to him than anyone or anywhere else. Women were made to feel guilty; it was their responsibility if a marriage fell into difficulties and it was their fault if it failed. Conduct book advice taught them to, 'Think not of the natural fickleness of man, but tremble lest the world suppose that the husband's infidelity proceeds from our own want of attractions to hold him faithful.' (Mary Robinson, *The False Friend,* 1799) The absolute classic for me was from Fordyce's *Sermons* of 1766. I think it is worth quoting at length:

> *I am astonished at the folly of many women, who are still reproaching their husbands for leaving them alone, for preferring this or that company to theirs, for treating them with this or the other mark of disregard or indifference; when to speak the truth they have themselves in a great measure to blame…* ***had you behaved to them with more respectful observance, and a more equal tenderness; studying their humours, overlooking their mistakes, submitting to their opinions in matters indifferent, passing by little instances of unevenness, caprice or passion, giving soft answers to hasty words, complaining as little as possible, and making it your daily care to relieve their anxieties and prevent their wishes, to enliven the hour of dullness, and call up the ideas of felicity,*** *(my emphasis) I doubt not you would have maintained and even increased their esteem… and your house might at this day have been the abode of domestic bliss.*

In other words, if they gave way to men in everything, ignored any unpleasant behaviour, waited on them hand and foot and did everything to please them, men would not leave their wives and look for pleasures elsewhere. With advice like that it is not surprising that some women complained about unfair treatment and their lives being similar to slavery.

There has been some speculation by modern day readers as to whether the conduct books and women's 'behaviour' were somewhat of a 'chicken and egg' situation. Were women behaving badly – as far as men, and even some of their own sex, were concerned – and so conduct books written to correct it? Or were conduct books written first and then women began to rebel against their restrictive recommendations? Certainly women did complain about their treatment. Fordyce obviously was aware of it and there are many examples of discontent in marriage, although most women still supported it as an established social and religious institution – but then they did have few alternatives for self-preservation unless independently financially secure.

There were several key areas for discontent – the drudgery of their role as wives, the abuse that some of them undoubtedly suffered, and the legal and social inequalities – including the sexual double standard – that allowed the situation to continue. If a woman accepted her role as a dutiful wife in the long eighteenth century, then it was necessary to accept a submissive, subservient position in her own home. According to the conduct books women were expected to endure whatever difficulties they faced in marriage. Knowing that someone would probably say it was their fault anyway, they would have to endure it. There were frequent references to parallels with slavery, being at a master's beck and call for whatever task was required. One wedding day was described thus, 'This morning began the slavery of Charlotte Danby and my horrid cousin, and left your Emily to her darling freedom' (Mrs Skinn, *The Old Maid,* 1771) Mary Wollstonecraft was to put it more forcefully, 'Is one half of the human species, like the poor African slaves, to be subject to prejudices that brutalize them, when principles would be a surer guard, only to sweeten the cup of man?' (*A Vindication of the Rights of Woman*, 1792) Mary Robinson was also to use the example when referring to an old man who had married a girl young enough to be his granddaughter, 'She had been purchased as the merchant buys the slave and her lot was more terrible than even that of the ill fated Negro.' (*Hubert de Savrac*, 1796)

Although I have found few examples of writing from lower class women, it is interesting to note that even some of them managed to write complaints about the life they led as wives. Mary Collier wrote *The Woman's Labour* in 1739 and a small excerpt will be sufficient to show that a few of her complaints may be just as valid for a working woman today:

No Learning ever was bestow'd on me;
My Life was always spent in drudgery:
And not alone; alas! With grief I find,
It is the portion of poor Woman-kind.

After working in the field all day she returns home to her husband and family:

We must make haste, for when we Home are come,
Alas! we find our Work just begun;
So many Things our Attendance call,
Had we ten Hands, we could employ them all.
Our Children put to bed with greatest Care
We all Things for your coming Home prepare:
You sup and go to Bed without delay,
And rest yourselves till the ensuing Day;
While we, alas! But little sleep can have,
Because our Children cry and rave;
Yet without fail, soon as Day-light doth spring,
We in the field again our Work begin...

The domestic work a woman had to do, whether aided by servants or not, was frequently a thankless task. One woman wondered whether wives were truly appreciated by their husbands:

Were it not for (our care of them) their Houses would be meer Bedlams, their most luxurious Treats, but a rude confusion of ill Digested, ill mixt Scents and Relishes, and the fine Furniture, they bestow so much cost on, but an expensive heap of glittering Rubbish. Thus they are beholding to us for the comfortable enjoyment of what their labour, or good Fortune, hath acquir'd or bestow'd, and think meanly of our care,

only because they understand not the value of it.
(Judith Drake, From an Essay in Defence of the Female Sex, 1696)

Not everyone felt such criticism was justified. Mary Astell was to comment that, 'The duty a woman was obliged to pay her husband was only a Business by the bye. Just as it may be any Mans Business and Duty to keep Hogs; he was not made for this but if he hires himself out to such an employment he ought to conscientiously perform it.' (*Some Thoughts on Marriage*, 1700) In other words she had chosen to marry, she knew her duty and should carry it out. It may not sound very sympathetic, but on a purely domestic level, at that time, the point was valid. If, however, her husband felt that fulfilling such a duty was all she was capable of, or treated her merely as his toy or plaything without respecting her, then that was another matter. Several writers were to refer to men as spoilt children, or the fact we ought to amuse them – as you shake a rattle to keep a child quiet (Mary Wollstonecraft, *A Vindication of the Rights of Woman*, 1792) – but there were rather more serious causes for concern.

As briefly mentioned earlier, one major criticism of marriage as it stood then was the fact that women were in a very vulnerable position and a husband could easily become a tyrant, and he had the law on his side. So in what form did the tyranny of husbands manifest itself, and why was so little done about it? For some the change in the behaviour of their chosen partner was to be a dramatic one, 'Where is there a Woman, who having generously trusted her liberty with a Husband, does not immediately find the spaniel metamorphosed into a tyger?' (Sophia, *Woman not Inferior to Man*, 1739) The key issue here was that in agreeing to marry, the law removed a woman's rights as an individual and gave them to her husband. He took over her property and her person and had full control over them. If a man was as considerate, loving, kind and thoughtful as a wife wished him to be, there may have been few problems. But what could happen if he wasn't? Let us begin with the notion of a wife being his property – on marriage everything she owned now became his. Maria Wollstonecraft was very much aware of the difficulties here, 'A wife being as much a man's property as his horse or his ass, she has nothing she can call her own... He may use any means to get at what the law considers his, the moment his wife is in possession of it.' (*The Wrongs of Woman or Maria*, 1798) The situation she foresaw reminds me somewhat of a poem about a toddler I read recently, 'If I want it, it's mine; if I see it, it's mine; if it's yours, it's mine...' For Charlotte Smith such a situation was a reality – her husband wasted their money, left her with the children and, when she was forced to write for money to maintain the family, he used to turn up to take the proceeds when she was paid. Much of her correspondence shows her distress and depression while facing such financial difficulties.

A wife was dependent upon the financial generosity of her husband and several authors who had direct experience of this (like Charlotte Smith and Mary Robinson) make references to husbands making light of financial resources while they were out, gambling for example, while the wife remained at home trying to make ends meet. The wife was also dependent upon him for any freedoms she wanted within marriage, for example paying visits to friends and family. If he did not approve or did not want her absent from home he was perfectly within his rights to refuse permission and there was little she could do about it. If allowed to go she would have not only needed transport, but also money and an escort – as it was unseemly for a woman to travel alone. Even Jane Austen relied heavily for much of her life on the kindness of her male relatives to take her and bring her home when she was on a social visit. If a wife chose to leave permanently, for reasons of unhappiness, her husband was perfectly within his rights to pursue her, and forcibly make her return to his home. He was also able to lock up his wife, even in a madhouse, and punish her in whatever form he thought fit, providing it wasn't life threatening – Maria Edgeworth gave the sadistically humorous example in *Castle Rackrent* of a husband first humiliating, then locking up his Jewish wife and only giving her pork to eat! (1800) A more serious example of abusive treatment of wives came from real life, where there is a record of an Old Bailey trial from the period where a Mr Veezey had imprisoned his wife *for years* without clothing or a fire. He had horsewhipped her and she had eventually flung herself out of a window. He was acquitted of her murder – because there was evidence of mouldy bread in the room, i.e. he had not starved her and he had not personally pushed her! (*Hardships of the English Laws in Relation to Wives*, Case 4)

A husband also became responsible for a wife's behaviour and, if he did not approve of it, he could correct it. Wife beating was never unknown and, after a legal decision in 1782, providing a stick did not exceed the girth of a man's thumb it was permissible to use it as a means of physical correction. Alternatively he could use his hand or anything else. Even a male novelist like Samuel Richardson, so supportive to women writers of the time, showed in his characterisation of a rake, Lovelace proudly proclaiming how in terms of tormenting, 'We begin, as boys with birds, and, when grown up, go onto women.' (*Clarissa*, 1747/8)

There are various examples of physical abuse towards women during the period. Mary Wollstonecraft's mother was badly beaten and Virginia Woolf made a well-known comment, that had Mary not witnessed such ill treatment her views on men may have been vastly different and her writing style less of a contrast to Jane Austen's. Frances Burney's sister Susanna was abused. She was forced to spend prolonged absences away from her family and friends and her son was deliberately sent away from her at home. Susanna also suffered various forms of direct mistreatment from her husband – not all of which was she prepared to describe to her sister. Even so, Frances did try to persuade her sister to stay in her marriage and only really intervened when Susanna became ill. It is possible that subsequently she felt guilty about this early lack of intervention – that is, after Susanna's death.

Reflecting situations from real life, and drawing attention to the predicament of women tied into such abusive relationships, women novelists naturally included such problems as drunkenness and physical violence in their work. When they occurred as directly narrated incidents in the text they were deliberately shocking. If Mr Munden was really angry he would throw objects at his wife and even killed her pet deliberately in front of her. (Eliza Haywood, *The History of Betsy Thoughtless*, 1751) Another such example was when the eponymous heroine Indiana did not want to accompany her husband to the colonies. First he locked her in her room, but after her escape from a window he grabbed her hair, threw her down and kicked his boot on her forehead. (George Sand, *Indiana,* 1831)

You may wonder why more was not done at this stage to protect women from abuse. In theory public opinion or the interference of relatives may have provided a safety net for abused wives, but the trouble was, just as in modern times, much of it could go on behind closed doors and a frightened woman would not want to risk further maltreatment by exposing her sufferings. Mrs Skinn highlighted the problem through the fictional experiences of Mrs Sandham. In private her husband struck her, called her 'shocking names' and generally abused her, but in public he behaved very differently. In this way he was able to prejudice her family and friends against her, and make her look foolish. It was only when he behaved badly in public, hitting not only her, but also her friend Emily who tried to assist her, that others intervened. (*The Old Maid*, 1771) The problem was simple; a husband 'might beat his wife, ill treat his servants, ruin his children, that's no-one else's business. Society only condemns deeds which are harmful to it.' (George Sand, *Indiana*, 1831)

A rather unsavoury side of being considered a man's property was the sexual element of marriage. Where marriage had been arranged for financial reasons and involved a significant difference in ages I had wondered how a young girl would reconcile herself to the physical attentions it would be her duty to receive. For Helisenne de Crenne, (pseudonym of a French author Marguerite Briet) writing as early as 1538, when 'the old man kissed her … it was as though a slug has dragged itself across her charming face.' (*The Torments of Love*) Hannah Cowley was to question what right old men had to claim ownership and possession over women's young bodies, 'Tis very odd no, that those ancients should take it into their venerable noddles, that a youthful bride is a proper appendage to their dignity.' (*A School for Greybeards*, 1786) Robert Bage, who has already been shown to have some sympathy towards women's difficulties, was also aware of the problem, 'Indeed my lord there should be a little affection, be it no more than sufficient to prevent a nausea.' (*Hermsprong*, 1796) This is somewhat similar to the eponymous Mary in Mary Wollstonecraft's novel where:

> *When her husband would take her hand or mention anything like love, she would instantly feel a sickness, a faintness at her heart, and wish involuntarily that the earth would open up and swallow her.*

After a shocking incident of brutality in *The Adventures of Betsy Thoughtless*, referred to briefly above, where her husband grabbed her pet squirrel by its neck, and smashed it against the marble chimney, Betsy flew out of the room saying she 'would never eat or sleep with him again.' (Eliza Haywood, 1751) I had not come across such a direct reference before where a wife refuses intimacy, but in reality a wife could be divorced for not fulfilling the conjugal rights of her husband. After all, an earlier judicial decision had been made by Sir Matthew Hale that rape within marriage was not a criminal offence – and that decision was not revoked until the law changed in the mid nineteenth century. The complaint that such marriages were no more than legal prostitution was raised by several important women writers during the period – Sarah Fielding, Mary Hays, Mary Ann Radcliffe and Mary Wollstonecraft to name but a few. Eliza Haywood too wrote similarly:

> *My husbands fondness increased for me everyday; but alas! The endearments of a man of his years are rather disgustful than agreeable; and I have often wish'd that as it is impossible that I should ever have any love for him, that he had less for me, in spite of the advantages I receive by it. (The History of Jemmy and Jenny Jessamy, 1753)*

For Mary Wollstonecraft, 'Personal intimacy without affection seemed to me the most degrading as well as the most painful state.' (*The Wrongs of Woman, or Maria,* 1798) Her own sister had indicated that she had suffered such sexual inconsideration and abuse in her marriage that eventually Mary and her other sisters helped to rescue Bess from her inconsiderate husband. I was very surprised to come across one reference in a novel, by a male author, where a father threatened to force a girl to have her marriage consummated with total disregard for her physical or mental state. (Robert Bage, *Hermsprong*, 1796) So far I have not yet come across a woman writer who went this far, although rape or forced sex within marriage were frequently mentioned.

Women were not supposed to have sexual feelings or passions in the same way as men, and so they were often disregarded when other people considered marriage for them. Women were discouraged from talking about this side of their relationship, but they were obviously aware of it – even if references were not generally as explicit as they were to become, both in Victorian times and later. Although this next quotation is from the 1860's and is therefore approximately thirty years after my period ends, it is still I think worth using to illustrate just how open women were to become with their discontent. It is one of the most shocking things I have ever read in my research of women's literature:

His arm is round my waist and he is brushing my arms and my cheeks, and brow with his somewhat bristly mustache as often as he feels inclined – for am I not his property? Has he not every right to kiss my face off if he chooses, to clasp me and hold me and drag me about in whatever manner he wills, for has he not bought me? For a first class pair of eyes warranted fast colour, for ditto superfine red lips, for so many pounds of prime white flesh, he has paid a handsome price on the nail, without any haggling, and now if he may not test the worth of his purchases, poor man he **is** *hardly used! As for me, I sit tolerably still, and am not yet actually sick, and that is about all that can be said of me. (Rhoda Broughton, Cometh up as a Flower, 1867)*

Shocking indeed. But it captures the idea of women as property and at least one woman's feelings about the sexual side of it extremely well. (Other problems regarding sex, particularly the question of the double standard, are to be considered in the next chapter.)

Many forms of tyranny and abuse within marriage come under the heading of mental cruelty, and there is an abundance of evidence that it existed during the period. Once again it had much to do with a man's opinion of women, and how much or how little he valued them. Some women writers like Charlotte Lennox had direct experience of it, others like Mary Astell witnessed it, even Jane Austen referred to it. Problems could easily arise if an intelligent woman had married a man who had less than her ability. Mary Robinson, writing under her pseudonym Anne Frances Randall, asked:

Supposing destiny, or interest or chance, has tied a man confessedly of weak understanding and corporeal debility, to a woman strong in all powers of intellect, and capable of bearing the fatigues of a busy life: is it not degrading to humanity that such a woman should be the passive, the obedient slave of such a husband?
(A Letter to the Women of England on the Injustice of Mental Insubordination, 1799)

Arbitrary decision-making could easily lead to a 'discussion' about alternatives and it was not uncommon for an argument to end 'because I said so'- no matter how insensitive or foolish the decision had been. Charlotte Lennox was supposed to have been a dutiful wife for many years, putting up with her husband's foibles without complaint, but in her work *Euphemia*, (1790) the cracks were beginning to show and there were many examples of real life situations that can have only come from experience. She discovered it was not worth arguing with him, or commenting on foolish decisions he had been responsible for. He would go into a rage if he were losing an argument, and just kept on pursuing her aggressively until she gave in anyway. Charlotte Smith had similar experiences with her husband and showed one of her male characters, Mr Vyvian, in similar vein, 'He contrived to do exactly what he could to make his wife miserable, and then quarrelled with her because she could not...always conceal her wretchedness.' (*Montalbert*, 1795)

Constant belittling and undermining are known nowadays to have disastrous effects on self-esteem; modern theorists and practitioners alike warn of the need for praise and encouragement, and not just during childhood. It is a valid point that unless you have experienced such negative, abusive treatment or witnessed its effects, it is easy to underestimate the damage it causes. As Amelia Opie wrote, 'Many a conjugal union which has never been assailed by the battery of crime, has fallen a victim to the slowly undermining power of petty quarrels, trivial unkindnesses and thoughtless neglect.' (*Adeline Mowbray*, 1805) Similar to the poem by Emily Dickinson quoted in my introduction was the line, 'Poor I was, an insignificant monosyllable that had no kind of meaning.'(Clara Reeve, *The School for Widows*, 1791) In the early eighteenth century Sarah Cowper kept a diary during her unhappy years of marriage to Sir William Cowper. In describing his behaviour where he was 'ever opposing and contradicting the most different harmless desires that may be, (and) must render himself but an uncomfortable companion,' she made a plea that must have been echoed by women throughout the centuries – 'O Lord give patience.'

Mary Astell gave a more thorough description of the problem:

To be yoked for life to a disagreeable person and temper, to have folly and ignorance tyrannise over wit and sense, to be contradicted in everything one does and says, and borne down not by reason but authority, to be denied ones most innocent desires for no other cause but the will and pleasure of an absolute lord and master, whose follies a woman with all her prudence cannot hide and whose commands she

cannot but despise at the same time she obeys them, is a misery none can have a just idea of but those who have felt it.
(Some Reflections upon Marriage, 1700)

There are obvious similarities here with the Atticus principle mentioned in my introduction – unless you step inside someone shoes you cannot fully appreciate what their life is like. Charlotte Lennox raised another interesting thought, 'To die for the man one loves is not such an act of heroism, as to chose misery with the man one has no reason to love, because it is one's duty.' (*Euphemia*, 1790) Mary Ann Hanway was to show a possible consequence of living under such a strain over a prolonged period of time – for Sir Denis did not value his wife and:

... had by his boisterous manners, ill temper and tyrannical disposition, occasioned her to die of that disease – a broken heart; which though not named in the bills of mortality, causes some thousands of his majesty's liege subjects to sink every year quietly into their graves. (Ellinor, 1793)

Mary Astell also warned that men must ultimately expect some reaction from women in such a long-suffering situation:

Can you expect woman to be entirely subjected to a man of corrupt nature? Will an ignorant weak woman have patience to bear continual outrage and insolence all the days of her life – unless you suppose her a very Ass! ... the Italians say, An Ass though slow if provok'd will kick. (Some Reflections upon Marriage, 1700)

But while women were obviously complaining about their treatment, they may have wondered what good could it do them if such legal decisions were made as, for example, one by Sir William Scott in 1790 which ruled that:

Mere austerity of temper, petulance of manners, rudeness of language, a want of civil attention and accommodation, even occasional sallies of passion; if they do not threaten bodily harm, do not amount to legal cruelty.

Mental cruelty did not seem to count; in a nutshell – 'Oh woman, poor subdued woman, thou art dependent mentally upon the arbitrary customs of man'. (Frances Burney, *The Wanderer*, 1814) Mary Robinson, writing as Anne Randall, raised a similar point:

> *Supposing that a woman has experienced every insult, every injury that her vain, boasting, high bearing associate man can inflict ... she has no remedy. She appeals to the feeling and reflective part of mankind; they pity but they do not seek to redress her, she flies to her own sex, they not only condemn, but they avoid her.*
> *(A Letter to the Women of England, 1799)*

Strictly speaking this comment did not apply to everyone – for apart from discovering sympathetic publishers like Joseph Johnson and Samuel Richardson, and a few supportive husbands like Frances Burney's Monsieur D'Arblay, I found some men not only openly supported women's emancipation, but also were actively prepared to put it in writing and put their names to it. William Thompson so respected Anna Wheeler's views on women's position in society, which were in accordance with his own, that he counted her as his co-author of the book, *Appeal of One Half of the Human Race, Women, against the Pretensions of the Other Half, Men, to retain them in Political and thence Civil and Domestic Slavery*. (1825) Her negative experiences of marriage played a significant part in the development of his work, and he acknowledged that although she had not actually written up her ideas, he was doing it for her. Later authors downplayed her contribution so I am not surprised if you have never heard of her. For Thompson and Wheeler marriage was a form of slavery, where men kept women under their domination for their own convenience, 'Home is the prison house of the wife, the house is his house with everything in it, and of all the fixtures most abjectly his, is his breeding machine the wife.' Thompson was ostracised by society for his pains, and Anna Wheeler conveniently forgotten.

What all these examples show though is that, far from completely accepting the status quo, courageous women in various forms were questioning the rights of men to abuse the authority they held in marriage, as well as their own lack of means to remove themselves from such situations. But as Mary Hays said, 'The greatest difficulty is to bring men to consider the subject with attention.' (*Appeal*, 1798). It was very much to men's advantage if women were dependent upon them for everything. It was even argued that if women had any form of financial independence – for example a personal allowance – it could have a negative effect on the marital relationship as it 'makes a wife independent, and destroys love, by putting it out of a man's power to lay any obligation on her that might engage gratitude and kindle affection.'(Samuel Richardson, *The Rambler*, No.97) In other words if a man did not have some power and control over woman, she would not necessarily find any reason to love him. Once again it could be argued that by providing for her, he was buying her affections, but he could also control her through fear. Fear of what the law could allow a husband to do, fear of being left without provision in marriage or maintenance, fear of being locked up in a madhouse, fear of public scandal or the shame of divorce. Women should not question the authority and precedence of the status quo.

In general only outspoken individual women like Mary Wollstonecraft were to comment so directly on 'the absurdity of the marriage laws, which, till divorces could be more easily obtained, was the most insufferable bondage'. (*The Wrongs of Woman*, 1798) Initially her work, *The Vindication of the Rights of Woman*, was popular and sold well, and her ideas had gained much support. However, after her death and her husband's revelations about her earlier relationships and illegitimate child, Mary's radical ideas became associated with loose or fallen women, and so it became dangerous for other women to openly support them. It was to be many years before Harriet Martineau, in her autobiography, was to emphasise the need for *virtuous* women to be upholders of radical ideas for them to carry weight, and thus be more likely to attract general support. She wrote, 'The best friends of the cause are the happy wives and busy cheerful single women who have no injuries of their own to avenge, and no painful vacuity or mortification to relieve.' (1877) Mary Hays was on safer ground, and probably spoke for many women when she wrote, 'The female sex should be protected by explicit and indisputable laws, from insult and oppression.' She had felt that women were denied the opportunity to tell the truth about the real situation in marriage for them, 'But man! tyrant man! ye cannot forgive that the lips should utter, what rises warm from the heart, if it does not chime in with your present feelings' (*Appeal*, 1798).

Lawyers themselves were to come under criticism too, not just the laws they operated. Charlotte Smith was not alone in her repetitive condemnation of lawyers and how in her situation they manipulated the law to their own ends at her, and her children's, expense. Her husband would have wasted any legacy left for her directly, but it took many years to actually obtain the legal entitlement bequeathed by her sympathetic father-in-law to her children. Lawyers seemed to enjoy using jargon and process to confound females less familiar with legal systems and they regularly appeared in negative forms in women's literature of the period. Only women who had supportive family members, or friends, who were themselves lawyers – like Elizabeth Bulwer Lytton (mother of the Victorian writer and politician, Edward Bulwer Lytton) and her brother – seem to have been in a position where they could make sure the law did actually protect them and directly benefit from it.

The actual legal reforms that were necessary to begin the improved status of women in marriage would not start to appear until the 1850's, where changes in property rules and infant custody gave married women some improvements in their situation. When Mary Robinson had raised the issue of a female's entitlement to inherit in her own right, in 1797, it was considered going too far. At the end of the novel, *Walsingham,* it was discovered that her hero, Sidney, was actually a female and had been dressed from birth and reared completely as a boy, in order to keep an inheritance that would otherwise have gone to a male relative. What a dreadful idea!

The 1850's were also to see major changes regarding abusive relationships for the 1853 Assault Act allowed that violent husbands could be convicted, and in 1857 the new Matrimonial Court recognised women's rights to be released from abusive marriages altogether. But until then, in spite of individual writers calling for the need for legal reformation, married women had to put up with the situations in which they found themselves. Besides which, religious and basic conduct book advice always told you not to make a fuss, to accept your punishment, to do your duty and look to the next world for an improvement in your circumstances. Eighteenth century books are full of such sentiments. Through one's sufferings in this life, one gained the approval of the Almighty and gained a place in Heaven. Life on earth could be awful, but things would improve after death. Hence,

'Rise above it then and prove yourself superior to the adverse difficulties which have befallen you,' (Hannah Foster, *The Coquette*, 1797) and on judgement day itself, 'the Laws for Equality will then be forever set Right and *She that humbleth herself shall be exalted*.' (*The Hardships of the English Laws*, 1735) Mary Astell herself explained the important role religion was to play for women during the period:

> *This makes her a sufficient compensation for all the neglect and contempt the ill grounded customs of the world throw on her, for all the injuries brutal power may do her, and is a sufficient cordial to support her spirits be her lot in this world what it may.*
> *(Some Reflections upon Marriage, 1700)*

With men being reluctant to change, and laws preventing it, progress would inevitably be slow, but to be fair some of the problems women faced have to be seen as part of the consequences of their own actions. This may be uncomfortable reading, but while women were content to lead limited lives, and accept low societal expectations of themselves, little progress for women overall would be made, and individual protests would stand out as exceptions to the norm and could thus be discounted. Let me explain this – if women in general accepted the role of subservience and the dominance of patriarchy, and trained their young families to accept the status quo then the system *would* be perpetuated. Mary Hays clearly pointed out that, 'All opinions degrading to women are founded in ignorance, supported by force of habit, by an authority once established, and *by the tacit acquiescence of the injured party*.' (*Appeal*, 1798- my emphasis) The very fact that women accepted this was taken as proof that they were really inferior. What few seemed to be aware of was that, while women made no negative comment or reaction towards abusive or inconsiderate behaviour, let alone unfaithfulness, they were, albeit unwittingly, letting the men get away with it. In one novel, *The Delicate Distress*, (Elizabeth Griffith, 1769) the wife even ended up volunteering to pay for a pension for her husband's mistress – so the mistress did not suffer when the husband regained his conscience!

Increased education gradually was to broaden women's horizons and show them possible alternatives to the lives they led. It would not always be the case that a woman 'was so ignorant of life that she thought resistance was impossible.' (*Indiana*, 1831) It is interesting to note that there was a slow but steady stream of books about how the laws affected women, written by women, from the early eighteenth century throughout Victorian times – just to raise women's awareness of the problems they could face. There was also an interesting question of logic posed:

> *When such laws were framed should not impartial lawgivers have first decreed ... to fix the national belief that the husband should always be wiser and more virtuous than his wife in order to entitle him with a show of justice, to keep this idiot or perpetual minor (i.e. woman) for ever in bondage? (Mary Wollstonecraft, The Wrongs of Woman, 1798)*

As education slowly raised the expectations of women, they began to realise that more was possible, even desirable, and began to make changes, however small, within the operation of their own family setting. Mary Astell had asked, 'What poor woman is ever taught she should have a higher desire than to get a husband? (*Reflections upon Marriage*, 1700) Outspoken individuals like Mary Wollstonecraft, Mary Hays and Mary Robinson, were well aware of this and wanted women to raise their expectations and achieve more of their latent potential. The first step was to have a greater level of self-respect, so that sheer drudgery or situations of abuse would not be acceptable. Others like Jane West and Hannah More wanted women to be more educated in order to fulfil their roles as wives more effectively, as I mentioned in an earlier chapter.

There was another handicap for the general progress of women, in that some women were reluctant to make changes. Within marriage they had found a niche where they could wield power, regardless of its limitations. For a strong woman, with or without a weaker husband, it was possible to rule over a domestic household. There were servants to control, decisions to be made, children to be reared and husbands to be managed. Mrs Skinn wrote:

> *I always said these imaginary lords of creation were mere babies, and I'm determined to have a pair of leading strings (baby reins) always ready for my mate ...that when I see him in the least inclinable to go astray, I may pin them on and set the little master right again.*
> *(The Old Maid, 1771)*

A highly amusing satire had been published in 1753, by Jane Collier, called *An Essay on the Art of Ingeniously Tormenting*, which showed various ways a woman could demonstrate power in petty ways over husbands and servants. Hence the advice, 'To master the art of tormenting, one must become a consummate manipulator, take pleasure in causing pain, and entertain only the most selfish views and wishes.' It is likely Jane Austen used this book when developing the character of Mrs Norris in *Sense and Sensibility*. According to the Essay, a wife could pick holes in everything her servants did, keep changing her mind and deny it, and regarding a husband there were an abundance of opportunities to make his life miserable. You could make him feel guilty if he went out, if he liked company take up sewing, if he liked women with traditional skills you could avoid them. You could be out of humour when your husband brought company home, or angry if he went out without you. And you could be troublesome if he let you accompany him. Women could just as easily become petty tyrants.

It was also said by some conduct book gurus that women could use their emotions to gain power over their husbands, and in this way gain some equality in the married situation, and this was in essence what many women wanted. Not in terms of power really but in terms of respect. To be treated fairly, to be a companion, not a slave. So many novels contrast caring, thoughtful male characters with unpleasant domineering inconsiderate ones that it is not difficult to appreciate the lesson that women writers were trying to teach. They wanted to be valued, to receive some understanding, to be appreciated for what they were and preferably to be loved as well. A husband could be a guide, a mentor, a teacher, and a lover. Men may well have been given authority in law to be dominant over their wives, but women felt such authority should not be abused, 'A good Husband would not desire the power of Horsewhipping, confining or Half Starving his Wife or squandering her Estate; a bad Husband should not be allowed it.' (*Hardships of the English Laws*, 1735) Mary Astell had already stated that if man was a tyrant he was not fit to be a husband. (*Reflections upon Marriage*, 1700)

A good husband would listen to his wife, and at least hear her opinions and enjoy spending time with her rather than, '...finding that her lord was either discovering the wit of his spaniel or had fallen asleep.' (Jane West, *A Tale of the Times*, 1799). If women were quietly, unresistingly, accepting subservience, then it would be easy for a man to believe he was a good husband because his wife never told him otherwise, for, 'Who among the lords of creation will contravert that opinion when they hear that his lady never contradicted him, and never found fault?' (*Ibid*) Mary Hays pointed out that if men tried to make women happy, not by silly flattery, but by genuine thoughtfulness, '...and above all by considering them as rational beings upon a footing with themselves, influenced by the same passions, and having the same claims to all the rights of humanity' (*Appeal*, 1798), then not only would women be happier in themselves, but men would also gain from their happiness.

Some marriages were very happy, for example that of Amelia Opie and her husband, John. In 1801 she wrote a letter to Robert Garnham saying, 'Indeed my husband is so fond of home, and I am so attached to his society, that the world has little to bestow capable of drawing me from my fireside without reluctance.' Similarly the author of the much quoted *Hardships of the English Laws* wrote, 'I thank God I have a husband who lets me be alive.'

It is important to point out that there were many variations within marriage – not all women suffered an unhappy marriage or even suffered to the same degree. Moreover women discovered quiet submissiveness took the sting out of many attacks. Eliza Haywood had commented that, 'Marriage is the great action on which our happiness depends' (*The History of Jemmy and Jenny Jessamy*, 1753), and much has already been said about how careful a woman needed to be in making her choice which was, after all, for life. If divorce was virtually unobtainable and separation generally unlikely, there were few choices. One could look forward to the death of an unpleasant husband and celebrate when the event took place. Alternatively one could make the most of the situation you found yourself in. In *Desmond*, Geraldine was asked, ' Why do you put on these fetters?' And the classic answer came, 'Because it is my duty.' (Charlotte Smith, 1792) Women may well have felt themselves bound by the serious promises they made and by adherence to the laws that bound them, but the following quote from *Indiana* is particularly significant as it summarised the situation for married women during the whole of the period:

> *I know I'm the slave and you're the lord. The law of the land has made you my master. You can tie up my body, bind my hands, control my actions. You have the right of the stronger, and society confirms you in it. But over my will monsieur you have no power. God alone can bend and subdue it. … you can impose silence on me but you can't stop me thinking. (George Sand, 1831)*

And these writings that I have cited, by women of the time, are testament to that.

Chapter Six
A Fall from Grace

An acquaintance of mine once commented that she found novels of the eighteenth century really boring. They all shared the same basic plots, had awful soulless heroines who were mind bogglingly dull, and who were so concerned with their virtue and appropriate behaviour that they all seem to have been cast in the same mould. It should be fairly obvious that I do not actually agree with this rather sweeping generalisation, although it is true that in real life females were supposed to live up to an ideal of virtue and submission – as you will remember from earlier chapters – their education and upbringing were geared to it. Until now I have made few direct references to sex itself, but it is a fundamental facet of human life, and emotions – particularly for women – play a major part in the process. However women at the time were not supposed to know anything about sex until they were married and were not even supposed to admit a preference for a man unless he had made a formal commitment of his intention to marry them. What some women writers tried to point out was that there was a danger in focussing so much on the virtuous and meek ideal image of woman – for it was not only being unrealistic, but it was also making women extremely vulnerable by being over innocent with regard to sex.

One of the major problems for women of the time – and for decades, if not centuries, after – was that there was a double standard regarding sexual behaviour in men and women. Through the consequences of their vulnerability women would discover this; they alone would then be punished and suffer accordingly. It was a completely different matter for the men. It was perfectly acceptable for a man to pursue a woman, to declare his love, and to try his luck sexually. It was considered normal for young men to have sex before marriage, and when married to continue to have mistresses and affairs at will. Men were different and did not have to live up to an ideal of moral perfection. In contrast a woman's position in society was based on her reputation and chastity – she had an ideal image to live up to.

When women writers created fictional accounts of young innocent girls who were easy prey to the pleasures of personal attention, flattery and gifts, they knew that there were several important lessons to pass on – but how could they effectively draw attention to the problems women could face if they strayed from the straight and narrow? Mary Hays had a simple answer, 'Why should we not paint (life) as it really is?' (*On Novel Writing*, 1797) Why not show how unrealistic and inappropriate the image of a virtuous angel was for a grown woman? Why not show the problems of women whose passions got them into trouble, why not show how society differentiated in its attitude to men and women's sexual behaviour, and why not try to do something about it? Some of these were radical ideas indeed and a far cry from the boring plots and dull women my acquaintance had considered. Perhaps she was reading the wrong books!

There are many important issues to consider here; but let us start with the concept of the ideal woman – this paragon of virtue and submission. I have already shown how critics reacted to women writing in general, because they were breaking out of the boundaries that society had seemingly set for them, and how some women did seem to suffer from a crisis of conscience in the performance of their work. For those women writers who dared to question the concept, precedence and authority of the ideal woman, it was a double crime against society because they were writing about taboo subjects. When women did write about love, passion, and sexual behaviour they frequently justified it by saying they were actually writing from a moralistic point of view, as a warning to young women, rather than offering a titillating or even semi pornographic experience. Eliza Haywood for example wrote in 1724, 'My design in writing this novel being only to remind the unthinking part of the world how dangerous it is to give way to passion...' (*Lasselia, or The Self Abandon'd*) and similarly Susanna Rawson proclaimed, 'If the following tale should save one hapless fair one from the errors which ruined poor Charlotte...' (*Charlotte Temple*, 1794) There were also warnings which verged on shock tactics, 'In her errors many participate; let them tremble, lest they do so in her punishment' (Harriet Lee, *Errors of Innocence*, 1786) and the exhortation 'Oh my dear girls…kneel down each morning and request kind heaven to keep you free from temptation, or, should it please you to suffer to be tried, pray for fortitude to resist the impulse of inclination…' (*Charlotte Temple*, 1794)

A young woman may fall for a seducer, she may suffer feelings of guilt for deserting home and family, but she would still experience the anxieties and pleasures of love before she received her just (!) reward and inevitable punishment. Eliza Haywood supposedly wrote with cautions in mind, but she also created sensuous, passionate tales that cannot have failed to raise the blood pressure of the young women who led rather limited lives in the eighteenth century. Popular in magazines and lending libraries such stories were eagerly devoured by young women, as they fed their imaginations, flattered them, teased them and led them on occasions to a satisfying climax, without anyone knowing what they had been through – albeit by proxy. In *Love in Excess* (Eliza Haywood, 1719/20) the women seem to positively throw themselves at the men – 'she sighed, she burned, she raged when she perceived the charming Delmont behaved himself towards her.' There was also a wonderful sequence of building sexual tension where in the heat of a summer night, a scantily clad female was almost won over and then there was an inevitable knock at the door, or footsteps heard in the corridor, intermingled with such commentary as, 'She now no longer doubted the Count's passion and trembled with the apprehension of what he might in time be tempted to do...'

Providing a moral ending to the tale, with suitable punishments and even death for miscreant females, may have been a way to try to satisfy critics, but it is also likely that authors like Eliza Haywood were providing a safe outlet for the sexual feelings and associated emotions of women, without them suffering any dire consequences in the process. In direct contrast to their popularity with the readers fiction like this was highly condemned by some contemporaries. Although James Fordyce, author of *Sermons to Young Women* (1766), claimed never to have read such books, he still felt totally justified in his censure of them:

> *What shall we say of certain books which we are assured (for we have not read them) are in their nature so shameful, in their tendency so pestiferous and contain such rank treason against the royalty of Virtue,*

> *such horrible violation of all decorum, that she who can bear to peruse them must in her soul be a prostitute, let her reputation in life be what it will?*

When Charlotte Dacre wrote about a fictitious woman who challenged the ideal by being a manipulative, aggressive and vicious sexual predator, the attacks were predictable, if a little unusual in terms of specific detail. Victoria the anti-heroine, or femme fatale, had resorted to making a pact with the Devil in order to get her man. In the process she had poisoned several characters, including her husband, murdered her rival by repeatedly stabbing her, and then had thrown her over a cliff. (*Zofloya*, 1806) One of her critics wrote:

> *Ladies of her description...have the seeds of nonsense, bad taste, and ridiculous fancies early sown in their minds. These having grown to maturity render the brain putrid and corrupt, and the consequence is the formation of millions of the strangest maggots that one can conceive...That our fair authoress is afflicted with the dismal malady of maggots in the brain is, alas, but too apparent, from the whole of her production...This malady of maggots is rendered more dreadful by its being infectious...It might be a charitable thing to have a hospital for the reception of these unfortunate people while under the influence of the disease... (Literary Journal, June 1806)*

I hope she ignored him – I enjoyed the book!

It does seem ludicrous to a modern reader that women should have been so pressurised into presenting a virtuous front, to be in such strict control of their passions and emotions, in order to satisfy societal requirements of them. Even in the conduct book novels women who were abandoned or mistreated by husbands hid their emotions in public – and then wept bitterly behind closed doors, became seriously ill with nervous feverish diseases, or poured out their hearts in a private diary or letters to a close female friend or relation. It almost looks as though women had to wear a mask of respectability in public – out vying each other in virtue and decorum – for the sake of maintaining this image of a perfect woman. It is not surprising therefore that women writers had to find ways of overcoming this social pressure and make some form of justification for their work, in whatever form they wrote.

Digressing slightly, it is worth noting that the subsequent Victorian extension of the ideal woman into the concept of the Angel in the House lasted for years, and continued to cause at least at least a matter of conscience for some women writers. Even Virginia Woolf, writing in the twentieth century, showed how she had been haunted by the image and finally overcame it:

> *I discovered that if I was going to (write) I should need to do battle with a certain phantom. And this phantom was a woman... The Angel of the House...it was she who used to come between me and my paper... It was she who bothered me and wasted my time...you may not know what I mean by the Angel of the House... She was intensely sympathetic... She was utterly unselfish... She sacrificed herself daily...if there was a draught she sat in it... she never had a mind or a wish of her own... Above all – she was pure. Her purity was supposed to be her chief beauty... When I came to write I encountered her with the very first words. The shadow of her wings fell on my page...I turned upon her and caught her by the throat. I did my best to kill her... Had I not killed her she would have killed me. She would have plucked the heart out of my writing... Killing the Angel in the House was part of the occupation of a woman writer.*
> *(Professions for Women, 1931)*

There are obvious links between the words of Virginia Woolf and the decision to confront society's image of the ideal woman during the long eighteenth century by woman writers like Dacre and Haywood. By demonstrating real feelings, sexual desires and the possible consequences of indulging in them, particularly outside marriage, they were able to offer alternatives to the stereotypical heroines – even if during the course of a novel such characters had to modify their behaviour, or alternatively die, in order to become socially more acceptable – and of course sell the book!

From real life too there were many examples of women who were open in their experience of passion and had to face the consequences. Mary Hays was very unfortunate in love. She was passionately attached to her first love John Eccles, but her family forbade her to marry him and, when they did eventually accept him, he tragically died before the wedding. She then suffered greatly from unrequited love for William

Frend and was in such a state that William Godwin – later to become husband to Mary Wollstonecraft – actually advised her to write about her experiences in order to cope. She was only too aware of how difficult it was to suppress real feelings and emotions – and was probably one of the first women authors to be conscious of the psychological damage such restraint could cause. Her subsequent fictional book *(Memoirs of Emma Courtney*, 1794) even included extracts of her own love letters. Mary's behaviour in pursuing the man of her dreams was humiliatingly satirised by another woman writer, Elizabeth Hamilton, who based the character Bridgetina Botherim on her, in *Memoirs of Modern Philosophers*, (1800). Women could be cruel sometimes.

Another example of where overt passion in a real woman was criticised was when one of Frances Burney's close friends decided that she had been a widow long enough, falling for a much younger man and then marrying him. To be a widow and remarry an older man – especially a widower who had a family of his own – was acceptable. To marry a younger man with no other apparent motive than physical attraction was definitely not. In 1783 Frances had heard that her friend Hester Thrale was about to say yes to a proposal from a young Italian musician, Gabriel Piozzi. She wrote back:

> *Oh, **think** a little before you utter it! You will say you have been thinking all this time,- no, dear madam you have **never** thought, you have distressed and horrified yourself not about **changing** your plan, but merely in a cruel anxiety to obtain **approbation** for it.*
>
> *That approbation will forever be withheld! The Mother of 5 Children, 3 of them as Tall as herself, will never be forgiven for shewing so great an ascendance of passion over Reason. **Somebody** you say shall be made happy,- ah that **somebody** will not be you!*

It was to be an end to their friendship.

In this letter Frances Burney raised a particularly important issue that was constantly being referred to by characters within the novels, as well as by authorial comments in the texts themselves. Could feelings of passion be overcome by reason? Could the mind really control affairs of the heart? Knowing that they were dependent upon men for their maintenance, position and welfare, and that their reputation was dependent upon their chastity and virtue, women were taught to counteract their natural desires. Take this from *The Coquette* (Hannah Foster, 1797):

> *Slight not the opinion of the world. We are dependent beings; and while the slightest traces of virtuous sensibility remain, we must feel the force of that dependence in a greater or lesser degree. No female, whose mind is uncorrupted, can be indifferent to reputation. It is an inestimable jewel, whose loss can never be repaired. While retained, it affords conscious peace to our own minds, and ensures the esteem and respect of all around us.*

Continuing in a similar vein I found this personal call for reassurance from a conversation between sisters in *Patronage* (Maria Edgeworth, 1814), 'Tell me that you approve of my exerting all my power over myself to do that which I think right.' Much has already been said on this in earlier chapters and it will be sufficient at this stage to call to mind all the conduct book authors had to say about how young girls should behave.

Of course the formula was not always successful. Although novels often found ways to stress the importance of good parenting, and frequently showed the problems that ensued if a mother was unable to guide her young daughters development, young people then, as now, did not always listen to their parents', guardians' or other 'expert' advice. Even assuming that if parents felt comfortable talking to their daughters about love, passion and sex – which somehow I very much doubt – there are some matters in which decisions are guided more by personal experience and choice. It was not enough to be told about good and evil, or be given advice that, 'We should not be overcome by that which our reason tells us is wrong. We should vigorously struggle to conquer and we should succeed.' (Rosa Matilda, *The Passions,* 1811)

Charlotte Dacre (writing as Rosa Matilda) had made use of a particularly strong image in this work when she wrote, 'The passions may be called the wild horses of the soul.' Mary Robinson, mistress of the Prince of Wales, was well aware of the problems facing a woman, and in *The False Friend* (1799) she exclaimed, 'What fool is woman while labouring under the influences of her senses! How useless is reason; how feeble the resisting faculties of her mind, when the stormy passions fasten on her soul.' She also described how easily overcome a woman's reason could be when in the presence of her lover:

> *Whenever my heart endeavours to shake off the fascination which holds it, he fastens the chain more securely by some kind and soothing attention; a look, a sigh, a word, will at any time counter the power of reflection, and deceive that heart that is the slave of his domain. (Ibid)*

Charlotte Dacre was also aware of how difficult the struggle could be between passion and reason, and warned, 'If our passions are to be overcome, it can only be by the *superior force* of our reason, but if our reason have *not* the superior force and our passions like a tide bear all before them, can we help it…?'(*The Passions*, 1811)

Once again women's writings were to show that unless you had experienced certain situations you could not really comment on them with understanding. Eliza Haywood wrote at length on the subject:

> *Methinks there is nothing more absurd than the notions of some people, who in other things are wise enough too; but wanting elegance of thought, delicacy or tenderness of soul to receive the impression of that harmonious passion, look on those to be mad, who have any sentiments elevated above their own, and either censure or laugh, at what they are not refined enough to comprehend. These* ***insipids,*** *who know nothing of the matter, tell us very gravely, that we* ***ought*** *to love with moderation and discretion, – and take care that it is for our interest,- that we should never place our affections, but where duty leads, or at least, where neither religion, reputation, or law, may be a hindrance to our wishes. – Wretches! We know all this as well as they; we know too, that we both do, and leave undone, many other things which we ought not; but perfection is not to be expected this side of the grave.*
> *(Love in Excess, 1719/20)*

However she too was aware of the consequences of giving in to passion, however impossible it was to avoid, 'Love my dear subverts the understanding and deprives us of our self control, robs us of our pride, overthrows our dignity, kills our souls with degrading jealousy, petty cares and vain regrets…' (*Ibid*)

So women were as susceptible to passionate feelings as men.

Outside of marriage some were tempted. Some were seduced; some were more willing than others. Some unfortunately were raped. Women in general had been brought up to trust men with their lives, but their education failed to teach them that not all men were actually trustworthy. Women writers were only too well aware of the facts and much of their concern lay with the groups of women whom they considered to be most vulnerable. Charlotte Lennox warned:

> *Unhappy state of youth and beauty. Left unprotected to the dangerous snares, which powerful vice is ever ready to lay for them. The most solid virtue is not always a sufficient defence against the artifices of men, whose rank and fortune supply them with various means for the ruin of unsuspecting innocence.*
> *(The Life of Harriet Stuart Written By Herself, 1751)*

Mary Ann Hanway similarly wrote this warning some years later:

> *We earnestly recommend to our fair readers, instantly to fly the object of their choice, who tries to sap their innocence and lull caution asleep by painting a fancied security, 'Let not such a man be trusted.'*
> *(Ellinor, 1793)*

One group of young women who were particularly vulnerable to the dulcet persuasive tones of a would-be seducer were those who were uneducated and had few dealings with the outside world in their sheltered upbringings. Words and gestures of love could be persuasive and it has been interesting to note how many authors have their men of the world, libertines, or rakes, make use of reasoned argument and logic to convince the young girl that she should actually have sex with him! These played on her emotions, and could range from 'if you really love me you would' or 'I will go abroad and you will never see me again', an awful tragedy for a lonely girl, to promises of marriage that never actually got fulfilled once the advantage had been taken. This is but one illustration:

> *Believe with me Julia, our love is fate. Let us no longer struggle against it, to our mutual destruction. While we pause and ponder and submit our right to be happy to the analysation of reason, the power of*

becoming so escapes us, and youth is consumed, and life is past in vain unprofitable struggles. Few are the roses scattered in our path to the grave; let us not sacrilegiously trample on them, but let us seek in each other the only happiness that is left us on the earth...Let us fly to some remote corner of the earth, where our love shall not be considered as a crime. Tis the laws of man which make it such, nature deems it none. (Rosa Matilda, The Passions, 1811).

George Sand underlined the point simply, 'She was so ignorant of life, she thought resistance was impossible.' (*Indiana*, 1831)

Some authors made use of secret marriages, which prior to the 1753 Act could take place with just promises exchanged between the happy couple, but an innocent girl would not have realised that by keeping it a 'secret' there was no proof it had taken place. She could easily be deserted and left to face the possible consequences alone. Secret marriages also had the advantage for the male that while the young woman stayed at home with her parents, thinking that she actually had a husband, the man could be flirting elsewhere and get formally married to another. Without her having knowledge of the laws involved, and being frightened of scandal and further shame, it is likely that such desertions of women were not unknown.

The other group of women who seemed to be somewhat vulnerable were those who had already been married but were unhappy. Possibly married too young to much older men, or married to men not of their choosing, from financial necessity or by forceful persuasion, such women could feel isolated, lonely and desperately unhappy. To find an apparently sympathetic male who was gentle, understanding and physically attractive could be tempting. Harriet Lee put it simply, 'A young married woman is the ideal victim of every libertine who approaches her' (*Errors of Innocence*, 1786). The anonymous author of *The Histories of Some of the Penitents in the Magdalen House* (1759), which had been set up to reform fallen women in 1758, had gone into more specific details:

A young woman who marries an old man brings her virtue into some danger and her reputation into more. Young men look upon the wife of an old one as part of their property: They may be disappointed of their conquest, but they generally make the trial. This exposes a woman to

> *frequent temptation. Age is seldom unaccompanied with peevishness; and the retrospection of a man's own folly...is not likely to let it lie dormant. Thus he, who can have no merit to a young girl but indulgence, becomes harsh and ill tempered; while every younger man is polite, attentive, assiduous and tender. The contrast is dangerous...*

But was it worth all the consequences of becoming a fallen woman? Naïve, innocent young women must have thought so at some stage of the process, but they had much to discover and to learn.

The idea of a woman being a paragon of virtue, an angelic upholder of morals, an object of adulation and worship has already been raised. It may have been an unrealistic image but it could have been a source of inspiration. From such a superior position though it is not difficult to see where the concept of the fallen woman, the fallen angel, came in. A perfect woman, set up on her pedestal, or at a celestial height, had a long way to fall when things went wrong. Too lively behaviour, or too many flirtations could lead to slander, scandal or a possible loss of reputation, but becoming a truly 'fallen woman' could have far more damaging consequences. During my research I kept coming across the following three lines, used as a quotation, from a play by Nicholas Rowe, published in 1714, called *The Tragedy of Jane Shore*:

> *In vain with tears the loss she may deplore,*
> *In vain look back to what she was before*
> *She sets, like stars that fall, to rise no more.*

Jane Shore was the mistress of Edward IV and also to other men of royal birth. Richard III later ordered her to do public penance for her promiscuity. Whenever I have found stories concerning fallen women some, if not all, of these lines seem to occur. It is not difficult to see why, and this does help our understanding of the double standard regarding sexual behaviour in men and women. If it was accepted that men were unable, or unwilling to take more control of their sexual needs and gratification, and were not subject to such stringent moral guidelines and controls, then it follows that there would be a more sympathetic or at least more tolerant approach to their sexual exploits that occurred outside wedlock. It was not the same for a woman.

As Delarivière Manley wrote in 1714 'What is not a crime in men is considered scandalous and unpardonable in women.' This double standard was to be a major issue for women. Mary Davys commented that in the case of a man, 'There are a thousand things perhaps not very innocent which I may act and no Notice taken of them, which in you would draw the Eyes of everybody towards you.' (*The Accomplish'd Rake*, 1727). It seems to have been commonly accepted that men had greater sexual needs than women and that these had to be satisfied whether married or not. Some men also had some rather strange ideas about women that would be bound to raise an eyebrow or two in the modern world. In the *History of European Morals* (1869), the Victorian historian W E Lecky suggested that prostitutes of the time were actually guardians of virtue because they kept wandering, but otherwise respectable, males from harming virtuous women. Over a century earlier, Colonel Mordaunt had suggested that, if there were not enough prostitutes to satisfy the males, then it would be perfectly acceptable to debase some respectable women – to make them into prostitutes, and then just explain to them what a sound job they were doing for England! (Colonel Harry Mordaunt (Bernard Mandeville) from *A modest Defence of public Stews; (ie prostitutes) or an Essay upon Whoring,* published 1724, taken from 1740 edition)

With all the emphasis on female virtue and moral rectitude it is interesting to note that even then sexually predatory behaviour by men was blamed on women. In *The Passions* (Rosa Matilda, 1811) Count Darlowitz put the blame firmly on his friend's wife Julia for his attraction and subsequent pursuance of her, 'Am I amenable for the impression you madest on me?' In earlier times men had been frightened of women's sexual behaviour but during the eighteenth century the mood had changed somewhat and even women's fashions could be blamed for luring men into bad behaviour. *The Lady's Magazine* of 1775 had a bachelor complaining, 'If girls are so imprudent as to commit such depredations on our sex (i.e. showing a cleavage or bosom in a low cut dress) they are certainly in great measure, the authors of their *own* misfortune.'

I still remember the invention of the mini skirt in the 1960's and judicial commentaries that blamed young women wearing them for the unwanted sexual attentions that were heard about in court. According to this theory women were responsible for men's predatory behaviour – men did not have to accept responsibility for their own actions. It does appear that during the long eighteenth century women did take on the moral responsibility, not necessarily by choice, in the matter of extra marital sex. As Charlotte Smith put it, 'Most unhappy woman, destruction hangs over you and it is only in your own power to escape it.' (*Montalbert*, 1795) It was their duty to take the moral lead, and it was their fault and their problem if things went wrong.

Time and again, when such sexual activities are referred to, male characters in the novels showed their total acceptance of the double standard and agreed, 'The cases are widely different. The worlds opinion affixes just disgrace to the vices in your sex, which in ours it views with more indulgent eyes.' (Mary Brunton, *Self Control*, 1810) Similarly 'He is not like a woman accustomed to view the smallest wandering of his ideas as a crime – he assumes and is granted an independence of conduct and opinion which in woman would not be tolerated.' (Rosa Matilda, *The Passions*, 1811)

Regarding young unmarried men 'sewing their wild oats', this is what one father told his daughter who was concerned about her fiancé's activities, 'Your simplicity and ignorance of the world make you attach far too much importance to (his) little irregularities.' (Eliza Haywood, *Love in Excess*, 1719/20) From the same novel there was a very clear example of the fact that what was acceptable in men's behaviour was definitely not so in women. First an authorial comment, 'Few men how ever amorous soever themselves care that the female part of the family should be so, and he was most sensibly mortified with it.' Totally ignoring his own games of sexual conquest the Baron D'espernay made the following outburst when he became aware of his sister's attempts to have a similar liaison with a Count, 'Thou shame of thy sex and everlasting blot and scandal of the noble house thou art descended from …' Need I say more?

When literary critics have discussed the development of the novel during the eighteenth and nineteenth centuries, I am not sure that sufficient tribute has been paid to the women writers regarding how much of a challenge they were making to the notion of the double standard. Apart from such typical fictional examples as those above, in her *Appeal to the Men of Great Britain*, Mary Hays included a French fable, which has been translated for me, kindly, by a friend. The fable may be recognised by some as a children's moral tale, but here it was pointedly directed at men. It concerned a young wolf that was strictly told how to behave by his father, and was told to be content with what he was given and not go off chasing the sheep, which were guarded by fierce dogs. However the young wolf realised his father was not abiding by his own words, clearly recognising the wool and blood of a sheep around his father's mouth. It was a matter of teaching the lesson 'Do what I say and not what I do'. The young wolf laughed at his father saying, 'Father I will do what I see you doing. YOUR EXAMPLE IS THE THING TO TRUST'.

For women readers there would be an obvious connection regarding the moral behaviour of men and the women themselves. Women were being constantly reminded of how to behave by those who behaved in a very different way. While the double standard was tolerated women were in a very vulnerable position, but the outlook would continue to look bleak, and women writers were only too aware of it. This next type of comment was by no means uncommon:

> *I feel that it is a vice that can never be suppressed, while he, who seduces a woman into guilt and shame, and abandons her to disease and poverty, obtains no other appellation by such villainy, than a man of gallantry, while he may be called a man of honour, tho' he breaks thro' ties of truth faith and humanity, in the destruction of one, whose greatest weakness was believing him incapable of the vileness to which she falls a sacrifice.*
> *(The Histories of Some of The Penitents of the Magdalen House, 1759)*

Here was a voice of discontent raised consistently, many times, by a whole series of women writers throughout the period – and indeed there is strong evidence of it continuing during the Victorian times in such works as *Jessie Phillips* by Frances Trollope, (1842/3); *Ruth* by Elizabeth Gaskell, (1853); and *Hidden Depths* by Felicia Skene, (1866). Some like Mary Robinson had queried how it was that men were still required to make formal oaths of fidelity and faith in church during the marriage service, while being perfectly conscious that they would not be required to keep them. (*Letter to the Women of England,* 1799) Others were to look back to the Bible and note how Jesus blamed both men and woman for such misdemeanours. (Mary Hays, *Appeal*, 1798)

To a certain extent it is true that when sexual encounters took place there was a fundamental difference for males and females – the female could be left with a problem. She may have conceived and she would be left literally holding the baby. This was centuries before the Pill and the sexual freedoms that are more acceptable today. In any sexual encounter there was the critical problem of possible pregnancy – whether the girl knew the facts of life or not. Contraception was not commonly understood and it was not to be until Victorian times that moves were made to educate and encourage the general public in its use. To be a fallen woman often meant to be the mother of an illegitimate child. In the days before DNA testing, proving fatherhood was a difficult problem. The father may be known, but all the trouble of getting him to first acknowledge the fact and then take responsibility for maintenance would then arise, and not every woman was prepared to face that.

In order to illustrate how the double standard could work it is worth giving a detailed example here. I have already mentioned how careful a woman had to be to try to preserve and maintain her own reputation. Betsy Thoughtless had already been warned, 'that a young lady more endangered her reputation, by an acquaintance with one woman of ill fame, than by receiving the visits of twenty men, though professed libertines.'(Eliza Haywood, 1751) In real life Elizabeth Inchbald, successful writer and playwright, had to be very careful when her friend, Mary Wollstonecraft, turned out to be the mother of an illegitimate child. Elizabeth withdrew her friendship in order to maintain her own spotless personal reputation. She had taken enough of a risk becoming an author and playwright and indeed, looking at one of her novels, *Nature and Art*, (1796) she had challenged the status quo with its double standard in a way that few had dared. In this work she was to show just how unfair the system could be towards innocent and vulnerable young women.

William, a rich and educated young man, planned to seduce Agnes, the daughter of a village cottager, who had been brought up to respect female virtue. She knew however that he would demand a particular 'pledge of her affection'. Unlike some he did admit he could never marry her because of his family and said it was a matter of her 'free choice' if she gave into him. In his eyes at least, 'for the consequences she will have herself and only herself to blame.' She became pregnant and tried to make contact with him, but he refused to have any more to do with her. Thus far the pattern of events was familiar, but Mrs Inchbald daringly took it a stage further. Agnes began her fall, seeking employment and losing it, trying to maintain the child she had initially abandoned at birth, later becoming destitute, even becoming a prostitute before she finally became involved in criminal and fraudulent activities. William meanwhile grew older, richer and became a judge, and then her judge.

When she was finally taken to court, he summed up the evidence, 'And every time he was compelled to press hard upon the proofs against her she shrank, and seemed to stagger with the deadly blow; writhed under the weight of HIS minute justice, more than from the prospect of a shameful death.' The verdict was guilty but it was he who placed the fatal black velvet cap on his head to pronounce her death sentence. She with a scream exclaimed, 'Oh, not from you!' In her written confession, read by him after her death, she forgave him, taking all the blame upon herself, and it was only then that he felt remorse – having been guilty of her seduction, refusing to help her, and ultimately forcing her into a situation where she had to undertake criminal activities in order to survive. He had then condemned her to death without pity. Elizabeth Inchbald may have had to play cautious in real life friendships, but it is quite clear where her sympathy lay. It is no wonder that the more outspoken Mary Hays was to write, 'What dependence can be had for justice, in any case where women are concerned, upon judges so partial, so criminally selfish?' (*Appeal*, 1798)

What was the situation with the law? Did it actually provide protection for women? The answer to this is rather complex but for the purposes of this book I will focus on a few elements. Prior to the 1753 Marriage Act, girls of 12 and boys of 14 could marry with or without parental consent, according to canon law. Banns were sometimes read, but they were not obligatory. At this time marriages could take the simple form of a promise, made anywhere – not just in a church – between the two parties, and thus promises could be reneged upon unless the marriage could be proven. Marriages could also take place in 'marriage factories' like the area of the Fleet prison in London, where age, willingness of the parties involved, and even the matter of being sober at the time, could easily be brushed aside in the interest of suitable payment of fees! Records could be forged or conveniently lost. This rather loose situation had left some young women abandoned after the event, with no evidence of a legal marriage, and those in favour of the 1753 Act felt that formalising the marriage procedure would at least mean it would be obvious and provable if a genuine marriage had taken place. Thereafter parental or guardian permission had to be obtained if the parties were under age, banns had to be read for three successive Sundays in the parish church, and with the church now becoming the only legal venue for a wedding (unless a special licence was obtained), an official record of the event would be made in its register.

However, even at the time, opponents of the Bill felt that women would still get entrapped by men's promises and would not change their sexual practices – i.e. they would still be tempted and give in! (Notice men's own sexual practices were not in question.) The records of the Parliamentary Debate show that some saw the Bill as 'one of the most cruel enterprises against the fair sex that ever entered the heart of man' and foretold that it would 'ruin a multitude of women'. These warnings were from those who had the foresight to realise that, if the bill was enacted, whenever a woman fell pregnant outside of marriage she in effect would become a whore and her children bastards. Later in history the situation would become even worse for women when, in 1834, the Bastardy Clause of the Poor Law Amendment Act completely absolved a man from any legal responsibility for his illegitimate offspring, making the woman totally responsible for the care and maintenance of such children until they were sixteen years old.

The original intention of the Marriage Act had apparently not been to protect the women who faced a lifetime of consequences, but rather to protect the richer men of the parish from having to face false claims from 'loose women'- and having to pay up. If families disowned their miscreant daughters, and they frequently did through shame and loss of their own reputation, unfortunate mother and child may end up in a workhouse – and that was neither a happy nor a comfortable situation to be in. Once again the law could be a good friend to the man involved.

Even before Hardwicke's Act of 1753 there had been a variety of criticisms of the laws regarding women. Mary Davys had already wondered, 'Why must a Poor Man be hanged for stealing a Sheep, and a Rich one escape, that takes away by Force or Trick what is much more valuable from us?' (*The Accomplish'd Rake*, 1727) This was a direct reference to young male members of the nobility who seemed to have a penchant for the ruin of young innocent girls and who got away with it. Her character Betty continued, 'I am resolved to make both himself and the World know what a Rogue he is; and I'll see him hang'd before he shall wear the Best Jewel I ever had and not pay a good price for it.' She was not talking about diamonds …

Mary Davys had referred to the double standard, in a similar vein, in an earlier work when one of her noble ladies, Amoranda, commented,

> *I wonder ..your Lordship does not get the House of Lords to endeavour to repeal the Law of Marriage: Why should you lawgivers impose on other people, what you think improper yourselves? Oh madam, said the Peer, there are politick reasons for what we do. (The Reform'd Coquet, 1724)*

Others too were to comment on how men had made the laws to suit themselves – at the expense of women. This was written anonymously in 1759, 'we may see the men made not only laws but customs. They have carved themselves out pretty lives. They the primrose path of dalliance led, while they would confine us to the thorny way.' (*The Histories of Some of the Penitents of the Magdalen House*) This particular book was important, as it claimed to be a true rendition of four of the individual case histories of women who actually entered the house set up for the reform and education of fallen women in London in the mid eighteenth century. Although written anonymously, it is likely to have actually been written by Sarah Scott who herself knew of one of the fallen woman who became a resident of the House. Another of the inmates was to comment on how the laws favoured the rich; when she faced desertion by her seducer and hoped to appeal to the law, his response was, 'The law, thou idiot…Know that money only can obtain justice; those who cannot buy must go without it; the redress of the law is out of the reach of poverty.'

Only recently have I begun to appreciate how much important social commentary these novels provide, on the laws themselves, at the time when they actually came into existence and the populace gradually felt their effects. When I first started my research I was aware of more general social criticism within the novels of course, but I am now learning to look more closely at the relation between specific Acts and the pertinent and timely observations or judgements within the texts. Let me illustrate this with a couple of relevant examples.

The Marriage Act as we know became law in 1753. *In the Histories of Some of the Penitents* (1759), the first case study gave details of a girl who asked her seducer for a contract when she left with him, as she was aware that she needed some form of legal protection. Although she obtained one, she foolishly destroyed it when he took her to the Fleet area for a marriage ceremony that she believed was legal. She was to learn her mistakes the hard way. Firstly the Act had made such marriages illegal, because they were not in church and no parental consent had been given – they were under age at the time. Also she had not known enough about the Act beforehand, 'I had heard the marriage act talked of, but had never attended to the purport of it; nor did I believe it could affect the validity of our marriage.' Her seducer amended her education by cruelly getting a servant to deliver a copy of the Act to her shortly after she discovered his deception, 'His servant brought the Marriage Act with his masters compliments and that he had sent it for me to peruse, for the clearing up of my doubts.' What a thoughtful way to let her know that she had not been living as his wife, but actually as his mistress, for the past few months!

This case study was supposed to be a true story. Even during the Parliamentary debate, before the Bill was enacted, Charles Townsend had stated his concern that such situations could arise, 'I am persuaded, that a few years hence many a young woman will be debauched under the pretence of a sham-marriage'. He forewarned that 'though those of the present generation may remember something of the law and be a little cautious' he predicted it would not always be so. He continued, 'The young women of the next generation will be as ignorant and regardless of it as they are now about our laws against wearing cambrics.' Young, innocent, and uneducated women could be easily misled by those able to manipulate the law; it was to be the undertaken role of many women writers of the period to keep repeating the warnings to their readers within the stories that they created. That sometimes therefore included direct references to the Acts themselves.

Earlier I mentioned the misery caused by the addition to the Poor Law of the Bastardy Clause in 1834. In her novel, *Cheveley*, published in 1837, Rosina Bulwer Lytton was to emphasise the cruelty of the amendment in her confrontation between the seducer and his unfortunate victim. He scorned her and thanked the parliamentarians who had let him off the hook, wiping him free from any responsibility whatsoever, for her or for their baby. While hiding in the bushes so she could not see him he threw a note at her feet which said, 'Woman cease to persecute me, the fittest place for you is a House of Correction. I suppose your father will disown you.. and as for your brat, thanks to the new Poor Laws you have no claim on me…' As in the case from the Magdalen House Penitents above, these examples were only a few years after the enactment of the laws concerned, and the suffering they caused is not difficult to imagine. It is no wonder that women were to complain about the laws created by men. As Mary Robinson put it in her *Letter to the Women of England* (1799), 'The laws are made by man; and self preservation is, by them, deemed the primary law of nature.'

For the woman who had fallen there were to be many problems for her to face. Although she may not have originally intended to leave home when she made her fatal decision, it was often necessary. An unmarried girl may have been forced to leave when her family disowned her, or she may have chosen to leave with her lover, or later to escape scandal if he deserted her. In doing so she lost her maintenance, her friends, her family, her security. For a married woman who had an affair the situation was little different – her husband could throw her out, or she may have chosen to leave with her lover, or found herself later abandoned when he became tired of her. Her decision too meant losing her home, losing her maintenance and often the most difficult part of all – losing her children. A wife lost all rights to her children when she left her husband's home. Her husband, though, could sue for damages, after all his property (i.e. his wife) had been damaged, and he could claim compensation through the courts for the 'criminal conversation' she had been engaged in!

For women in trouble there seems to have been a shock of realisation when they suddenly became aware of their full situation. It was as if one had awoken from a dream, ' I have indeed been long asleep and dreadful is such an awakening…'(*The Histories of Some of the Penitents of the Magdalen House*, 1759) No longer protected by father, husband or lover the woman stood alone, and apart from all feelings of shame and repentance she could feel very hurt, ' I did not then understand how soon a woman, who cannot possess a man's esteem, loses all regard when he ceases to love her. But to be left with such indifference…' (*Ibid*) There was also the realisation that if a man was not bothered about leaving her, then he would not have even cared about how she would fare for herself or the poverty he may have been condemning her to.

Charlotte Smith summed up the situation for many, 'After long deliberation, I saw no way to escape the disgrace which was about to overwhelm me but hiding myself from my own family and all the world.' (*Emmeline*, 1788) But what was she to do – having abandoned family, friends and contacts, who would vouch for someone they did not know? People would have no reason to trust such an unknown woman with their property or young family and would be reluctant to pay for a servant or governess without references. Mary Wollstonecraft was to provide several illustrations of this in her novel *The Wrongs of Woman* (1798) and named the additional problem,'A man with half my industry, and, I may say, abilities, could have procured a decent livlihood'. It was to be even more difficult if there was an illegitimate child in tow. Mary Davys emphasised the point, when in her novel an unmarried mother was offered marriage she replied,'No, I will never think of Marriage, even that will never retrieve my lost Credit, the good natured World knows my Fault, and it will be sure to keep it in continual Remembrance.' (*The Accomplish'd Rake*, 1727) In the next chapter I will be considering further the problems women from the middling and upper classes faced when they did try to be self supporting – whatever the circumstances of their own particular situations.

We already know the law could not be relied on for its support of fallen women. But what of society itself? Unfortunately, the double standard ensured that fear of scandal and slander meant that many women deliberately avoided tainting their own reputations, by having only negative associations with fallen women, in case they should be tarred with the same brush. Mary Hays in *The Victim of Prejudice* (1799) showed how servants, tradesmen, previous friends and prospective employers could all condemn such an unfortunate woman for her actions, and even if she did manage to find safety where she was unknown, in time her true situation would be frequently found out and the woman was forced to move on. She summarized the situation:

> *Unable to labour, ashamed to solicit charity, helpless, penniless, feeble, delicate, thrown out with reproach from society, borne down with a*

> *consciousness of irretrievable error, exposed to insult, to want, to contumely, to every species of aggravated distress, in a situation requiring sympathy, tenderness, assistance – From whence was I to draw fortitude to combat these accumulated evils?*

This was later followed by the fundamental plea on behalf of all such women:

> *I only sought the bare means of subsistence... surely,* ***I had a right to exist****! For what crime was I driven from society?*

It is unrealistic to say that it was only women who recognised the inequality here. There were some men who had not only had sympathies with the plight of such women but who also were not afraid to voice their opinions in public. Dr Dodd acknowledged this in his sermon of 1759 when talking about the fallen women who sought refuge at the Magdalen Hospital:

> *And it is well known how much harder that case, in this particular, is with the female sex than with our own. One false step forever ruins their fair fame; blasts the fragrance of virgin innocence and consigns them to contempt and disgrace. While the author of their distress may triumph in his villainy! And shame to human nature – not be branded with one mark of reproach for the ruin of a fellow creature.*
> *(An Account of the Rise, Progress and Present State of the Madgalen Hospital, for the reception of Penitent Prostitutes. Together with Dr Dodd's Sermons, 1770)*

Later William Thompson, working with Anna Wheeler in the early nineteenth century, noted, 'in almost all cases where the evil or vice can be made to fall on a woman and the enjoyment can be reserved for the man, such an arrangement of pain or pleasure is made.' (*Appeal of One Half of the Human Race*, 1825). They also showed concern for the neglected illegitimate child and again the abdication from any responsibility by the father of it. This was their verdict:

> *Disgrace and privation, by way of punishment, are inflicted on the unoffending child, who could have committed no offence, on whom*

> *therefore punishment by way of reformation or intimidation is thrown away, while in the way of example it strikes not fathers or any men capable of becoming such: on the contrary it relieves them from the fear of punishment by throwing all its burden on the shoulder of others ... the real criminal holds up his head and smiles, if not glories, while the victim only is punished.*

They too were to question the law, and indeed the legislators themselves, and raised the all important question – how can legislators have claimed to represent women if they failed to assess their needs fairly, ascertain what they wanted or took any notice of situations from their point of view? Valid points, but somewhat premature at that time... Few women had considered even gaining the vote – let alone being consulted on what was to be discussed in parliament.

There were however other fundamental points to consider which could have more immediate impact on the fate of fallen women, and it was to these issues that women writers turned their attention. It was too easy, and far too simplistic, just to blame men for the double standard within society and the way fallen women were treated because of it. Once again women did have to take part responsibility for the way the double standard continued for so long, and had such a devastating effect upon the lives of those unfortunate women affected by it. Society is made up of both men *and* women and, regardless of the law, much of the damage done to fallen women was by the attitudes of society itself – shown through the thoughts, words and deeds of other men, women and even children. I have already shown some of the ways women could be cruel to each other- by snubbing them, refusing to give them aid or by blaming their negative circumstances purely on the unfortunate women themselves. Occasionally female characters would directly question woman's inhumanity to woman, 'Is it possible there lives a wretch who would destroy the buds of renovating virtue, at the moment when they are struggling amidst the poisonous weeds of vice; whom and what was your enemy?' and the reply, 'Woman, that cruel torturer of her frail sex.' (Mary Robinson, *Walsingham*, 1797)

Even though it is likely that by such unpleasant or cruel behaviour women were trying to protect or enhance their own self-image as virtuous, pure and even 'model women', to modern readers it may seem very uncharitable indeed, and more in line with the 'I'm all right, Jack' school of philosophy. However it wasn't just their own actions that could be damaging – women could also make sure their households, families, friends and acquaintances acted in the same way and thus were responsible for creating a snowballing effect.

These actions helped to perpetuate the system by allowing the man, who was *at least* partly responsible for an unfortunate woman's plight, to avoid taking any blame for it. The system was also aided and abetted by those women who continued to encourage the behaviour of a libertine, by socially accepting him, while still condemning the female concerned. The following was written anonymously in 1759, 'If such a man shall be caressed by his own sex and admired *by the other* (my emphasis) can we wonder that he goes on?' (*The Histories of Some of the Penitents of the Magdalen House*) Maria Edgeworth in the early nineteenth century was to make a similar comment,

> *I am persuaded.... that if women would reprobate young men for such instances of profligacy and cruelty, instead of suffering such conduct to go under the fine plausible names of gallantry and wildness, it would make a greater impression than all the sermons which could be preached. (Patronage, 1814)*

At the same time it has been noteworthy how frequently fallen women took on all the blame themselves, forgiving their lover everything, and thus, unwittingly perhaps, they too helped contribute to a system that perpetuated itself by the very attitudes of the people, like themselves, within it. In *The Passions*, Julia felt so guilty about the thought of having an affair – even though she never actually totally betrayed her husband – she wished the punishment of society upon herself. 'Let society point at me as a mark, may I be shunned, unpitied by the pure and good and spurned with contempt by the unworthy.' (Matilda Rosa, 1811) Typically, of course, she totally forgave her husband's best friend who pursued her repeatedly and refused to give her up or leave her alone. It must have been all her fault...

By focussing on the plight of fallen women in general, these female writers looked in varying degrees at the faults in society, which contributed to the problem, including some very hypocritical attitudes that existed within some of the fundamental institutions of society itself. One such example was with Christianity. England was proud of being a Christian country and often proclaimed itself as such – yet in the matter of fallen women such beliefs seem to have fallen, like the unfortunate women, by the wayside. Long gone for many was the belief in Christian forgiveness – in spite of the sinners obvious remorse and attempts to do penance, the reality of the situation was often that one mistake meant a punishment for life. One such penitent, Mary, was told for example, 'What is called in your sex, honour and character can, I fear, never be restored to you, nor will any asseverations or future watchfulness (to adopt the cant of policy and superstition) obliterate the stain.' (Mary Hays, *A Victim of Prejudice*, 1799) This lesson was reinforced even more forcefully later in the novel when her lover:

> *... hinted that society would, with inexorable malignity, hunt me from its privileges ...the consolations of a spotless fame were forever denied me; that the prejudices of the world, unrelenting to my sex, would oppose to all my efforts insuperable barriers...toils and snares would beset my paths and inevitable destruction ultimately overwhelm me.*

Women writers drew attention to the hypocrisy of proclaimed practising Christians in different ways. Even Jane Austen was to comment ironically on it. Look back at *Pride and Prejudice*. Mr Collins was a member of the clergy. After the elopement of Wickham and Lydia Bennett – even after they had been pursued by Darcy and forced to marry – Mr Collins advised her parents, 'You ought certainly to forgive them as Christians, but never admit them into your sight or allow their names to be mentioned in your hearing.' Jane Austen's pointed remark was, 'That is his notion of Christian forgiveness.'

Another reminder to Christians who failed to have a more sympathetic approach to fallen women came from both Mary Hays and Susanna Rowson. In her *Appeal*, Mary Hays had recalled the Gospel story where a woman had been proven to be adulterous. She was brought before Jesus to be judged, 'And ...does he not put all her accusers to shame and to flight by a simple, and unexpected appeal to their consciences, by bidding him who is free cast the first stone?' (1798) Susanna Rowson too was to make a similar authorial comment in her first novel:

> *Surely, when we reflect how many errors we are ourselves subject to, how many secret faults lie hid in the recesses of our hearts, which we should blush to have brought into open day...I say, my dear Madam, when we consider this, we surely may pity the faults of others...The world would deride and scoff...(at) an unfortunate female who has once strayed into the thorny paths of vice, (and) would gladly return to virtue...'tis a very unfeeling world, and does not deserve half the blessings which a bountiful Providence showers upon it. (Charlotte Temple, 1794)*

Mary Robinson too was to ask, 'If none will feel for those who err, where are we to hope for reformation?' (*The Natural Daughter*, 1799) and anonymously had come the loud cry 'Shall we be more rigid than He?'(*Histories of Some of the Magdalen Penitents*, 1759)

Women writers like Mary Wollstonecraft, Mary Hays, Sarah Scott, Charlotte Smith, Elizabeth Inchbald, and Susanna Rowson – to name but a few! – all had personal knowledge and/or family experience of the sufferings of abused and fallen women. Due to these experiences, they were to call for a more sympathetic, humanitarian approach to unfortunate women through emotive experiential writing that raised many of the issues that were likely to have been faced when in such a situation. A striking contrast to the norm was shown in the behaviour of one Christian family, for when faced with the problem, the father began, 'We are Christians, and will endeavour to receive the evil as becomes us...' And a close male family friend reaffirmed, 'What if thou hast been faulty, thou art not the first; God has forgiven thee I am sure; and let him that hath no sin cast the first stone.' Elizabeth Helm also made this simple authorial exhortation during the course of the same novel, 'The villain Edwin succeeded in his infernal purpose. Daughters of chastity condemn not – but pity!' (*The Farmer of Inglewood Forest*, 1796)

Several women were to consider the notion of 'There but for the grace of God, go I'. In 1753, Eliza Haywood had her virtuous, leading female character, Jenny, pose the question:

> *How can I be certain that in the same circumstances I should not have acted in the same manner as poor Sophia has done? I have been defended from the misfortune that has befallen her; – first by my fathers care...and afterwards by the well proved fidelity of the man ordain'd*

> *for me:- had I been left to my own choice, who knows what might have happened. (The History of Jemmy and Jenny Jessamy)*

Mary Hays later wrote in similar vein,'If I have more purity of heart and conduct than these unfortunate sisters, have I not more cause for thankfulness than triumph? Can I lay my hand upon my heart and say what would have been my conduct in precisely the same circumstances?' (*Appeal*, 1798). More poignant still was this exclamation by one Christian mother,' Forgive her? ... Oh, yes, whatever be *our* errors, is she not our child? And though bowed to the earth even with shame and remorse, is it not our duty to raise the poor penitent, and whisper peace and comfort to her desponding soul?' (Susanna Rowson, *Charlotte Temple*, 1794)

When Charlotte Smith used the example of Lady Adeline as a fallen married woman, instead of scorn and rebuke, her leading female characters heard her story,'...with tenderest pity, and made them both anxious to give her all the consolation and assistance she was now capable of receiving.' (*Emmeline*, 1788) Surely this was a far more Christian attitude and one supported by Mary Ann Radcliffe who believed, 'These poor young women, who have through extreme necessity been driven to criminal and unlawful pursuits, are not to be despised or sunk beneath our care, but cherished and supported, in order to reclaim their wicked course of life.' (*The Female Advocate*, 1799) A far better example of Christianity would have been the ability to say simply and honestly, 'I am not ashamed of having rescued a penitent from too severe contumely and restored a valuable member of society.' (Ann Plumptre, *Something New*, 1801)

Just as women writers were to make use of the technique of getting a vital message across through the mouthpiece of strong, positive, respected male role models in their novels – for example when supporting the call for women's education, or a more sympathetic relationship in marriage – so too were they to use the technique with regard to fallen women and their unfortunate children. Charlotte Smith made use of this in a speech by the highly respected Lord Montreville to his wife who did not want their son to marry the illegitimate (and therefore poor) Emmeline. Lady Montreville was determined to send Emmeline out of the way to France and have her confined there until her son was forced to marry another woman. Lord Montreville spoke sharply to his wife:

> *... nor should you, Lady Montreville, in the heat of your resentment forget that you are a woman- a woman too whose birth should give you a liberal mind, and put you above thinking of an action as unfeminine as inhuman ...Surely, as a mother who have daughters of your own, you should have some feeling for this young woman, not at all their inferior, but born in circumstances for which she is not to blame... (Emmeline, 1788)*

Similarly Sarah Fielding used the eponymous hero David Simple to comment on one libertine, 'And is this man respected in the world? Will men converse with him? Should he not be drove from society and a mark set upon him that he might be shunned and despised?' (*The Adventures of David Simple*, 1744)

Concern too was shown for the poor father of seduced girls, and the feeling that something ought to be done about the perpetrator of the crime, rather than letting him get away with it again and again:

> *Gracious heaven! When I think on the miseries that must rend the heart of a doating parent, when he sees the darling of his age at first seduced from his protection and afterwards abandoned, by the very wretch whose promises of love decoyed her from the paternal roof – when he sees her poor and wretched, when fancy paints to me the good old man stooping to raise the weeping penitent, while every tear from her eye is numbered by drops from his bleeding heart, my bosom glows with honest indignation, and I wish for power to extirpate those monsters of seduction from the earth.*
> *(Susanna Rowson, Charlotte Temple, 1794)*

Not all women writers agreed with going this far in terms of direct punishment of men, or even the excessive emotional content, although many were to agree with the basic principle– something ought to be done. Put simply by Mary Brunton, 'It is he who ought to shrink, it is he who ought to tremble, yet it was (she) who trembled' (*Self Control*, 1810)

Although few writers were keen on men being directly punished for seducing women, some like Mary Wollstonecraft agreed that men should take on the responsibility for maintenance, at least of the resulting illegitimate children, and she particularly felt that the

Magdalen House, and other such asylums established for the reformation of fallen women, were not proper remedies for the situation – justice was necessary. (*A Vindication of the Rights of Woman*, 1792). Few would have openly agreed with her.

As it was socially acceptable for men to engage in sexual activity outside of marriage, it was rare to find women writers having men actually showing real remorse for any extensive period, or making true amends for the damage they had caused. A few fictional men even tried to hide the evidence. In *Memoirs of Emma Courtney,* (Mary Hays, 1796) Emma's husband, having had an affair with a servant, tried to abort the resultant foetus and then, as that was unsuccessful, tried to poison the sickly babe with drugs. He, like other guilty men, showed remorse, conveniently, only at the end of his life when it was too late to have taken responsibility publicly, and the damage to the woman had already been done.

Continuing the Christianity theme, one authoress, Sarah Scott, had actually dared to challenge the men to think about Judgement Day itself:

> *Did you reflect but one moment, on another bar, before which you will be summoned, you would see there could be no excuse for violating the laws by which you are there to be tried. If you could justify yourself to the world, or to the women of whose folly you take advantage, by the fallacious arguments which you have so ready for that purpose, such cobweb sophistry cannot weaken the force of an express command. (Millenium Hall, 1762)*

Always one to make a suitable, though apparently less judgemental comment, Jane Austen wrote:

> *That punishment, the public punishment of disgrace should in just measure attend his share of the offence, is we know not one of the barriers, which society gives to virtue. In this world the penalty is less equal than could be wished, but without presuming to look forward to a juster appointment hereafter (i.e. Gods judgement) we may fairly consider* ***a man of sense*** *(my emphasis)...to be providing for himself no small portion of vexation and regret – vexation that must rise sometimes to self reproach, and regret to wretchedness. (Mansfield Park, 1814)*

In other words, in the world, at that time, one had to rely on man being punished by his conscience alone – and of course privately hope that he would receive his just deserts in the after life!

Practical help was being given, gradually in the guise of reformatories or establishments like the Magdalen House in London, where a fallen women would not only be taken care of, but also given retraining, so that she could in time regain her independence by doing a steady job like being a servant, or working for a seamstress. However in order to benefit from such charity she had to give up her child – and not everyone wished to do so. She was also supposed to feel suitably guilty and penitent, although in the *Histories of Some of the Penitents of the Magdalen House* (1759) some inmates only said they were penitent in order to gain admittance. Hardly surprising really... It was still very much taken for granted that it was the woman's fault – there was still the emphasis on her mistake, her fall and her need for redemption.

As a fundraising ploy for the Magdalen House it had been said, in both newspapers like *The Times* and propaganda articles, that middleclass women who did fall were in grave danger of becoming actual prostitutes – rather than just fallen women trying to survive honestly. Something had to be done to help them. Amelia Opie was well aware of this when she wrote:

> *In my opinion mistaken writers of both sexes, have endeavoured to prove that many an amiable woman has been forever lost to virtue and the world, and become the victim of prostitution, merely because her own fault was treated with ill judging and criminal severity.*
> *(The Father and Daughter, 1801)*

Women certainly feared the evils of prostitution, and many of the novels cited show to what extent women tried to avoid them and earn some form of honest living, even though they had lost everything else. Eliza Haywood showed this before the Magdalen House was even set up, 'Heavens to be a common prostitute – to earn precarious bread by being the slave of every man's licentious will. What is digging in the mines? What is begging? What is starving compared to this?' (*The History of Miss Betsy Thoughtless*, 1751)

Not everyone supported the enterprising and philanthropic gentlemen responsible for setting up the House. Even the *Histories of the Penitents* gave the example of one virtuous local landlady commenting on its establishment, 'I have no patience with the gentlemen who give encouragement to such wickedness: Starving is too good for them.' The conservative Hannah More, who had very set attitudes regarding behaviour and virtue in young people, was very clear in her opinion when she stated harshly:

> *Be not anxious to restore the fallen penitent against the laws she has so grievously afforded and remember that her soliciting such a restoration furnishes but too plain a proof that she is not the penitent your partiality would believe.... To restore a criminal to public society is perhaps to tempt her to repeat her crime, or to deaden her repentence for having committed it.*
> *(Strictures on the Modern System of Education, 1799)*

Was it right that fallen women should be condemned forever, or should they have been helped to rejoin society? People differed in their opinions, often being guided by their own personal knowledge and experience – or lack of it. Many of the writers included in this chapter tried to draw attention to the double standard, and through their own direct and indirect experiences of the problems that it caused for many, tried at least to raise people's awareness of the realities of the situation – the despair, the degradation, the suffering, the misery and the isolation of the fallen women. They knew there would be no easy solution. They were aware that it would be difficult enough to change people's attitudes, let alone the laws that helped enforce them. Even so, in different ways, to different extents, according to their own beliefs and assumptions, they could not only warn women of the dangers, but also start to make pathways towards a better future for those who did succumb.

Unfortunately negative attitudes towards fallen women would continue for many years – even when I lived as a teenager in Chelmsford, Essex in the promiscuous 1960's, I remember my mother talking about the home for unmarried mothers there. Just as in the eighteenth and nineteenth centuries the girls there were still the ones to blame. However as far as many of the women writers of the period were concerned, they at least could say, 'I am not of that tyrannical virtue, who condemn all that part of my sex, unhappy enough at one

time in their life, to deviate from its path.' (Mrs Skinn, *Old Maid*, 1771)
They could also look forward to the time that Felicia Skene could envisage when, eventually, 'These matters want looking into by someone who had the power to put them right.' (*Hidden Depths*, 1866)

Chapter Seven
A Woman Alone

According to Richard Steele writing in the eighteenth century periodical *The Spectator*, a woman's role was easily defined, 'All she has to do in this world, is contained within the Duties of a Daughter, a Sister, a Wife and a Mother.' (April 2, 1712) As I have already shown this view was held in common with many of both sexes; the place and function of women in society was largely defined by their relationship with significant males. However to view women in such limited terms was to turn a blind eye to a problematic situation – how was one to consider women who did not fit into this broad pattern? What of those women who, for whatever reason, did not have a relationship with a significant male – those who had no father, or husband or even brother to guide or protect them? What prospects did life hold for them? Even the philosopher Rousseau could offer them no suitable role or place. It was much easier for them to be dismissed or totally ignored. Frances Burney illustrated the point when her character Lord Merton said, 'I don't know what the devil a woman lives for after thirty: she is only in other folk's way.' (*Evelina,* 1778) According to this notion a woman had only a limited period of usefulness in her life. It was her duty to marry and have children, after that she had little to contribute and spinsters were thus a complete anomaly.

Certainly there were many references in literature to single women aged twenty seven and over who were considered old maids, left on the shelf, unwanted and unloved, and serving no useful purpose. Such women were often portrayed as embittered, sour, grumpy, 'hateful old cats' and even 'spiteful witches'. They were failures; they had no man to provide for them and they had failed to win a husband of their own – whether through lack of wealth, status or beauty – and so they were subject to mockery and derision by those who had little or no understanding of their situation. The negative image of an old maid could be quite a disturbing one. In 1711 the future Lady Mary Wortley Montague wrote in a letter:

> *I have a Mortal Aversion to be an Old Maid, and a decaid Oak before my window, leaveless half rotten, and shaking its wither'd Top, puts me in Mind every morning of an Antiquated Virgin, Bald, with Rotten Teeth, and a shaking of the Palate.*

Rather than be subjected to such negative attitudes, it is perhaps understandable why some women persistently tried their luck in the marriage market and in their desperation did not necessarily make wise choices. Mary Astell described the situation:

> *... for the poor lady...having spread all her Nets and used all her Arts for Conquest and finding that the Bait fails where she would have it take, ... and growing every day more and more sensible that the respect which us'd to be paid her, decays as fast as her Beauty; quite terrified with the dreadful name of* ***Old Maid,*** *she flies to some dishonourable Match as her last, tho' much mistaken Refuge, to the disgrace of her Family and her own irreparable Ruin.*
> *(A Serious Proposal to the Ladies, 1694)*

Jane Austen was to refer to a somewhat similar situation in *Pride and Prejudice*, (1813) where Charlotte Lucas was only too ready to pick up Mr Collins on the rebound from his rejection by Lizzie Bennett, rather than face being an old maid. Charlotte knew that he 'was neither sensible nor agreeable; his society was irksome and his attachment to her must be imaginary. But he would still be her husband.' For Charlotte such a marriage was still a far more preferable option than being an old maid without a home of her own. In another Austen novel one poor old maid, Miss Bates, was made fun of by the eponymous heroine, who then commented harshly, 'if I thought I'd be (like her) I'd marry tomorrow.' (*Emma,* 1816)

Some, of course, were unable to catch a husband, no matter how hard they tried, and could 'be reduced to the uncomfortable and mortifying situation of my poor forlorn Aunt Patty who has been praying for an husband any time these twenty years; and all to so little purpose, I don't believe she will ever pray again.' (Mrs Skinn, *The Old Maid*, 1771) Humorous though this particular example may seem the issue was a serious one and the prospect of living alone, without the protection of a male or the benefit of his income or status, was not just of concern to those women who became too old to gain a husband. Many women found themselves in the same unenviable position through circumstances beyond their control – through bereavement, family illness or tragedy, the failure of business and so on. While it is true that some women were fortunate enough to benefit from legacies that provided them with independent means, my concern is not with them at present.

For those females who had been raised in the middling or even upper classes, with an emphasis on accomplishments rather than a real education that could have enabled them to make their own way in the world, to find they had lost everything must have been devastating indeed. When a husband died, unless he had made provision for his unmarried daughters, they along with the wife were likely to find their financial circumstances seriously altered. They could even be homeless. Sons who had been educated for a trade or profession could go out into the world and earn a living; they may even have inherited property and estate. Women, as a rule, were less fortunate. Jane Austen, along with her mother and sister, had had to move to ever-cheaper properties in Bath after the death of her father as they found it increasingly difficult to make ends meet. Charlotte Lennox was but one author who was to draw attention to the plight of widows when she warned:

> *You have alas! many evils to struggle against. Poverty is a more dreadful monster than any Hercules overcame: and to bear it with patience, to preserve our integrity, our independence of mind; in a word, to fall with dignity, is to be a greater hero than he was. (Euphemia, 1790)*

With the benefit of hindsight it is easy to be critical of the times, and wonder why on earth people did not foresee the difficulties that could lay ahead for women – if the men on whom they were dependent should suddenly become unable to provide for them. Surely it was foolish to assume that all daughters would be able to make successful marriages and be adequately provided for, and that widows would manage on whatever was left behind. I was amazed to find that Mary

Hays had actually raised some of those important issues when she had written the following letter to the editor of *The Monthly Magazine* in 1797. It is worth quoting from at length:

> *The greatest proportion of young women are trained up by thoughtless parents, in ease and luxury, with no other dependence for their future support than the precarious chance of establishing themselves in marriage; for this purpose (the men best know why) elaborate attention is paid to external attractions and accomplishments, to the neglect of more useful and more solid accomplishments ... Might not a part of the time wasted in the acquisition of beliefs and frivolous accomplishments, be devoted to the attainment of some ingenious art or useful trade by which a young woman might hope to gain an honest and honourable independence and be freed from the disgrace of bartering her person to procure a maintenance.*

She then went on to severely criticise the parents who, in effect, had let their daughters down, 'Every parent having a family of daughters for whom it is not in his power to make a suitable provision is guilty of cruelty and vice, when he hazards their being exposed, helpless and unprotected to the world.'

Mary Hays was not alone in placing the blame firmly with the parents of young girls who failed to prepare them for some of life's adversities. Mary Ann Radcliffe was to write in a similar vein:

> *When the parents die and leave them what can be said in behalf of such parents? Can their easy compliance with the fashion of the times form any apology for such a mistaken conduct? – This surely cannot be called true paternal affection, to entail upon these helpless young creatures such a succession of misery as must eventually ensue?*
> *(The Female Advocate, 1799)*

Although in *Pride and Prejudice* Mrs Bennett who, while acting in common with other mothers of the time, is much laughed at for her obsession with marrying off her daughters, at least had been showing some concern for their future well being.

In other novels of the eighteenth and early nineteenth centuries a sick or dying parent would acknowledge that there was no provision for the daughters of the family, and had only started to worry about their future when it was too late for any remedial action to take place. Maria Edgeworth, who has already been shown to have very strong theoretical and practical ideas regarding education for girls, did acknowledge that while some parents had 'sufficient kindness and foresight to provide, in point of fortune, for their daughters', they still failed to realise that if the young women were to remain single they may wish to have achieved something more in their lives than empty headed accomplishments. (*Letters to Literary Ladies*, 1795) However in a later novel (*Helen*, 1834) she too could be found making the point that no plans were being made for the future of unmarried women...

> *She is young to know sorrow...How cruel of her uncle (ie her guardian) with all his fondness for her, never to think what would become of her the moment he was dead; to breed her up as an heiress and leave her a beggar, and to struggle with difficulties to which she is quite unsuited, both by nature and education.*

Mary Lamb had raised the point that it was unfortunate that there was no way to predict in advance which daughters would fail to acquire husbands, and thus secure their own livelihood, so that parents could focus on properly educating those girls who would need to go out in the world. These parents:

> *...would feel it a duty incumbent on themselves to strengthen the minds, and even the bodily constitutions of their girls, so circumstanced, by an education which, without confronting the preconceived habits of society, might enable them to follow some occupation now considered above the capacity or too robust for the constitution of our sex.*
> *(Letter to the British Ladies Magazine, 1815, On Needlework)*

She also gave a nice twist to her argument by asking what boy's parents would bother to spend a fortune educating them and training them, if it was most likely that by the time they were twenty they would be living off the wealth of their marriage partner?

A number of women writers had made more direct calls to the girls themselves to raise their own standards and expectations, so they were more prepared for unknown future needs. As early as 1694 Mary Astell had asked, ' How can you be content to be in the World like Tulips, to make a fine shew and be good for nothing?' (*A Serious Proposal to the Ladies*) Mary Wollstonecraft in particular was strongly in favour of girls using their brains and developing into rational beings capable of earning their own living, 'How much more respectable is the woman who earns her own bread by fulfilling any duty, than the most accomplished beauty.' (*A Vindication of the Rights of Woman*, 1792) She had a warning for those who preferred the life of ease, decorative accomplishments, and being admired for beauty rather than skills or personality:

> *Proud of their weakness however, they must always be protected, guarded from care, and all the rough toils that dignify the mind. If this be the fiat of fate, if they will make themselves insignificant and contemptible, sweetly to waste life away, let them not expect to be valued when their beauty fades. (Ibid)*

These girls in particular would have found it very hard if their safe world collapsed and they had to rely on their own resources.

Mary Ann Radcliffe believed that there were plenty of women like herself who would willingly try to make their own way in the world, in spite of an inappropriate education or upbringing that had never allowed for the possibility of them having no future provision, particularly if they suddenly found themselves in dire need:

> *What numbers of helpless and destitute young women there are, who seeing themselves neglected and despised by their connections....would gladly endeavour, through necessity to make up the deficiency of their parents neglect by putting themselves forward in the world, in order to obtain a support. (The Female Advocate, 1799)*

She was very conscious of the difficulties they could face, as during the course of her own working life she tried being a governess, teacher and companion, as well as more unusually attempting to run a shoe shop and a cake shop. She knew only too well that for some of those who tried to be independent,

> *... alas to their sorrow, they quickly see it is not in their power; for under the present circumstances, the world is not their friend, nor the*

> *worlds laws... What was not effected by their parents, cannot possibly be obtained by an inexperienced young woman. (Ibid)*

Several specific references have been made in the quotations above to the 'upbringing' rather than the 'education' of these females, which in effect handicapped their chances of success. Women from the middling and upper classes could be so protected from the world, with little experience of dealing with situations by themselves, that they lacked the skills in order to gain a job and even the methods of finding one – beyond word of mouth. They also could have very little knowledge of the financial issues that would so suddenly affect them. Frances Burney had referred to the 'painful timidity, that to the inexperienced and modest, is often subversive to the use of the very talents which it is their business and interest to display.' (*The Wanderer*, 1814) Women had been taught that they should not put themselves forward, or sell their talents for money, and that they should always retain an air of submissive modesty and obedience. Within the marriage market such attributes, along with beauty, social standing and preferably wealth, placed a young woman in high regard. When her luck ran out, however, previous family status and values could count for little.

Sarah Fielding had this to say on the matter:

> *Alas there is no situation so deplorable, no condition so much to be pitied, as that of a gentlewoman in real poverty. I mean by real poverty, not having sufficient to procure us necessaries, for good sense will teach people to moderate their desires and lessen their way of living and be content. Birth, family and education become misfortunes when we cannot attain some means of supporting ourselves in the station they throw us into; our friends and acquaintances look on it as a disgrace to own us. (The Adventures of David Simple, 1744)*

Charlotte Lennox also showed her awareness of this when she had her heroine, Henrietta, state, 'It was not indeed easy to form any plan for my future subsistence, which would not subject me to a situation very unfit for my birth.' (*Henrietta*, 1758)

The theme continued throughout the century. Charlotte Smith later was still raising a similar point when Lucy Marchmont said, 'But I must not, says family pride, go into business, for I am descended from people who were of great consequence two hundred years ago, and of still more in the last century. Ah dear, my ancestors will *now* do nothing for me... What then are we to do?' (*Marchmont*, 1796) Mary Hays was to show a more emotional response, in the form of anger, in her fictional work:

> *Cruel prejudices! – I exclaimed – hapless woman! Why was I not educated for commerce, for a profession, for labour? Why have I been rendered feeble and delicate by bodily constraint, and fastidious by artificial refinement? Why are we bound, by the habits of society, as with an adamantine chain? Why do we suffer ourselves to be confined within a magic circle, without daring, by a magnanimous effort, to dissolve the barbarous spell?*
> *(Memoirs of Emma Courtney, 1796)*

More objective than angry, Maria Edgeworth had her own version of the problem in the early nineteenth century, and through it she referred to the fatal double standard that ran through so much of society at the time. This is from *Patronage* (1814):

> *How much temper and strength of mind are necessary, to enable women to support the loss of wealth and station! – A man who has received a liberal education may maintain himself with honour by the exertion of his abilities in respectable professions, and in a variety of employments, which are allowed to be gentleman like. In doing this he continues to be on a footing with his equals in birth; his personal merit and mental qualifications ensure him admission into the first societies; but a woman, by the caprice, the cruelty of custom, is degraded by the very industry which should obtain respect, and, if unmarried, she loses the prospect of being suitably established in life.*

Underlying all of these issues was the awareness of a single key point, 'The Principle by which alone man can become what man is capable of being, is independence.' *(Mary Hays, Memoirs of Emma Courtney, 1796)* Without that independence single women could face a grim future. In those days there was no welfare state, no system of benefits to cover the basic needs of widow, spinster or female orphan. The lack of work opportunities for women of the middling classes, or an inability to obtain work within those limited parameters, for example through advanced age, disability, infirmity or youth, were among the main causes of them being forced them into a dependent situation when disaster struck.

It was also suggested in Mary Hays' novel that there was a direct link between the great fear of dependence and the infamous career of prostitution – with women sometimes left with little to choose between them:

> *Hapless woman! – crushed by the iron hand of barbarous despotism, pampered into weakness, and trained the slave or meretricious folly!- what wonder that shrinking from the chill blasts of penury (which the pernicious habits of thy education have little fitted thy tender frame to encounter)...and to escape the galling chain of servile dependence, (thou) rushest into the career of infamy from whence the false and cruel morality of the world forbids thy return and perpetuates thy disgrace and misery. (Ibid)*

Mary Ann Radcliffe had referred to this link in *The Female Advocate* (1799) – but I have found few other direct references to it elsewhere – only the possible link between fallen women and a downward spiral into prostitution that was mentioned in the previous chapter.

With few working opportunities available to her, one of the greatest fears for a single woman was being left completely dependent on the good will and generosity of other family members or friends, or even bare acquaintances. Although some no doubt really benefited from the arrangement of being taken into another's household on a permanent footing, with all basic needs of board and lodging taken care of, and personal needs too, like clothing, there was no guarantee that such humanitarian aspects as love, affection and even respect would be part of the bargain.

Scattered amongst novels by a wide variety of women authors are references to the distress that the fear of dependency evoked. These are just a few examples: 'The small pittance bequeathed to me was insufficient to preserve me from dependence. – *Dependence!* I repeated to myself and I felt my heart die within me.'(Mary Hays, *Memoirs of Emma Courtney*, 1796) 'How dreadful is that woman's fate who is born to dependence... I sicken at the prospect before me.' (*The False Friend*,

Mary Robinson, 1799) Charlotte Smith too had written, 'There is something so pitiable in the situation of a little unprotected old being who is forced to eat the bitter bread of dependence,'(*The Young Philosopher*, 1798) and she had even written a poem about it:

Dependence! Heavy, heavy are thy chains,
And happier they who from the dangerous sea,
Or the dark mine, procure with ceaseless pains,
A hard earned pittance – than trust to thee.

So what could go wrong if one was unfortunate enough to find oneself in a dependent situation? You do not have to search for long to find examples in both fiction and non-fiction. Accepting dependence meant a loss of dignity, any independence in terms of action and choice, a need for submission and acceptance, and frequently an obligation to remain eternally 'grateful'. Mary Robinson had this to say on the subject, 'Where fortune frowns, where necessity propels, the proudly enlightened mind is frequently condemned to bear the insolence of wealth, the pomp of pity, and the pang of smothered indignation.'(*The False Friend*, 1799) Jane Austen used the example of Fanny Price in *Mansfield Park* (1814), who as a dependent was frequently patronised by her Aunt Norris and constantly reminded of her lowly position and obligation of gratitude to the family. This was said openly in front of her, 'I shall think her a very obstinate, ungrateful girl, if she does not do what her aunts and cousins wish her – very ungrateful indeed, considering who and what she is.' Fanny also had to face the awkwardness of family activities, which did not necessarily include her, and found it very uncomfortable. When they decided to put on a family play:

Everybody around her was gay and busy, prosperous and important, each had their object of interest, their part... She alone was sad and insignificant; she had no share in anything; she might go or stay, she might be in the midst of their noise, or retreat from it... without being seen or missed. She could almost think that anything would have been preferable to this. (Ibid)

It is not hard to imagine the difficulties that had to be faced with the arrival of a not necessarily loved, or wanted, relative on a permanent basis – both from the perspective of the dependent person, or the family due to receive her. Examples can be found from real life, shown in personal correspondence of the period, where the dependent woman concerned had not been impressed by the behaviour and comments of the family towards her. In 1736 Marthae Taylor for example complained to her niece that she had been tossed 'from wig to wall,' when age and infirmity meant that she needed to live with a relative. She complained that only the immediate members of the family – whether husbands, wives or children, received any consideration or affection. Whether she contributed anything positive herself to the household, in terms of love, care, or completing minor chores is uncertain, but undoubtedly she felt neglected. In a similar letter written some thirty years later Mary Allsopp had written to a friend that she did not think she deserved to be treated so badly by her relatives. She was prepared to mention her unhappiness to the relatives concerned, but no attention was paid to her complaint, indeed her nephews actually 'seemed deaf' when she told them of the 'miserable situation' she was in. One had to be grateful for being taken in as a dependent, but it does not seem to have been an ideal choice.

As I have mentioned before, male members of a family received preparation for life's difficulties in the form of education, general experience and going off to work. In many situations they were then left with financial responsibilities for the female members of the family when the father died. In the late seventeenth century for example a woman named Anne Chaytor wrote to her brother,

> *I could never speak to you anything concerning my fortune before you married, but always relied on your good nature which I always found, and still do – though it is generally seen that people's kindness is much taken off from their relations when they have once got a wife.*

For anyone who has read *Sense and Sensibility* (Jane Austen, 1811) such a complaint may sound a little familiar. In this novel when Mr Henry Dashwood died he relied on his son John to take care of his step-mother and sisters, as they were not actually covered in his will. The son was aware of his obligation and was willing to carry out his father's wish – it was the actions of his wife that prevented it. By persuading her husband that their own children would miss out, she justified an ever-decreasing amount to be given to his female family members until she virtually justified them receiving nothing at all. The hardships that she was so keen to inflict upon them would no doubt have been totally unacceptable to her – but she was quite happy to dish them out to someone else! Returning to Anne Chaytor's case above, she did want to marry and had to remind her brother of the portion due to her. He decided to only give her half of it, keeping the rest for himself, and then pretended it was a gift out of his own kindness! From her earlier comments I wonder how much his wife had to do with it...

Throughout my research I have come across many examples of women being deliberately unpleasant, even vindictive, towards other women, in order to promote themselves and enjoy the feeling of power and control. Possibly the clearest example of this is in one of the situations of dependency where a woman became a 'companion' to another wealthier, frequently single or widowed, woman. In this situation the vacancy may have been advertised through word of mouth, one to another, so that the companion may have had no idea of the nature of the woman to whom she had become committed. A poor woman may have had no choice but to take the position anyway, if her situation had been really desperate, and in her role as companion a woman could be required to do anything, whether she liked it or not.

Women writers were to make regular use of the tragic plight of such a female throughout the eighteenth and nineteenth centuries in order to expose the tyrannical situations that such unfortunate women could face. During her lifetime Frances Burney, like Jane Austen, was to make many close observations of people's behaviours and had some interesting comments to make on the subject of companions. This is how one of her characters, Mrs Ireton, was to describe the job specification:

> *I meant a person who could be of some use, and some agreeability; a person who could read to me when I was tired, and who when I had nobody else, could talk to me, and find out a thousand little things for me all day long, coming and going, prating or holding her tongue; doing everything she was bid; and keeping always at hand. (The Wanderer, 1814)*

In itself that may sound fairly harmless but you could gain a clearer idea of what was really involved from a conversation held between Mrs Ireton and a friend Mr Giles:

> *'I thought I had engaged a young person, who would never think of taking such a liberty as to give her own opinion; but who would do, as she ought, with respect and submission, whatever I should indicate...'*
>
> *'Why that would be leading the life of a slave... Tell a human being that she must only move, to and fro, like a machine? Only say what she is bid, like a parrot, employ her time, call for her talents, exact her services, yet not let her make any use of her understanding? Neither say what she approves, nor object to what she dislikes? Poor pretty young thing.' (Ibid)*

Other authors too were aware of the misery of dependent, over used and abused companions. Sarah Fielding's character Cynthia had stated in a similar vein, 'I was to have no passions or inclinations of my own, but was to be turned in to a piece of clockwork, which her ladyship was to wind up or let down.'(*The Adventures of David Simple*, 1744) Mary Ann Hanway wrote of Lady Dy's companion who was expected to make up all her hats and clothes, superintend the household accounts, embroider court dresses, keep her company when she was dining alone, wash and clean her pet birds, wash and comb the dog, and so on. When the poor companion did dare to complain that she did the same work the servants did, without their wages, Lady Dy thought she was grossly impertinent. Indeed, 'The superlative happiness ever attending the situation she was placed in, was to be as totally overlooked by the female part of her ladyship's visitors as if she had not been present.' (*Ellinor*, 1798)

There was a less than flattering nickname associated with a companion – a 'toad eater'. Sarah Fielding clearly explained the use of the term and its connection with dependency when she wrote:

> *It is a Metaphor taken from a Mountebanks' Boy's eating Toads, in order to show his Master's Skill in expelling Poison: It is built on a Supposition, (which I am afraid is too generally true) that People who are so unhappy as to be in a State of Dependence, are forced to do the most nauseous things that can be thought on, to please and humour their Patrons. And the Metaphor may be carried on yet further, for most People have so much of the Art of tormenting, that every time they have made the poor Creatures they have in their power* ***swallow a Toad****, they give them something to expel it again, that they may be*

> *ready to swallow the next they think proper to prepare for them: that is when they have abused and fooled them… they grow soft and good to them, on purpose to have it in their power* ***to plague them the more****. (The Adventures of David Simple, 1744)*

Sarah Fielding was a close friend of Jane Collier, the author of *An Essay on The Art of Ingeniously Tormenting*, a highly amusing satirical work that I have had occasion to refer to earlier in this work. It is quite possible that Mary Ann Hanway, Frances Burney and Jane Austen may have come across this satire themselves. It is not difficult to see similarities between sections of their work and a very interesting section within it, on having a companion and how to make life totally miserable for her. The fun would begin by first choosing a companion who was not below the rank of a gentlewoman – so you could feel good yourself about relieving such a woman in distress, and positively revel in the daily tributes of their eternal gratitude. It was important to choose a woman who was not high-spirited but rather one who was meek, gentle and tender hearted because, 'If she has spirit enough to despise your insults…all your sport is lost; and you might as well shoot your venom at a marble statue in your garden!' (*The Art of Ingeniously Tormenting*, 1753)

For someone with malicious tendencies there could be distinct advantages in having a companion rather than another ordinary servant. In some ways the two positions were similar, although there were some significant differences between them:

> *She receives wages, and the humble companion receives none; the servant is most part of the day out of your sight, the humble companion is always ready at your hand to receive every cross word that rises in your mind: the servants can be teased only by yourself, your dogs, your cats, your parrots, your children; the humble companion, besides being the sport of all these, must, if you manage rightly, bear the insults of all your servants themselves… (Ibid)*

To a certain extent one can understand the motives of someone *taking up* a position of being a companion, but looking across the novels I think the motives of some of the women *choosing* to have a companion, which was generally an unpaid position, must be a little suspect at the very least. Several authors, Frances Burney included, suggested that such women chose to have a companion in order to gloat over someone in a less comfortable position than them. Mrs Ireton, whom we have already met, 'was all impatience to display to a new dependent, her fortune, her power and her magnificence.' Charlotte Lennox showed a similar example, when her eponymous heroine confirmed to a friend that in her previous position, 'You have guessed truly… It was to gratify her pride, to have the daughter of a gentleman subjected to her bounty, that made (Lady Manning) so solicitous of having me with her.' (*Henrietta*, 1758)

It is hardly surprising that with such a negative image associated with being a companion, or indeed a family dependent as Fanny Price was in *Mansfield Park*, women feared losing their independence. It was not just a case of being homeless, or lacking financial status or income, or having to work for a living, it was much more personal. If unfortunate enough to be placed with an unsympathetic 'lady' the poor companion could be in for frequent personal attacks. Left with few possessions, her looks, her behaviour, her manner could be all that she had remaining and as such became prime targets for attack. Many authors have referred to the constant humiliation in such a situation, being forever reminded of all one has lost, and all that one can never hope to have again, as well as being told of the need to be grateful. From *The Art of Ingeniously Tormenting* again, while it was suggested that you could insult the companion over her dress, better still, 'One thing be sure not to omit, although it is everso false is to tell her, and in the plainest and grossest terms, that she has, (oh shocking accusation to a fine girl!) sweaty feet and a nauseous breath'. How mean!

Furious scolding and being abusive were good, but apparently insulting taunts were better. You could mortify a companion in public by drawing attention to her situation and could cause a real emotional upset by being sympathetic about the loss of her parents, and then rub it in that she did not have them anymore. In spite of all this abuse of course a companion was unlikely to leave unless she preferred poverty and the workhouse. To prevent any risk of this it was necessary to occasionally sweeten up the victim – and reinforce the obligation to be grateful again. There is an obvious connection here between this alternating pattern of behaviour and the toad-eating sequence that I mentioned earlier.

It is easy to see how Jane Austen may have got her inspiration for Mrs Norris in *Mansfield Park* and Frances Burney for Mrs Ireton in *The Wanderer.* However it would be foolish to dismiss these incidents and examples as purely fictional entertainment. Undeniably there were women of the period who *were* forced into difficult positions of dependency by their lack of independent financial means and the limited opportunities for getting suitable employment. The author of *The Art of Ingeniously Tormenting* had known this only too well. Jane Collier and her sister had to face life as homeless spinsters and relied on the support of friends to help them. They were only too aware of the evils of dependence and Jane drew attention to both the sufferings of those affected and the malicious, vindictive nastiness that could be imposed upon them by thoughtless 'superiors'. Charlotte Lennox though raised a valid point in *Henrietta*, when the heroine was offered a position as companion to a countess who had befriended her. Henrietta had already made it clear she preferred the idea of being a servant to that of being a dependent because she 'was not of a temper to be easy under great obligations.' The countess reassured her:

> *I know your generous scorn of dependence,* ***but it is the unworthiness of the donor only that can make the benefits sit heavy on a mind like yours****: there is often as much greatness of soul in receiving as in conferring benefits, and when true friendship, is the motive for giving, it is pride not generosity to refuse. (Henrietta, 1758)*

Unfortunately I have found little evidence for women being happy in the long-term situation of a dependent companion, but I can accept that there may have been some that were so, providing the temperaments of companion and mistress were compatible. Certainly in the situation where friends supported each other it could be so. Jane Collier had gone to live with her friend Sarah Fielding for a period of time after her own mother and brother had died. Later she was to live with the family of Samuel Richardson, a well-known writer/publisher of the time. So she knew from personal experience how supportive friends and acquaintances *could* be in times of need – but her satire is very useful in showing the reverse of the coin.

Of course, it would have been so much easier if women had been able to work freely for a living, and had their education and training prepared them for it. Mary Wollstonecraft had known that, 'A proper education would enable a woman to support a single life with dignity,' and a widow, even if she had not been left 'a sufficient provision', would at least be in more of a position to look after her own children. (*A Vindication of the Rights of Woman*, 1792) From the illustrations of dependent situations above one can perhaps now understand why Ellis in '*The Wanderer*' (Frances Burney, 1814) decided to change her dependent position with Mrs Ireton for 'an honourable, however fatiguing, exertion of her talents and acquirements with which she had been endowed by her education.' At this stage the thought of working and being self-supporting may have seemed more preferable, however the reality of the situation – that is finding a suitable position and keeping the job – could be somewhat different.

Bearing in mind the limitations regarding most women's education at the time, it was natural that women of the middling classes should look for situations where they could survive on what little knowledge or experience they had. Mary Brunton made this lack of choice clear through her character Ellen, 'What channels had the customs of society left open to the industry of woman? The only one which seemed within my reach was the tuition of youth.' (*Discipline*, 1814) This point was also raised by Mary Wollstonecraft who had commented that, 'The situation of governesses (was) the only one in which even a well-educated woman, with more than ordinary talents, can struggle for a subsistence; and even this is a dependence next to menial.' *(The Wrongs of Woman, or Maria,* 1798)

In Ellen's situation above, fictitious though it may have been, she initially felt she had been fortunate, 'I felt myself less dependent when I recollected my thorough knowledge of music, and my acquaintance with other arts of idleness.' For those parents who only valued accomplishments for their daughters she would at least be an appropriate candidate. But even she had had her doubts about the realities of the situation, and her own ability to deal with it, 'When indeed I considered how small a part of the education of a rational and accountable being I was after all fitted to undertake, I shrank from the awful responsibility of the charge.' For Adeline Mowbray, in a similar fictional position, it was easy to be more realistic, 'I had seen enough of the world to know that it would be difficult to obtain the office of teacher upon the mere strength of my acquaintance with what I pretended to teach.' (Amelia

Opie, *Adeline Mowbray*, 1805) Charlotte Smith made a brief reference to one elderly governess who had never had the benefit of a good education and could only have limited expectations regarding the performance of her role. The pitiful situation was summarised very poignantly, 'As she knew nothing, she could teach nothing; but she was careful of the children's health.' (*The Young Philosopher*, 1798)

From the brief examples above one can begin to appreciate the real problems facing women when they did go out into the world, and to anticipate some of the situations they would face if they did take up a position in education, as governess, school mistress or even 'headmistress' of a small school of their own. In novels at least it was not uncommon for a woman to take up a position some distance from her home. To move away from home was always a learning curve – and not always a happy one. However there was one advantage in doing so for women who suddenly had to go out in the world to earn a living. It was at least one way to avoid the embarrassment and possible humiliation in the area where one was known, particularly if you had to take up a teaching position in the very circles you used to move within. This is how one character, Ellen, described the situation, 'To meet scorn in the glances of once envious rivals, and pity in the eye of once rejected lovers, would have furnished exercise for more humility than I had yet attained.' (Mary Brunton, *Discipline*, 1814)

Once she had arrived at her new 'home' there could be all sorts of problems waiting in the wings for a governess – particularly if she was young and/or pretty. Ignoring any questions of education for a moment, there were the problems of relationships with the family – adults included. If for example the governess was well educated, and the mistress of the house was not, there could be problems of jealousy that could result in the undermining of her position in the house. It was not just a question of showing the servants you looked down on the poor governess and encouraging their neglectful behaviour towards her. It was also extremely easy for the mistress of the house to undermine any work done with the children there, by countermanding instructions that the governess had given, finding fault with her in front of the children and letting them off any punishment due to them for bad behaviour, by excusing it. It could be the art of tormenting all over again. Mary Ann Hanway drew attention to the similarity of position for governesses, humble companions or poor relations by saying, 'They are all treated with uniform cold neglect by all the domestic establishment, who are very quick at adopting the manners and opinions of their superiors.' (*Ellinor*, 1798)

The other problem of course could be to do with the husband. If he was not strictly moral in his behaviour it could be very uncomfortable if not dangerous being a young and innocent governess living in his house. The wife could feel jealous at the very least and use this as another excuse to be unkind; the governess could be unfairly dismissed whether she was 'in trouble' or not. In *Millenium Hall*, Miss Mancel was advised to remain a little longer in school, even though 'her understanding and attainments were far superior to her years' for 'her youth would be a great impediment to her in any undertaking'. One of her masters indeed advised her that, 'she must not expect, while her person continued such as it was, that a married woman would receive her in any capacity that fixed her in the same house of her husband.' (Sarah Scott, 1762) Sometimes older governesses were deliberately selected for a position, regardless of their previous experience, as they would pose no threat to the mistress of the house.

Socially the governess could be in a difficult position too. Women writers with personal knowledge or experience of the job– like Mary Wollstonecraft, and later Anne and Charlotte Brontë – referred to the loneliness that was often felt by governesses who were in a somewhat isolated position, living in a strange limbo between the family above stairs and the servants below:

> *Alone in large mansions, I say alone, because they had no companions with whom they could converse on equal terms, or from whom they could expect the endearments of affection, they grew melancholy and the sound of joy made them sad.*
> *(Maria or The Wrongs of Woman, 1798)*

Jane Fairfax, in the novel *Emma* had put off becoming a governess for similar reasons:

> *With the fortitude of a devoted novitiate, she had resolved at twenty one to complete the sacrifice, and retire from all the pleasures of life, of rational intercourse, equal society, peace and hope, to penance and mortification for ever. (Jane Austen, 1816)*

Elizabeth Elstob, in her personal correspondence of the mid eighteenth century, was to raise a point that was commonly referred to in women's literature of both the eighteenth and nineteenth centuries regarding the lives of governesses. It was the question of time; free time. For a governess could be required to look after her charges for virtually all the time they were awake, and remain in their rooms, or alone in her own, when they were asleep. There were no unions, no agreed codes of conduct, and no negotiable contracts. If you were employed you did as you were told – or you left. So Elizabeth Elstob commented, 'I have less time than I ever had in my life to command because it is not my own.'

The primary function of a governess was to be responsible for the education of the children in her charge, and this could include moral education as well as the more standard subjects, but unless she had previous experience whether in a working capacity, or from years of experience in her own familial setting, success was not guaranteed. I expect you are familiar with the old adage, 'Those who can, do; those who can't, teach.' Unlike some I had always known I wanted to be a teacher, made suitable subject choices towards my desired profession during school years, obtained an honours degree and postgraduate teaching qualification, then taught for fifteen years. The problems I faced in the classroom were little different to those faced by women throughout the ages who have taken up teaching in some form or another. However I had some major advantages – I had received a good education and followed it up with professional training, and my personal motivation was not financially based. I believed I had a vocation. They say you learn on the job, you learn by experience. In teaching this is most certainly true.

Not everyone however is suited to teaching – and for those who are not it can be very difficult to cope, even if you felt it was your only option. Elizabeth Elstob, mentioned above, was not suited to the task and found it very difficult. She wrote, ' I have no time to do anything til six at night when I have done the duty of the day and then am frequently so fatigued that I am obliged to lie down for an hour or two.' She also complained, 'When my school is done my little ones leave me incapable of either reading, writing or thinking, for their noise is not out of my head till I fall asleep, which is often too late.'

Mary Robinson described the situation for her character Mrs

Morley who 'thought of gaining a livelihood by the dull drudgery of diffusing knowledge in a seminary of fashionable education.' She was engaged as a teacher in a boarding school where:

> *Here indeed her patience was put to the trial, by the stupidity of some; the infantine impertinence of others; the budding pride of the high-born; the pert vulgarity of the low; while the dawning consequence of the wealthy, and the confirmed arrogance of the dull minded presented to her view a little phalanx of future tyrants... (The Natural Daughter, 1799)*

Frances Burney had referred to the 'dull and dry labour of teaching' although her character Ellis acknowledged that as:

> *... it was a profession so preferable to all others... she bore patiently and cheerfully the minute mechanical, and ear-wearing toil, of giving lessons to the unapt, the stupid, the idle, and the wilful; for such, unhappily are the epithets most ordinarily due to beginners in all sciences and studies. (The Wanderer, 1814)*

This was to be repeated some thirty years later by Anne Bronte in her work, *Agnes Grey*, which was largely based on her own early teaching experiences, when she wrote, 'Irksome as my situation was, I earnestly wished to retain it.'(1846)

Rather than being a governess in someone else's home, a more risky educational venture was to either join someone else's, or consider setting up a school of one's own. For this one needed premises, whether within a room of your own dwelling or a separate establishment, one also needed educators and one needed a clientele. Schools could vary in their rate of success, and in what were considered to be the criteria of success. Some were to emphasise the feminine accomplishments discussed earlier, some were to provide a more worthwhile educational experience. Some were more geared towards childcare and basic skills for the young – others were providing little more than somewhere to offload unwanted children. It is known that the school run by the spinster Hannah More and her sisters was very successful in its time, and helped provide her with an income which, along with the profits of her books, meant that she was one of the few highly successful single women of the time.

It is uncanny reading the women's literature of the period and seeing just how many issues raised in their works were taken up later, particularly during the Victorian era, in the attempts to raise the status of women's education, and create professional training for them, as well as to see how many are still real issues of education today. These points were raised within the context of novels and serious works alike, and were considered from the perspective of those women, like the untrained governesses and school mistresses, who had to face them. Frances Burney may never have been a teacher herself, although she did observe her father teaching music and had many opportunities to see other teachers in action. In spite of the fact that these words are in the text of a novel, her comments on the science of teaching are significant:

> *Wide is the difference between exhibiting that which we have obtained only for that purpose (e.g. performing an instrument) from the power of dispensing knowledge to others… But to disseminate knowledge, by clearing that which is obscure, and explaining what is difficult; to make what is hard appear easy …to lighten the fatigue of practice, by the address of method, to shorten what requires study by anticipating its result; and demonstrating effects to expound their cause: by the rules of art to hide the want of science; and to supply the dearth of genius by divulging the secrets of embellishments; these were labours that demanded not alone brilliant talents…but a fund of scientific knowledge. (The Wanderer, 1814)*

Ellis, the would-be teacher in question, did not feel she possessed it.

In other words in order to do the job properly women had to be better educated themselves, as well as understanding what the job required. For a woman alone, facing the prospect of earning a living for the first time, the lack of these skills could cause real difficulties. The extract above had been written in the days before the general appreciation of the importance of different teaching and learning styles, multi-sensory teaching, accelerated learning techniques and so on. Yet Frances Burney, albeit unconsciously, seems to have been aware of them. Similarly Maria Edgeworth was a writer of novels, yet she had ample experience of teaching from the educating of her father's many children. She wrote education textbooks that would help parents, teachers and governesses in their task, but she was also very aware of the need for professional training for women teachers and a recognised qualification at the end of it. Her recommendation to parents regarding the appointment of a governess is worth noting. Parents should appoint 'some person of enlarged and philanthropic mind' and should ensure that she had 'a sound discriminating and enlarged understanding' and should also know 'whether her mind be free from prejudice; whether she has steadiness of temper to pursue her own plans; and above all, whether she has that species of integrity which will justify a parent in trusting a child to her care.' (*Practical Education,* 1798)

Maria Edgeworth was not alone in realising the importance of education, and other authors like her understood how easy it was for some parents to delegate all responsibility for their children on to the shoulders of other people (the governess for example), and then criticise only them for all the shortcomings. I am sure anyone from the National Union of Teachers or any similar organisation would be only too amused to read the following extract, especially when they realise it was written over two hundred years ago:

> *Schools are fluctuating and uncertain; a parcel of gossips will sit in judgement upon them and their conductors. Schools are talked up, and talked down, by those who know nothing of their requisites, or the real government of them. Parents are weak and partial: in that case, they are offended that their children are exceeded by others. Are there others, who are careless and indifferent towards them? They will exonerate themselves of all blame, by throwing the whole of their faults upon their preceptors and governesses. The conducting of a seminary of education is an arduous and laborious undertaking; it is not duly estimated, nor sufficiently rewarded. Those who devolve upon others the important charge of education, do not sufficiently consider their obligation to those who discharge it faithfully, and who are to acquit themselves of a most serious duty to society in general, and their families respectively.*
> *(Clara Reeve, School for Widows, 1791)*

For those who were dedicated teachers, in whatever form, the responsibility of educating the young was a serious business. From the same book Mrs Darnford, acting as a governess, summarised her feelings thus, 'I have undertaken an important charge, and I am obliged to perform the duties of it. I am accountable to your friends, to you, and to myself; and I cannot be pleased with myself if I do not.'

In spite of the dedication of some of them, women educators did not have a very high status in society, and writers like Maria Edgeworth realised that this had a direct link with their financial remuneration for the task. Jane Austen too was to point out that teaching was hard work and women teachers should have been better rewarded. Referring to her novel *Emma* again, when the eponymous heroine heard about Jane Fairfax's plan to start working as a governess, the subject of salaries was raised, 'Ah, madam...if other children are like what I remember to have been myself, I should think five times the amount of what I have ever yet heard named as salary on such occasions, dearly earned.' (*Emma*, 1816)

Mary Wollstonecraft had noted the inequality between the sexes for financial remuneration when educating the young. She had pointed out, 'When a superior education enables (women) to take charge of the education of children as governesses, they are not treated like the tutors of sons.' (*A Vindication of the Rights of Woman,* 1792) Maria Edgeworth had taken this consideration a stage further – male tutors were not only given a far higher wage, but they could also gain positions, for example within the church, that would ensure they were looked after even in their old age. Governesses and women teachers were poorly paid and were unable as a rule to put by for that eventuality. (Maria and Richard Edgeworth, *Practical Education,* 1798) Sick, elderly, unemployable single women could look forward to poverty and the grim prospect of the workhouse. In the mid to late nineteenth century such issues were to be taken more seriously – women were being trained for their educating role and benevolent associations would help out with the problems of being old or sick. Maria Edgeworth's suggestion that women teachers should receive greater remuneration for their efforts, so they could look after their own needs later in life, fell on mainly deaf ears at the time.

It is true that I have focussed at some length on the situation of a working governess, or schoolmistress, rather than on other occupations that may have been undertaken by women left alone in the world. This is mainly because there is such an abundance of information and evidence available, both in fiction and non fiction, which covers so many issues pertinent, not only to the difficulties a woman faced when actually working, but also to all the other interrelated problems she faced throughout her life, which have been raised in previous chapters. The vast quantity of literature on this subject did not by any means diminish as time progressed during the nineteenth century. It has even been said that the governess story has almost become a genre in itself, like crime fiction, or romance, with so many women writers concerned with the subject, although a great number of whom are little known to modern readers. Classics by the Brontë sisters, like *Jane Eyre* and *Agnes Grey* are more famous, but it has to be remembered that they too were written with the benefit of experience.

One other occupation that was occasionally mentioned in women's literature was that of sewing, which could be taken in and completed at home for a fee, or completed in a workroom belonging to a seamstress, mantua maker and so on. (A mantua was a fashionable loose gown worn open over a petticoat, usually made of expensive material like damask or brocade.) Occasionally women tried to go it alone and set up a shop but without previous experience, knowledge of the business itself and sufficient capital to set up and run one, such a decision would be likely to be rather risky. There was also the added problem, mentioned occasionally by such authors as Frances Burney, where the well-to-do were very slow in paying their bills anyway, thinking mistakenly that the traders/workers involved would be honoured by the fact that such prestigious people were in debt to them.

For women capable of plain sewing, or even fancy work – with embroidery, for example – the work was poorly paid and not always easy to come by. As it was regarded as a respectable occupation many women were to consider it as an option in their hope of avoiding dependency, however it could mean long hours for little return, as well as the risk of ruining their eyesight in inadequate lighting. Frances Burney was one of the authors who pointed out that sewing for a living had various drawbacks, 'She was deadened by uninteresting monotony... the unvarying repetition of stitch after stitch, nearly closed in sleep her faculties, as well as her eyes.' (*The Wanderer,* 1814)

One of the other issues raised by concerned women authors of the time was that many of the tasks that had previously been performed by women were increasingly being taken over by men, and so it was becoming harder for women to find work. Their recommendation was that women should support each other by giving their business to those women who were trying to earn a respectable living through such trades. If they could actually afford to buy their own clothes they should do so, rather than do any of their own sewing at home, in order to give out as much work to needy women as possible. Mary Ann Radcliffe and Priscilla Wakefield both agreed in this area and felt that women should even refuse to be served by men in shops that dealt with women's needs. In theory these ideas were very supportive of women's issues, but I am not sure whether their views had any effect at the time.

Just in passing, it is worth mentioning here that of course one type of work that single women chose to take up in order to support themselves, and their relatives if necessary, was that of writing. As I have already covered this topic in considerable detail in an earlier chapter it is not necessary to add much to it at this stage. Suffice to say it was an increasingly popular option as women took over a greater percentage in the publishing market, particularly in the production of novels.

For some women the fear of dependency or the need to undertake paid employment did not arise. Apart from the occupations I have mentioned above many other spinsters were forced into a different occupation, which also prevented them from gaining any real independence, financial or otherwise, as they had to take up positions of care or nursing within their own families. An only daughter, the eldest daughter if she remained unmarried, or the youngest if all her siblings had gone, could be left as the primary carer of elderly parents – a full time occupation. I have found various references to the call of duty, or comments such as, ' How could I leave my mother?', 'How could I leave my father?', or 'She could not think of leaving him…' scattered amongst texts of the time.

We do not know, however, if all such daughters accepted their responsibilities and filial duties with equal meekness and good grace. There are occasional references to being left behind when the rest of the family were able to leave home, or comments like, 'Sometimes indeed I … really think I am living to no purpose.' (*Letter from Elizabeth Carter to her friend Catherine Talbot*, 1751) One real life example where there were problems was in the case of Mary Lamb, the sister of the writer Charles Lamb. As an only daughter she had ended up being responsible for caring for her elderly parents and her two brothers, as well as having to deal with looking after any new additions to the household. It may have all been too much pressure for her because one day in 1796, apparently out of nowhere, she turned on her mother and stabbed her violently, as a result of which the mother died. The verdict was insanity – and although Mary spent time going in and out of asylums for periods during the rest of her life, her overall situation did change. People started paying attention to her needs, and indeed she successfully joined forces with her brother in the writing of *Tales from Shakespeare* (1807), which is still available for children today. One can guess that this literary success would not have been possible if she had been forced to remain in her full time occupation as family carer.

Jane Austen spent much of her adult life, as companion, carer, nurse or useful aunt to her extended family, but seemed to have accepted her situation more willingly. Although for much of her life she did not have money of her own, particularly after the death of her father, her personal correspondence shows she was delighted when the situation did change as her first few books were published. The letters even show how concerned she was to make sure she gained what she felt she was entitled to, and her displeasure when she did not. A little bit of financial independence was indeed worth having! Jane had initially written for pleasure, for family entertainment, not to support her family, and she did not abandon her role as family carer in spite of success. She was described as being 'a good aunt', but it is important to be aware of the other perspective, and that being for many years she was very much at the beck and call of whichever family member wanted her services as an extra pair of hands.

Throughout this chapter I have been considering situations where women alone found themselves in difficult circumstances. However as the life of Jane Austen illustrates it would be inappropriate to give the impression that spinsters and widows were a totally doomed species. It is true that under the right circumstances women alone could be happy, even successful. There were writers like Hannah More who had financial independence from a combination of sources – the school, her books and even a small income from the man she did not marry. She had the financial and social freedom to be active in society and was well respected by many of both sexes. Another writer, Anna Seward, was a successful poet and literary correspondent, who as eldest daughter of a widower, had remained to nurse her senile father until he died when she was over forty, and it was no longer necessary for her to marry.

Single women could gain satisfaction from philanthropic ventures like Sarah Trimmer who organised poor girls into attending Sunday Schools, or Priscilla Wakefield who established a Female Benefit Club and a Penny Bank for children, and a group of women, more commonly known as The Bluestockings, who were to gain pleasure from their intellectual pursuits. These women will come under greater consideration in the next chapter.

In 1810 a leaflet had been published about a silk spinner who had spent her last twenty-five years alone. The pamphlet recorded her saying:

> *It is a fine thing to live by oneself. They tell me you should have somebody with you, but unless they be very agreeable, a body had better be by oneself.*
> *(The Happy Spinster of Lancashire or The Story of Poor Blind Ellen)*

These real life examples of success or contentment were reflected in the fiction of the period with such comments as:

> *I am not ignorant that young women totally destitute of fortune as we are have no chance of marrying...well, it is very sad to be sure, to be predestined old maids: but a million of others live single, and I am sure there are such who are living happier, and more quietly and comfortably than many women who have families.*
> *(Charlotte Smith, Marchmont, 1796)*

There was also Jane Austen's simple comment in her early work *The Watsons* (1805), 'I could do very well single.' Similarly the image of the merry widow is not unknown in fiction, whether celebrating freedom 'to enjoy pleasures she had been debarred' during years of unhappy marriage, or having the determination 'to act at last according to my inclination.' (Elizabeth Helm, *The Farmer of Inglewood Forest*, 1796) These were particularly true if widowhood was accompanied by financial independence.

Unfortunately however, women had been brought up, conditioned, if you like, into believing that marriage was the only way forward and that to become an old maid was a dreadful thing. I found this example, written in the 1780's by John Bennett in a conduct book for young ladies, which predicts a miserable future for a spinster:

> *A single woman is particularly defenceless. She cannot move beyond the precincts of her house without apprehensions. As she goes down the* ***hill*** *of life, her friends* ***gradually*** *drop away from her, like the leaves in the autumn, and leave her a pining,* ***solitary****, creature. She wanders through a wild bustling world, uncomfortable in herself, uninteresting to others, frequently the sport of wanton ridicule, or a proverb of reproach.*
> *(Letters to a Young Lady on Useful and Interesting Subjects, 1789)*

This was hardly an encouraging or cheerful prospect, and unlikely to bring comfort to those who failed to gain early success in the marriage market. Also John Bennett certainly did not seem to credit such unmarried women with any strength and inner resourcefulness – and implied that a spinster could be extremely vulnerable if she dared to leave her house without protection. What women writers could do in their works was to show a more positive image of, and attitude towards, single women, and thus try to alleviate the situation as envisaged above. One way was by showing single women as intelligent, resourceful and capable individuals who would make good role models for others. Works such as *The Governess* (Sarah Fielding, 1749), *Millenium Hall* (Sarah Scott, 1762), and *The School for Widows* (Clara Reeve, 1791), show how women were capable of running successful business ventures, community care schemes and educational establishments without the interference or support of men. There will be more to say about their utopian schemes too in the next chapter.

Another way was by drawing attention to the connection between the negative sneering attitude of society to spinsters and the crotchety behaviour of those spinsters who had found themselves in unhappy, uncomfortable circumstances and who were mocked for it:

> *I am firmly persuaded the old maid, generally speaking, would be an unpretending quiet animal, were she left to herself. It is the insults, the festering little wounds, the thoughtless level at her which rouse her to bitterness... When we consider the sly innuendoes, the open insults and thousand nameless taunts, that are strewn in OUR thorny path, it can scarcely excite wonder that the old maid is sometimes roused to retort.*
> *(The Spinsters Journal, by A Modern Antique, 1816)*

It was a very good point. Women in adversity were often humiliated by society. The connections between cause and effect for their situations were rarely made, and particularly not by members of the opposite sex. The double standard regarding sex and the fate of the fallen woman is but one further example; limited educational opportunities for girls and the low expectations of women's abilities provides yet another. Like many other women writers Mary Ann Radcliffe and Mary Wollstonecraft worked to support themselves, and their writings give us a real feeling of some of the situations that had to be faced by women in general. Time and again such writers were to argue that there were many people placed in far better situations than they were, who did not have a clue about the sufferings of others – unless they had had direct related experiences or allowed themselves to be informed by those who did know. They knew it was critical that those who held the power for change should be properly informed. This was from the Preface of *The Female Advocate*:

> *The subject of the following pages is an attempt to delineate the situation of those poor, helpless, females whose sufferings, from a variety of causes, are too grievous to be borne…unless some friendly hand take up the pen, how can those, who are enabled by fortune and prompted by compassion, stretch forth the hand of clemency to distresses, of which they have never heard. (Mary Anne Radcliffe, 1799)*

Of course it was possible that nothing would change, or that some considerable length of time would elapse before it did, but these women writers could hope at least for the development of more sympathetic attitudes towards the plight of the single woman left alone, whether spinster or widow. By looking more closely at the novel, *Emma*, by Jane Austen, one can see a clearly laid out example of this process of education. For most of the novel Emma's attitude towards the spinster Miss Bates was quite derogatory, and she also went out of her way to be unkind to Miss Bates' niece Jane Fairfax who seemed to be likely to end up in a similar position. It was left to Mr Knightley, the well-respected gentleman of the novel, to reprimand and educate Emma. (Note the use of a significant male character again to get the message across!) After being particularly cruel towards Miss Bates in public, Emma was asked bluntly by him:

> *How could you be so unfeeling to Miss Bates? How could you be so insolent in your wit to a woman of her character, age and situation? ... She is poor, she has sunk from the comforts she was born to; and, if she live to old age, must probably sink more. Her situation should secure your compassion.*

In time others too could learn from Emma's lesson.

Chapter Eight
Woman on the Move

Looking back at the earlier chapters I find it amazing that I knew so little about a subject that really does concern me – in both senses of the word! There is no doubt in my mind that throughout the long eighteenth century women reviewed the circumstances of their lives, developed their own opinions and found ways to give voice to their discontent. The work of the women writers provides adequate contemporary evidence of that. Although there were many perspectives to the different problems they identified for women, with hindsight it is possible to look back and identify common causes of complaint. Society had very set notions of the role and nature of women, and when those limited views were challenged, whether by radical or more apparently conservative women, the very boundaries which seemed to restrict women's behaviours were gradually to be tested, and ultimately would be broken. During this chapter I will be looking at some of the different forms these challenges took.

I think it would be stretching a point though to assert that all of the women writers mentioned here were 'feminists', or even 'early feminists', because apart from the fact the term was only coined during the nineteenth century, at least some of the women cited in this work would have been horrified to be personally associated with such a radical notion. It is probably safer merely to acknowledge that the roots of feminism can be traced back at least as far as the beginning of the eighteenth century, as many of the points in this chapter will serve to illustrate. For countless women at the time the issues were about the detail of their *own* lives, and the desire to make them more satisfying *personally*, rather than the direct confrontation between male and female that we tend to associate with modern feminism. The fact that radical women of the period commented on the lack of shared identity amongst women, the lack of solidarity, as well as the willingness of some women to assert themselves over and against less fortunate members of their own sex, shows that *in general* women may well have seen their problems in individual terms. It was thus felt, by some at least, that there was a real need for women to wake up to the reality of their situation, before they could be motivated to do something about it – let alone working together for a common cause.

Some authors did register surprise that it had taken so long for women to notice they were being oppressed. Mary Ann Radcliffe was to ask, 'Yet how astonishing is it, that the oppressions of these men, who are the authors of so much mischief, should have so long passed unnoticed?' She had a very strong opinion regarding the various causes that could have given rise to them – 'A want of reflection, from its being a precedent of long standing; a wilful blindness; through avaricious views, or a downright want of understanding!' (*The Female Advocate*, 1799)

Others like Frances Burney showed an awareness of the conflict a woman could feel when faced with the choice between accepting, and following, traditional customary views regarding women, and taking a more radical pathway. Thus one heroine Ellis observed:

> *... the strong conflict in the mind of Elinor, between ungoverned inclination, which sought new systems for its support, and an innate feeling of what was due to the sex that she was braving, and the customs that she was scorning. (The Wanderer, 1814)*

Mary Hays, too, was to comment on how her own habits as a woman could contribute to the difficulty:

> *Hemmed in on every side by the constitutions of society, and not less so it may be by my own prejudices – I perceive, indignantly perceive, the magic circle without knowing how to dissolve its powerful spell. (Memoirs of Emma Courtney, 1796)*

Elizabeth Hamilton's radical and outspoken 'feminist' Bridgetina Botherim described the constraints more visually:

> *... chained by the cruel fetters which unjust and detested custom has*

> *forged for my miserable and much injured sex, I am not at liberty ... Barbarous fetters! Cruel chains! Odious state of society. (Memoirs of Modern Philosophers, 1800).*

While it is true that she was personally critical of such outspoken and extreme opinions, Elizabeth Hamilton was obviously aware that such feelings did exist and gave Bridgetina the opportunity to give a much more rational explanation for her outburst:

> *Would you have me conceal my sentiments in conformity to the pernicious maxims and practices of the world? But what so much as the dread of censure has cramped the energy of the female mind? (Ibid)*

Once again linking back to the limitations of traditional female education, another fundamental criticism was the lack of real personal achievement it was possible for a woman to attain during her life. Mary Wollstonecraft was not the only one to feel that there was a real waste of talent with regard to the possible contribution of women to society. She knew little would be achieved by women while the emphasis was on female beauty and accomplishments, and commented, 'If we revert to history, we shall find the women who have distinguished themselves have neither been the most beautiful nor the most gentle of their sex.' (*The Vindication of the Rights of Woman*, 1792) Ann Plumptre's character Olivia made comparisons to knights in shiny armour going off to battle, adventure and glory, while she had to:

> *... tamely seat myself in a tame side saddle, canter my steed for an hour or two over the smooth shorn lawn, or along the even gravel road, and then return home dull and indolent as I went out, again to betake myself to my paltry feminine employments. Thus must I crawl through life, at the end of which I shall not have performed one exploit worthy to hand down my name to far removed posterity. (Something New, 1801)*

Unfortunately by emphasising the gentle nature of women, their natural aptitude for caring, their apparent willingness to serve and obey, men were only focussing on the certain aspects of the female character that suited them and thus, according to various works of the time, both misjudging their abilities and exploiting them. I was highly amused to find out that Jane Austen was so incensed by the irritating and suffocating misogynist manner of one of Frances Burney's characters, Dr Marchmont from *Camilla*, that at the end of her own copy of the book she actually scribbled the following postscript, 'Since this work went to press a circumstance of some assistance to the happiness of Camilla has taken place, namely that Dr Marchmont has, at last, died.' I like Jane Austen!

With men underestimating the potential ability of women, their own superiority was easy to assume and assert. As early as the end of the seventeenth century women were arguing:

> *Men look upon us to have very little interest in the public affairs of the world, and therefore trouble us very seldom with their grave serious trifles, which they debate with so much earnestness among one another. They look upon us as things designed and contrived only for their pleasure, and therefore use us gingerly, as children do their favourite baubles. (Judith Drake, Essay in Defence of the Female Sex, 1696)*

The comparisons could be even worse, 'In his dealings with men, Sir Patrick was a man of honour; in his dealings with women completely the reverse: he considered them as a race of subordinate beings, made for the service and amusement of men; and that if like horses, they were well lodged, fed, kept clean, they had no right to complain.' (Amelia Opie, *Adeline Mowbray*, 1805) Similarly Sophia was to comment, 'That they are our masters they take it for granted; but by what title they are so not one of them is able to make out.'(*Women Not Inferior to Men*, 1739)

Increasingly questions were being asked, albeit sporadically, that were to dispute the claimed right of man to superior status. Frances Burney queried, 'Why for so many centuries has man alone been supposed to possess not only force and power for action and defence, but even all the rights of taste?' (*The Wanderer*, 1814) There were even occasional appeals to God, 'Gracious creator of the human race! Hast thou created such a being as woman…for no better purpose? Can she believe she was only made to submit to man, her equal … can she consent to be occupied merely to please him?' (Mary Wollstonecraft,

A Vindication of the Rights of Woman, 1792); and from *The Female Advocate* in 1799 a challenge to both men and women:

> *... since these men have become apostates from Christianity, why any longer suffer their arbitrary power to be a subterfuge for fraud and oppression... let them appear and shew cause why they are entitled to oppress these poor women, in order to enjoy indolence and ease.*
> *(Mary Ann Radcliffe)*

Within the text of novels the issue was occasionally to be debated in direct conversation. This was part of a heated argument from *The False Friend*:

> *'I preach and shall never fail, to feel those precepts which have been inculcated by one who now sleeps in the grave (Mary Wollstonecraft) ...but whose monument is built on the immortal basis which supports the right of women. On the illustrious name of their departed champion I will bestow that eulogy which should be the glory of our sex though it may expose the tyranny of men.'*
> *'Preposterous... woman is merely a domestic creature, take her from the humble avocations of life and she becomes ...'*
> *'Your equal.' (Mary Robinson, 1799)*

This was to be a major issue for outspoken women in the long eighteenth century and a harbinger of the whole debate in the centuries ahead: the question of equality between the sexes. In a similar argument in *The Wanderer*, Ellis angrily spoke about the Rights of Woman, 'Rights, however, which all your sex, with all its arbitrary assumption of superiority, can never disprove, for they are the Rights of human nature; to which the two sexes equally and unalienably belong.' (Frances Burney, 1814) Mary Astell had clearly stated her fundamental belief in women's equal rights to knowledge and learning as early as 1694 in her *Serious Proposal to the Ladies*, and many were to agree with her during the course of the eighteenth century. Mary Robinson believed strongly that, 'We were born to be the associates, not the slaves of man.' (*The False Friend*, 1799) She had much to say on this particular issue within the book, which in fairness, I ought to acknowledge was written after she had had some very negative experiences with men. Hence for example:

> *Man is an envious as well as an overbearing creature; he shrinks at the idea of equality, where Time and that pernicious tyrant Custom has authorised his power to govern. Where women were confined to the dull occupations, men were mere despots; not loved but feared; blessed but not blessing. We may have broke the spell which manacled the mind; we are no longer the vassals of our imperious help mates;* ***we dare think*** *(my emphasis) and we at length assert those rights which nature formed us to enjoy. (Ibid)*

Occasionally male characters could be used to express how women wished they would act:

> *Let the superiority given us appear in the superior good we do; for while our lives are as trifling and useless as those of the other sex, we ought to be ashamed to esteem ourselves above them, and should act more judiciously, in not laying claim to superior talents, without we make proper use of them. (Sarah Scott, The History of Sir George Ellison, 1766)*

Of course the classic text on the Rights of Woman is Mary Wollstonecraft's *Vindication* – but to quote solely or even extensively from this text at this point would be to give the impression that she alone had strong feelings about the subject during the period – and that would be a terrible mistake. Let it suffice to say that there are many references to her work during the course of this book – and hers is well worth a read in its own right.

Women who did believe in the equality of the sexes could be severely critical of those who accepted unquestionably the right of a patriarchal system to dominate their every move, and who were prepared to live the lives of pampered, idle women. In 1739 Sophia had expressed her hope that 'while women have any spirit left, they will exert it all in shewing how worthy they are of better usage, not by submitting tamely to such misplaced arrogance.' (*Women Not Inferior to Men*) Mary Wollstonecraft seemed very conscious of the time the whole process of change would inevitably take – as women themselves were very much part of the problem. Hence, 'It will require a considerable length of time to eradicate the firmly rooted prejudices which sensualists have planted; it will also require some time to convince women that they act contrary to their interest on a very large scale.' (*A Vindication of the Rights of Woman*, 1792) Later Frances Burney's character Juliet was to refer to:

> *You, and such as you, tame animals of custom, wearied and wearying plodders on of beaten tracks... There are fools, I know in the world, who suppose me mad already! only because I go my own way; while they poor cowards, yoked one to another, always follow the path of their forefathers; without even venturing to mend the road...*
> *(The Wanderer, 1814)*

Sometimes the criticisms, although sounding funny to a modern reader, must have shocked the contemporary ones in their directness – with little or no attention paid to a person's sensitivity – for example referring to a particularly poor choice of marriage partner, 'Heavens! Where was the woman in you, when you contended to yoke yourself to such a numskull? Not one little bit of the spirit of contradiction? – oh fie...' (Mrs Skinn, *The Old Maid*, 1771)

Apart from questioning the very nature of patriarchy, the assumptions on which it was based, and the willingness of (some) women to comply with them, women writers had a crucial role to play in the development of women per se. For in their works they were to challenge the stereotypical images of traditional woman, and test out ideas of what it was theoretically possible for women to be. Just to give one example – while it is true that, in the context of a regular novel of the period, a feisty young woman may have to have been 'reformed' before she could end up with her male (i.e. her husband) as a reward, during the process a reader could be exposed to a completely new image of female behaviour. The 'heroine' could show new use of language, new actions being taken, the exposure of weaknesses not registered before and the discovery of new innate strengths. It has been a fascinating area to explore – with some very amusing incidents, which I will share with you shortly. Of course it has to be mentioned that although some of the 'challenging' characters may not have been approved directly by the authors themselves, it has been generally easy to see where the sympathies lie, or where at least mixed feelings existed. The very fact that both radical and 'conservative' writers included them showed an awareness of the ongoing debate about the nature and role of women, and their own participation in it.

Let us start with the idea of language – and the expectation that women would be submissive in their dealings with father, husband etc – in all areas of their lives. There are various examples of where women, in fiction at least, were not prepared to accept the assumption of male superiority of knowledge, or the apparent control that it gave over their lives. Sometimes women did have more relevant experience and knowledge. Take Betsy Thoughtless for example:

> *She had a very good regard for her brothers, but did not think it their province to prescribe rules for her behaviour; – she looked upon herself as a better judge in what manner it would become her to act, than they could possibly be, as having lived more years in London than either had done months, and if she was willing to be advised, would not be directed by them.*

Then again later in the book, 'The thought of having any disagreement with them was dreadful to her, yet the putting a constraint on her inclinations to oblige them was no less so…'(Eliza Haywood, *The Adventures of Betsy Thoughtless*, 1751)

Another area of claimed superiority was of classical knowledge, and Charlotte Lennox raised this in *A Female Quixote* in 1752. A little explanation is necessary here. Arabella spent much of her time reading, and was prepared to get into an argument with Mr Selvin who, 'affected to be thought deep-read in History, and never failed to take all the Opportunities of displaying his Knowledge of Antiquity, which was indeed but very superficial.' She challenged him regarding the Grecian springs of *Thermopylae* of which he had never heard. Not only was he disconcerted but also:

> *The Shame he conceived at seeing himself posed by a Girl, in a Matter which so belonged to him, made him resolve to draw himself out of this Dilemma … yet he maintained that she must be Mistaken…*
>
> *Arabella, who could not bear to be contradicted in what she took to be so incontestable a Fact, reddened with Vexation at his unexpected Denial.*
>
> *It should seem, said she, by your Discourse, that you are unacquainted with any material passages, that passed among very illustrious Persons there…*

> *I think, Madam replied he with great Self-sufficiency that I am pretty well acquainted with everything that relates to the Affairs of the Athenian Commonwealth.*
>
> *You are mistaken, Sir, said Arabella.*

She then proceeded to give him a mini lecture on it, much to his embarrassment, in front of several other important visitors. He submitted, 'I protest, Madam…casting down his Eyes in great Confusion at her superior Knowledge in History, these Particulars have all escaped my notice.' Women after all were supposed to keep their knowledge hidden – presumably to avoid any such embarrassing incidents!

This is not the first example I have come across where the assumption of greater knowledge, which provided at least one basis for male superiority, had been challenged, with either the male providing false claims to his learning – or the female actually knowing more about the subject in question. Jane Austen was to make several important comments regarding the knowledge that men had gained, particularly from books that men had written. The comment about there being hardly any women in history is well known, but she also asserted, 'It is very tiresome: and yet I often think it odd that it should be so dull, for a great deal of it must be invention.' (*Northanger Abbey*, 1818) In *Persuasion* she stretched the idea a little further when, in a discussion with Anne, Captain Harville said that he could prove his point by reference to books. Her comment is highly significant, 'Yes, yes, if you please, no reference to examples in books. Men have had every advantage of us in telling their story. Education has been theirs in so much higher a degree; the pen has been in their hands. I will not allow books to prove anything.'(1817) At least in this work I have tried to allow women to have the opportunity of telling their side of the story!

Similarly it has been refreshing to find intelligent, spirited, female characters challenging the lectures they received regarding behaviour, as if they were too simple to be able to work out the dangers for themselves. This was from Charlotte Smith – Miss Goldthorp, a financially independent young adult, was staying with her aunt and uncle. He, Dr Winslow, had very traditional views about women. They argued:

> *'A young lady's reputation, my dear niece, a young lady's reputation is like... is like a sheet of the finest white paper – it must not have the least, the minutest blot or stain – it has justly been compared to... to... to...'*
>
> *'To a fiddlestick', cried the young heiress, 'for God's sake my dear Dr Winslow keep all this commonplace stuff for your parishioners at Gandersfield Green; it may do well enough for May-day girls and love sick dairy maids and may keep them from the* ***false arts of perjury lovers****, who woo them, with a Sunday posey all set round with sweet marjoram, and win them by half a pound of gingerbread and a cherry coloured top knot from the fair; but do not, beseech you, my nunky now, do not lecture* ***me****...' (The Young Philosopher, 1798)*

Many female authors were to show the importance of being self confident, assertive, determined and capable women. This is just a taster of how some of their characters reacted to the assumptions of men and very much believed in their own capabilities:

> *Lady Arabella had charming spirits. She laughed at the vanity of men, creatures who supposed themselves of any consequence... she was a free and independent being and accountable to no-one for her actions, which were the result of her opinions, and no one had any right to scrutinise the opinions of others. (Jane West, A Tale of The Times, 1799)*
>
> *I wish you.. would recollect I am not a child; that I am now my own mistress... really one must consider oneself a little.*
> *(Charlotte Smith, The Young Philosopher, 1798)*
>
> *You have taught me that to confide in the heart of man is to lay up stores for sorrow, henceforth I rest on myself.*
> *(Mary Hays, A Victim of Prejudice, 1799)*
>
> *Now you must know, that I am as firmly determined as yourself and as my resolutions are infinitely more consequence to me, than yours can be, I shall most strictly adhere to them.*
> *(Mrs Skinn, The Old Maid, 1771)*

And once again male characters were used to reinforce the message:

> *You have talents, cultivate them and learn to rest on your own powers... You are capable of standing alone and your mind by so doing will acquire strength.*
> *(Mary Hays, The Memoirs of Emma Courtney, 1796)*

Certainly, in fiction at least, women did stand up to men, and at times in quite dramatic form. Mrs Skinn may be one of the relative unknowns of women fiction writers of the period, but she was the source of some fabulously relevant quotations. Typical stories of the period had poor, defenceless, young women being pestered, pursued and frequently abducted in order to gain control of their persons and/or their fortunes. Such heroines would go weak, collapse, faint and offer no resistance. With Mrs Skinn the heroine had far more important things to do... When Mr Clayton dared to make a pass at his wife's friend Emily, she was not afraid of direct confrontation. She was after all staying with her friend during her lying-in, i.e. when she was having a baby. Apart from calling Mr Clayton's behaviour despicable, she had a real go at him:

> *This is the way you would recommend yourself to my esteem, by making yourself the most detestable monster human nature can produce? A married man! – Married to the most amiable, the most deserving of women – For shame, MR CLAYTON, – recollect yourself.*

When she told him to leave he asserted that he was sure she would not tell his wife about it, as it might distress her. She replied vehemently, 'How dare you? Insolent as you are, says I, make use of her name as a warrant in so vile a cause: instantly unhand me...' Within two pages he was at it again, so she took things a stage further, and making an original use of her needlework scissors – normally used for more feminine, docile occupations – she stabbed him in the hand, saying to her maid, 'Don't you think they are a pretty kind of weapon my dear... Never go without a pair in your pocket.' (Mrs Skinn, *The Old Maid*, 1771)

The poor girl seemed to be beset by danger; later on she was abducted by Lord Wilton, who wanted to force her to marry him, in order to gain control of her fortune. Once again she started disdainfully, first mocking and then attacking him:

> *Did you think my contempt for you before was not sufficient, but you must take such pains to make me despise you ten thousand times more thoroughly... I am very resolute, you can neither intimidate me with your threats, nor your impertinence. Insolent and wicked as I know you to be, and capable of the vilest purposes, I fear you not at all... you could not hit upon a worse person in the world to play the fool with... Really Lord Wilton you will cut a mighty silly figure in this affair, don't you begin to feel yourself a little awkward? You never appeared mighty wise. Prithee man, take my advice and be convinced, you are naturally ridiculous enough, without taking pains to appear more the ideot than you already are.*

Somewhat exasperated she resorted to shooting him – unfortunately she missed – but at the beginning of the next volume when she tried to leave and he tried to prevent her, she picked up a knife, struggled with him and managed to cut his hand and arm badly. Just to rub salt in the wound, she then humiliated him further in front the maid, 'Observe him Kitty, observe how despicable a being, is that thing called lord, when divested of those mental and material ornaments which bespeak the man.'

Not surprisingly she did escape – even though she had to jump out of a first floor window, and although she did hurt her ankle, it did not impede her.

Mrs Skinn was not the only writer to have her heroine challenge the audacity of wicked men, others too have climbed out of windows, (Mary Robinson, *The False Friend*, 1799; George Sand, *Indiana*, 1831) or used self defence to avoid being assaulted (Mary Brunton, *Self Control*, 1810), however her examples are clear attacks on the stereotypical passive woman so often praised in books of the time. Charlotte Smith too, had one character, Medora, abducted – twice in fact, although both times she did escape. Even though she was frightened, she too clearly informed the abductor that she thought him a fool, and he should take her home. She was no feeble heroine, and unlike countless others in similar situations kept her wits about her:

> *... after the first flutter of my heart had subsided, and I began to comprehend the character of the man in whose power I remained still*

it is true, under considerable terror, but not to such a degree as to deprive me for a moment of my recollection and presence of mind.
(Charlotte Smith, The Young Philosopher, 1798)

Another writer, Clara Reeve, chose to show an abused wife reacting with anger and violence when her husband had offered her sexual favours to a Lord in return for some privileges for himself. She was so exasperated to discover this, that when he gave her a glass of wine, she knocked it out of his hand and smashed it. Furious about his maltreatment of her, she did not forgive him or forget his behaviour – she packed her bags and left home. (*The School for Widows*, 1791)

I discovered recently that, in her youth, the writer Maria Edgeworth had shown much independence of spirit – she too had thrown tea in someone's face when annoyed, she knew how to escape by climbing out of a window, had trampled on new hot bed frames, and even cut out squares from her aunt's sofa cover! Apparently these ideas used in fiction were not totally without precedent in real life!

So women were being shown in a new light, prepared to stand up for themselves a little and even, in theory, to fight back. Judith Drake had referred to male critics of the female sex as 'a sort of ungenerous Adversary, that deal more in Scandal than Argument and when they cant hurt us with their Weapons, endeavour to annoy us with their Stinkpots. Let us see therefore if we cant beat them with their Ammunition, and turn their own Artillery upon them…' (*An Essay in Defence of the Female Sex*, 1696) We have already seen how ridicule and general humour have been used in certain circumstances but challenges could come in other forms too.

Take, for example, the conduct book guide to putting up with bad behaviour in a husband – normally the expectation had been that the wife would ignore it, put up with it or even blame it on herself. This was not always the way in fiction. Clara Reeve had some original ideas. Mrs Darnford had a problem with her husband's gambling, and when he came home in the early hours of the morning he was afraid of her reproaches, and asked for comfort instead. She was kind but the following morning tried unsuccessfully to get the full picture. First she read a tale to him about how a noble wife took over her husband's debts, sorted out the household expenses and where they were to live, and showed him how to behave himself. A week later she took him to the theatre to see the famous actress Mrs Siddons in a tragedy, where rather than committing suicide the characters should have faced up to their problems. She then took him to a play called the Gamester – and the moral was obvious even to him! Later he became angry so she said, 'If I had given him pain, it was in order to save him from greater; and I hoped there would come a time when he would thank me for it.' (Clara Reeve, *The School for Widows*, 1791)

From another example in the same book Mrs Strictland had actually created a contract – as part of a planned reconciliation with her estranged husband. He had been cruel, thoughtless and unjust in a situation where, 'Poor I was an insignificant monosyllable that had no kind of meaning.' With her standing up to him, circumstances changed, and she set the contract. He was to pay her agreed allowance on time, without her being forced to ask for it. She was to be allowed her own personal maidservant, and to have the freedom to visit, and be visited by, respectable neighbourhood gentry, as well as to write to her friends, guardian, and family. Henceforth he was to behave with complaisance, kindness and courtesy towards her. Apparently small demands indeed, which would greatly improve her own domestic situation – but I had never come across a woman formally dictating terms before!

The issue of finance itself, and of money that belonged specifically to daughters and wives, has already come under some scrutiny elsewhere in this work. Some female fictional characters were shown to be very keen to keep a strict control over their own money – rather than hand it over meekly to the nearest male. Frances Burney had illustrated how men thought 'girls knew nothing of money, and ought not to be trusted with it' but Cecilia, the eponymous heroine, was not satisfied with her guardians plan to pass the inheritance from her uncle directly to 'a good husband', bypassing her completely. She asserted, 'The £10,000 bequeathed I regard as peculiarly my own property, and therefore think myself at liberty to dispose of it as I please.' Her guardian was not amused. (Frances Burney, *Cecilia*, 1782) In a similar vein Miss Goldthorp was to say:

> *I do not mean to marry until I have been sometime my own mistress...not quite three thousand a year, though it is not a very great fortune, gives me the right to please myself, which I assure you I intend*

> *to do...having a house of my own and living my own way...I cannot give up my own freedom.*
> *(Charlotte Smith, The Young Philosopher, 1798)*

Apart from wanting to take a little more control of their own lives there is evidence that women of the middling, and even some of the upper classes, were wanting a little more from life than the rather stifling and limited domestic and/or leisured role they were required to perform. Mary Ann Radcliffe had stated clearly, 'Women were ultimately designed for something better.' (*The Female Advocate*, 1799) In modern literary criticism there have been many references to the 'mask', which women had to wear over their feelings at the time, so that for all intents and purposes they appeared respectable, conformist and submissive women – yet as we have seen a different picture appears in private writings and the contents of novels. The evidence is there once you know where to look. Mary Hays wrote very succinctly about women, 'For it is very clear, that they are not what they ought to be, that they are not what men would have them be, and to finish the portrait, that they are not what they appear to be.' (*An Appeal to the Men of Great Britain*, 1798)

When Frances Burney tried a little experiment in role-play in the early pages of *Camilla* it must have jarred one or two readers. To humour his niece on her birthday, while still a young child, old Sir Hugh allowed her complete control over him:

> *She metamorphosed him into a female, accoutring him with her fine new cap, while she enveloped her own small head in his wig; and then, tying the maids apron round his waist, put a rattle into his hand, and Eugenia's doll upon his lap, which she told him was a baby that he must nurse and amuse. (1796)*

He stayed in this ludicrous role for some considerable time much to the huge amusement of the household – even the servants found ways to peep and thoroughly enjoy the grotesque spectacle that he created.

However it was only a role he played for the afternoon – even allowing for his weakness while he recovered from illness, he had put aside other interests for the duration of those few hours only. A few women writers had noticed that women too played a role, a domestic role that was expected of them, wearing a mask to hide their thoughts, emotions and real abilities, but this mask was gradually to be set aside as women expressed themselves more in thought, word and deed. Maria Edgeworth made this point quite clearly when Lady Davenport stated:

> *And yet, she added, after a moment's pause of reflection, to how few can my character really be known! Women cannot, like men, make their characters known by public actions. (Helen, 1834)*

To return to Sir Hugh, when he had had enough the game was over, and he could resume other activities. The domestically based role for women was not so easily put aside, and yet women did find ways to do so.

In spite of the need to hide their true natures, one thing that women seemed to find difficult to do was to subdue their minds; intelligent women wanted to think, wanted to learn and make suitable use of their learning. Mary Ann Hanway described the personal importance of this for one of her characters, Harriet:

> *It is most true that I cannot condescend, by low and debasing arts, to mask the energies of my mind, and sink myself, in my opinion, below that point of perfection in the scale of human nature, to which I proudly aspire. (Ellinor, 1798)*

Self-esteem was apparently becoming important to women, and their own personal achievements would help them raise it. Long before the above book was written Sophia wanted:

> *... to exhort all my sex to throw aside idle amusement and to betake themselves of the improvement of their minds, that we may be able to act with that becoming dignity our nature has fitted us to, and without claiming or valuing it, shew ourselves worthy something from them (ie men), as much above their esteem, as they conceit themselves above us. (Woman not Inferior to Man, 1739)*

Mary Robinson categorised three types of women in the eyes of men and pointed out clearly why some men hated clever women:

There are but three classes of women desirable associates in the eyes of men: handsome women, licentious women and good sort of women, – the first for his vanity, the second for his amusement and the last for the arrangement of his domestic drudgery. A thinking woman does not entertain him; a learned woman does not flatter his self love, by confessing inferiority; and a woman of real genius, eclipses him by her brilliancy. (A Letter to the Women of England, 1799)

I have already shown that many women did have to use their intellects to write, to teach, to set up schools and so on. This however only covers some of the activities that intelligent women engaged in. During the last chapter I mentioned a group, commonly referred to as the Bluestockings, whose members were educated, intellectual, and mainly conservative women. Apart from literary concerns, these ladies were also trying to raise moral and intellectual standards of the time. During a period of lapse social and sexual standards, particularly among the higher classes – whom the Bluestockings thought should have been setting a better example – these women were not interested in frivolous gambling, drinking, partying or other forms of loose living. Copying the better parts of the French salons that some had witnessed on visits abroad, these high society women and their friends hosted evening entertainments that offered intelligent polite conversation, discussions of literary writings, and current, even political, events. One example of their literary work was in the defence and promotion of Shakespeare as a national treasure, after the French writer Voltaire had had the audacity to slate him!

The interesting point about their social gatherings is that they included both men and women, with both sexes being held in mutual regard for their contributions. Individual merit therefore counted; rational friendships could take place between men and women without the interference of sexuality. It was a forum for intellectual exchange. In contrast with more radical women the Bluestockings took pride in stating they took no active part in political affairs, preferring to take politics as more of a spectator sport. It is possible that you may now recognise a few names of some who were associated with the group – although not all could be counted as key members of it – Frances Burney, Elizabeth Carter, Ann Collier, Sarah Fielding, Catherine Macaulay, Elizabeth Montagu, Hannah More, Sarah Scott, Anna Seward– even Mary Wollstonecraft.

It cannot come as a surprise that even the virtuous Bluestocking women were to be criticised by some of both sexes, for their presumption in daring to speak out on any public matters, let alone political affairs, or risking any opinions more associated with radical thinkers. Over time the reference to Bluestockings, or a person being 'blue' became pejorative terms. In their defence Amelia Opie wrote:

> *I think it incumbent on all those women who are really bluestockings, to dare to be themselves, and to shew by joining seasonably and modestly in intellectual converse, that all females of cultivated minds are not pedants or precieuses, and they love information for its own sake... (Detraction Displayed, 1828)*

The Bluestockings, however, were also great believers in mixing their own opinions with practical applications of their ideas, so supported each other in times of need, promoted not only each others writings, but also those of other women, and were very keen to participate in philanthropic activities, again encouraging other women to do so. Sarah Scott had reaffirmed the right of women to get involved in such activities:

> *... if any people have a right to turn reformers, you ladies are best qualified, since you begin by reforming yourselves; you practice more than you preach, and therefore must always be listened to with attention. (Millenium Hall, 1762)*

Women of the middling classes and above were in just the right position to do so, with resources and time to spare, especially if they were single or no longer had the domestic responsibilities of marriage and family. These women were able to have a significant impact with their individual projects during the period, particularly with regard to the poor and lower classes, and when such noteworthy and well respected, virtuous women as Hannah More took part, others were bound to be influenced and follow her lead.

Although some of their projects aimed to contain the poor, for example by providing training schools which would keep the lower classes safely and happily in their lowly social positions – as Hannah More had done, the Bluestockings and other writers were to be critical of some of the attitudes to the poor, shown by members of the upper classes who had little to do with them. Jane West made reference to this when Lady Arabella said:

> *When I have seen several little dirty starved naked children peeping out of those dirty smoky hovels which stand by the road side, I have often thought it would be a great mercy to shoot them, as one does worn out horses. (A Tale of the Times, 1799)*

Frances Burney had tried to point out the need to be more aware of the problems poor people had to face in *The Wanderer*. Hence, 'Were ye to toil with them but one week, to rise as they rise, feed as they feed, work as they work, like mine then your eyes would open.' (1814) Women writers also realised that the very actions and ignorance of the upper classes made a direct contribution to the situation of the poor. Elizabeth Hamilton had previously noted:

> *Great folks do not know the degree of misery they often inflict by their carelessness; they are too highly exalted out of the sphere of their fellow creatures to cast a thought upon the difficulties of those who are to earn their bread by labour. I myself know of ladies who never refuse to open their purses to charity, but who if they had paid their tradesmen with punctuality, might have preserved some honest families from ruin. (Memoirs of Modern Philosophers, 1800)*

Frances Burney agreed, 'I think you should neither eat your meat, nor drink your beer, nor sit upon your chairs, nor wear you clothes, till you have rewarded the industrious people who provide them.' (*The Wanderer*, 1814). Charlotte Smith had also considered the situation of the poor in her political novel *Desmond* (1792), believing that where situations of extreme poverty and wretchedness existed some form of change at government level, not just temporary individual assistance, was necessary, 'If governments be for the benefit of the governed, not the governors, surely these complaints should be heard?' The response of the aristocrat who felt threatened by this suggestion was predictable:

> *I insist that there is no cause for complaint in England; nobody is poor unless it be by their own fault; and nobody is oppressed. As for the*

> *common people ... what were they born for but to work? They have no rights, they can have none, but to labour for their superiors; and if they are idle tis their own fault, and not the fault of the constitution, in which there are no imperfections, and which cannot by any contrivance be made better. (Ibid)*

Elizabeth Hamilton perhaps held the key for many women when she wrote:

> *The government ought – but, alas! I cannot dictate to the government. I have not the power to dictate to the government. I have not the power to influence the makers of our laws. But cannot I do something towards the relief of a few of these unhappy individuals? Let me see... (Memoirs of Modern Philosophers, 1800)*

Herein is contained the essence of individual women getting involved in philanthropic activities of the time – regardless of general restrictions or codes of behaviour. Women did find ways to make change, to get involved and where necessary to justify their involvement. This ranged from small gestures of visiting the needy poor close to home, to writing about possible alternative social set ups which could act as both remedy for, and prevention of, social evils – particularly for women – and even in rare cases to set them up in real life.

Fictional examples of alternative societies came in various guises, whether educationally based as centres of learning, mutually supportive and independently financed communities or even commercial enterprises. In contrast to utopias considered by men at the time these societies were set within real life, close to home. In these communities women who were not catered for by society, single women, widows, the elderly, even the handicapped, could find a home and a new purpose in life, without men. Mary Astell considered an educational community, a college for women, in *A Serious Proposal for the Ladies* (1694), an idea that was taken up by later women writers too. Clara Reeve imagined a *School for Widows* where a group of widows proved themselves to be resourceful, capable of supporting themselves and living useful lives. Sarah Fielding thought of a mixed benevolent society that was economically successful in *The Adventures of David Simple* (1744). Sarah Scott based her ideas of a responsible Christian female community at *Millennium Hall* (1762) on Mary Astell's ideas, and her sequel *The History of George Ellison* (1766) showed how these ideas could influence other people, and encourage them to copy her principles – at least in theory! Of particular significance is the fact that Sarah Scott was involved in the setting up of a woman's community in 1768 at Hitcham, in Buckinghamshire where, with the support of her sister Lady Elizabeth Montagu and many of her friends, she did apply her theoretical ideas of benevolence to the disadvantaged in society. Even though the project was short lived she too was a woman on the move…

Although it was more acceptable for women to involve themselves in philanthropy, as has been mentioned above, scattered throughout novels of the period are comments regarding the involvement of women in other activities, with some women stating for example, 'Far be it from us to meddle with politics – we have quite enough to do with manners and morality.' (Maria Edgeworth, *Helen*, 1834) Moral issues certainly did concern the Bluestockings, amongst others, and many women were to be involved in the evangelical movement, which promoted better religious practice from both the laity and the clergy. To be involved in activities because of one's moral duty may have been tolerated by the male sex, at times even promoted, yet one area that was generally taboo was the field of politics.

It has been previously noted that it seemed necessary that women should clearly deny any interest, let alone involvement, in political activity. Any such participation would have been unfeminine at the very least, because politics was seen solely as a man's domain – or so I had previously understood. Charlotte Smith had noted, 'We have always been taught that women should never advance a step into the field of politics.' (*Desmond*, 1792) As a radical thinker she was to ignore such lessons and had much to say on the subject; we will return to her in due course. During the course of my research I discovered ample evidence that some women in real life did ignore such didacticism, or found ways and means to justify getting round it. They did get directly involved in politics in a variety of ways and, when such women challenged traditional notions regarding their capabilities and their roles, they were to discover new strengths and their contributions were to be significant.

Men around them were to start to realise their worth at last and, although they made use of females for their own ends, at least women were able to satisfy their own needs in the process. Take one of my favourite women of the time, an upper class lady, Georgiana, Duchess of Devonshire. I was taken by surprise when I first heard about her involvement in politics – she was a very popular public figure, and could easily draw crowds. She was fascinated by the subject of politics and knew much about it. She too had written a novel exposing the evils of the society she lived in, (*The Sylph*, 1779) and criticised the marriage laws as they affected women. She was a close friend of the Prince of Wales, a keen and very active supporter of the Whig party, and a good friend of the politician Charles Fox. She was a key part of his election campaign for Westminster in 1784, leading a ladies party onto the hustings in his support, using her personality to win favour with the people, and even using her own carriage to collect voters. She was said to have had a winning way with people, a way to make them feel special as if their opinions really mattered to her. Why was I not surprised to find that one of her direct descendents was Diana, Princess of Wales?

For a while when I first encountered Georgiana I felt I was being haunted… coincidence or fate I could quickly spot her picture in bookshops, find an odd reference in a newspaper or within a television programme. I found her in totally random places I visited; when I took my son to see the local historic Chiswick House, not knowing it had any associations with her, it turned out to have been one of the Duke's residences. She had thrown her political parties there, helped in the garden design and there were many pictures of her on the walls. A few months later I visited the Tea and Coffee Museum with a friend who was visiting in London, and there was a contemporary etching of Georgiana on the wall – this time entertaining the Prince of Wales and giving him tea. Even then I felt she was trying to tell me something.

Georgiana had a mixed reception from the press. They either loved her or hated her. The criticisms were predictable. The *Morning Post*, 8th April 1784, stated:

> *The Duchess of Devonshire's attendance at Covent Garden, perhaps will not secure Mr Fox's election; but it will at least establish her pre-eminence above all other beauties of that place, and make her a standing toast in all the ale houses and gin shops of Westminster… Ladies who interest themselves so much in the case of elections, are perhaps too*

> *ignorant to know that they meddle with what does not concern them, but they ought at least to know, that it is usual, even in these days of degeneracy, to expect common decency in a married woman.*

Within the space of a paragraph she had been compared to a prostitute (the beauties of Covent Garden), mocked for her popularity amongst the poorer classes, had her intelligence insulted and her morality questioned. She was particularly mocked at one point for her allegedly kissing a butcher in exchange for his vote – but I cannot remember ever hearing of one male politician being slated for when they hugged a granny or kissed a baby! Many political etchings poked fun at her sexually as 'women should not get involved in politics', but a significant number too were to poke fun at Charles Fox for his dependence upon her. There are several of him riding piggy-back on her, for example as he entered Parliament for the first time. She had played a major part in his success – even though, or rather perhaps because, she was a woman. Just to illustrate the point, before the election was over she had a miscarriage and her mother took her out of London to recuperate. Charles Fox and the Whigs called her back, as they needed her popularity to win the day. She returned; Charles Fox won his seat. The political etchings may have made fun of her – but they also reflected, and contributed to, her popularity, portraying her image as a successful woman of the time.

Georgiana was not the only woman to support campaigns for election – some of her family and friends were, for example, involved in Fox's campaign and other women supported a rival, William Pitt. Women had involved themselves in canvassing for elections previously in the past, where a direct family member or close family friend was up for the position. What was radical about Georgiana was that she took part without feeling the need for any of those justifications, and her participation was clearly necessary to Charles Fox and the Whigs.

Other political issues too had drawn long term interest from women, throughout the whole period, in one form or another. As circumstances changed and more events took place and became publicised, women's opinions could develop, change and become more widely known. At times they could even find themselves being used, while feeling useful, in support of other campaigns and even major political events, like the introduction of Bills into Parliament. Let me give you a specific example. In recent years there has been a revival of interest in the subject of slavery, especially with the bi-centennial anniversary of the abolition of the slave trade in this country in 2007. However, it certainly came as rather a surprise to me that this subject had provided a real key area for *women* in the past, with many of them taking an active part in related political activity, and in the process learning much about themselves. Slavery is a huge topic and I have to acknowledge that, even as far as women have been concerned with it, after I had found there was more than enough evidence to prove my point, there was yet still more to discover...

In the process of reading many novels of the long eighteenth century I had come across short references to plantations in the West Indies, the wealth derived from the slave labour there, and occasional references to rebellion, or the threat of it. Much of the wealth of the landed gentry in Britain was due to its connections with trade and the use of slavery. Very few women here had direct experience of it, so many had not really questioned the moral concerns regarding slavery, and had enjoyed the life of luxury and ease in England that their male relatives had obtained for them. Of course, it was possible to have mixed feelings regarding the source of the wealth while still enjoying its benefits! However the situation was changing, and the question of abolition arose many times, and this is reflected once again in the women's literature during the period.

For some, slaves were a subhuman species and neither required, or deserved, consideration in their treatment. Plantation owners who thought this tended to use their beliefs as a justification for their cruel and vindictive behaviour towards their own slaves. Some women writers were quite prepared to expose such behaviour and use it to highlight the obvious link between hatred of the owners and the negro race – as well as indicating possible ensuing rebellion when the slaves reached breaking point. Dorothy Kilner wrote a tale about a runaway slave boy, who had been severely maltreated and was rescued and brought to London to start a new life. The slave trade came under severe censure:

> *Nor can it be wondered at, when they poor wretches, are torn from every comfort, from freedom, country, relatives and friends, bound and forced by cruel whippings on board of vessels, and carried off from every thing*

> *they hold dear and valuable in life;- when the parent is torn from his family, the father from his child, the husband from his wife, the child from its parent, and separated under the agonizing idea that it is not only for ever, but that it is to become, to be sold, the slave of a foreign, distant and cruel master; When every tie that God and nature has sacredly cemented is thus torn asunder, and all by white men professing themselves Christians, can it be wondered at, that they should imbibe the strongest prejudices against the whole race of whites... (The Rotchfords, mid 1780's)*

What is perhaps most surprising about this criticism of theoretical Christianity, is that it comes from a children's book – but where better to start attacking prejudice and cruelty in society? Other women writers showed agreement with her views. Hannah More, for example, had pointed out that the evil slave trade had been carried out by men claiming to be Christians, and wanted to make it clear that that this was not a valid claim – true Christians did not behave like that to fellow men:

> *....he has learn'd to dread the Christians trust;*
> *To him what mercy can that God display,*
> *Whose servants murder, and whose sons betray?*
> *Savage! Thy venial error I deplore,*
> *They are* ***not*** *Christians who infest thy shore.*
> (*The Black Slave Trade*, 1788)

In another of her poems, a Negro woman slave was to describe the humiliations she suffered on the journey, such as being made to dance for the sailor's entertainment, and made many references to beatings and other physical abuse, stating:

> *Poor and wounded, faint and sick,*
> *All expos'd to burning sky,*
> *Massa bids me grass to pick,*
> *And now I am near to die.*
>
> *What, and if to death he send me,*
> *Savage murder though it be,*

British laws shall ne'er befriend me,
They protect not slaves like me.
(*The Sorrows of Yamba, or, the Negro Woman's Lamentation*, 1795)

Perhaps the most poignant line of her anti slavery poetry was the succinct statement:

But they are still men and men should still be free.
(*Slavery, A Poem*, 1788)

Elizabeth Inchbald had raised the whole question of colonialism and native insurrection, 'You have heard the savages of our party put our whole party to death... I was broken hearted for my comrades; yet upon the whole, I do not know that the savages were much to blame – we had no business to invade their territories! And if they had invaded England, we should have done the same by them.' (*Nature and Art*, 1794) Charlotte Lennox too had already forewarned that if insurrection took hold in one plantation 'the danger would be very great' and quickly spread. (*Euphemia,* 1790)

Acknowledging the poor treatment that some slaves received from their masters, Sarah Scott had created a humanitarian plantation owner called Sir George Ellison who, while still dependent on slave labour, introduced a radical scheme for slave management. This included giving them each possession of a cottage with a small piece of land to cultivate for their families, free time, holidays, care in ill health and even education for the young. His slaves knew when they were well off – but slaves they remained. (*The History of George Ellison*, 1766) Later a condensed version of this book was brought out called '*The Man of Real Sensibility'* which removed his noble status but put greater emphasis on 'Mr Ellison's attitudes towards slavery and general benevolence towards the poor'. Right at the beginning of the book was the key comment that he hated the cruelty 'used up on one part of mankind, as if the difference of complexion excluded them from the human race.' A key point, with which others were to agree:

What strange offence, what aggravated sin?
They stand convicted of a darker skin...
(*Hannah More, The Black Slave Trade*, 1788)

People were becoming aware of the fact that slaves were humans, and possibly, just possibly, they might have some rights as such.

Lucy Peacock was one woman who looked on the slaves as not only being humans, but also having rights to spiritual equality – a consideration that some women were to take on very seriously as the justification for their involvement in the campaign for abolition. Her narrator in *The Creole* (1787) stated, 'Surely my dear madam, we have no right to tyrannise over and treat as brutes those who doubtless one day will be made partakers with us of an immortality.' For she believed in 'the cultivation of that universal spirit of philanthropy which teaches us to embrace all mankind as brethren, the children of one father.' Righteous though this sounds, there were some ulterior motives hidden here – if slaves were better treated and were educated in Christian notions, and were persuaded or even forced to abandon any other religious beliefs they held, they would learn to believe the principles of accepting one's place in this world and working towards the next. In so doing slaves would become less of a threat to their owners, insurrections would become less likely, and the need to abolish slavery could safely be postponed to some vague time in the future, and meantime profits could continue to be collected.

One of the more radical supporters of married women, Mary Ann Radcliffe, compared the life and treatment of slaves with oppressed women in England. While she was not alone in recognising that there were parallels in terms of loss of status and personal freedom, sexual bondage and lack of rights, it was none the less shocking to read her views on the subject:

> *What are the untutored, wild imaginations of a slave, when put in the balance with the distressing sensations of a British female, who has received a refined if not a classical education, and is capable of the finest feelings the human heart is susceptible of. A slave through want of education has little more refinement than cattle in the field; nor can they know the want of what they never enjoyed or were taught to expect...how much greater pleasure must it give the feeling heart to patronise the poor unfortunate woman of our own nation, who labour under the worst kind of slavery, and must continue to languish under the fetters of a painful bondage, till death, or the kindly hand of interference has severed the chain. (The Female Advocate, 1799)*

Although she appeared to dismiss the concerns of foreign slaves, many people, both men and women, were concerned about their fundamental treatment, as well as the slave trade in general, and had been trying to do something about it for a considerable length of time. Yet because of the link between the powerful, prosperous landowners and gentry, and the use of not just cheap labour, but free labour, which had contributed significantly to their wealth, there was reluctance for them to do anything about it – for as long as they could get away with it! Somehow more people had to be made aware of the horrors of slavery, and raise the issue in the eyes of the public, so pressure could be brought on parliament, and laws could be changed. Attempts had been made as early as 1788 (remember the Abolition Act was not passed until 1807) and even then women had been used to make their valuable contribution.

Women were notorious for their caring attitude and their emotional sensitivity, and were to make good use of both in the campaign for abolition – particularly through their poetry. I have already used a couple of examples by Hannah More – but her early contributions were of particular significance. Renowned and valued for her involvement in literary, philanthropic and Christian activities, Hannah More had actually been asked by the Abolition Committee to contribute a written piece on slavery, timed to be ready for the opening of the parliamentary debate, when the Abolition Bill was to be introduced in May 1788. Like Georgiana, Duchess of Devonshire, she was asked to do this because she was popular and, in her case, well respected – so it was likely that the publicity regarding her involvement would do much to encourage others to join the campaign.

Hannah More was well aware of the importance of the timing of the release of her poem, and like other campaigners must have felt very frustrated when the debate was quickly postponed, 'to collect more evidence'. It was another procrastinating technique used by those in power who did not want change. Well aware of the continued, ongoing distress of the situation, like other female campaigners she had stressed the horror of slavery from a woman's perspective – the experiences of family separation, emotional disturbance, physical abuse and so on – and used highly emotive language, in order to gain wider appeal:

See the dire victim torn from social life
The shrieking babe, the agonising wife!
She, wretch forlorn! Is dragged by hostile hands,
To distant tyrants sold, in distant lands....
By felon hands, by one relentless stroke,
See the fond links of feeling Nature broke,
The fibre twisting round a parents heart,
Torn from their grasp and bleeding as they part.
(*Slavery, a poem*)

Helen Maria Williams, who was to make significant contributions in other political areas that will be considered shortly, wrote poetry to mark significant events in the history of abolition. She was delighted when in 1788 a Bill was passed which limited the number of slaves that could be transported on a single shipload. At this stage she was full of praise for Britain's lead in its work to end the notorious slave trade,

O, first of EUROPE'S polish'd lands,
To ease the Captive's iron bands!
Long as thy glorious annals shine'
This proud distinction shall be thine:
(Poem On The Bill Lately Passed For Regulating The Slave Trade, 1788)

In 1791 when she was leaving Britain to live in France, she was to show her disappointment with the continuing scandal of the slave trade and the failure of the abolition movement. She was most taken with the new French Republic that now seemed to be taking up the cause,

Y*es GALLIA, haste! Tho' Britain's sons decline*
The glorious power to save, that power is thine;
Haste! Since, while BRITAIN courts the dear bought gold,
For which her virtue and her fame are sold,
And calmly calculates her trade of death
Her groaning victims yield in pangs their breath;
Then save some portion of that suffering race
From ills the mind can scarce endure to trace.

Oh whilst with mien august thy Leaders scan,
And guard with jealous zeal the rights of man.
(*A Farewell, for Two Years, to England. A poem*)

These poems were not just published in a collection, years after the events. They, like those of Hannah More and others, were published shortly after being written, so they could be read and discussed. Just as women's novels of the period were to be important for the spreading of ideas, regarding women's issues for example, so too were poems particularly to be used for propaganda purposes in the fight for abolition. So often, just as in novels, women worked on their sewing – when involved with the anti slavery movement they could, for example, pop a Tract or poem into a sewn workbag which was then sent to influential women, in the hope they would take up the cause. Maria Edgeworth and even Princess Victoria were sent them.

Many of the women we have encountered elsewhere had something to say about slavery or the African race. I discovered Georgiana, Duchess of Devonshire, continuing to get in everywhere, had written a poem that stressed their humanity. The famous explorer Mungo Park had related an incident of kindness shown to him by one African village woman, which Georgiana put into a poem, which was included in his book *Travels in the Interior Districts of Africa 1799*, and was then set to music for popular appeal. This is from the chorus:

The White Man shall our pity share;
Alas, no wife or mother's care
For him the milk and corn prepare…

Go, White Man, go; – but with thee bear
The Negro's wish, the Negro's prayer;
Remembrance of the Negro's care.

Mary Wollstonecraft too had made an important contribution in the battle against slavery. In a collation of literary extracts she put together in 1788, to help young women develop their reasoning and intellectual abilities, slavery was one of the major topics included. Like Dorothy Kilner, she had realised the importance of educating the young – in order at least to try to reduce the continuation of unreasonable prejudice in future generations. The readings were by both men and women, and only a small fraction was of her own composition. There were extracts from the Bible, where Joseph was sold as a slave when his brothers wanted to get rid of him, and the captive Israelites were unable to sing a song in a strange land. There was the story of Mr Inkle a trader en route to the West Indies, who got shipwrecked in America, seriously attacked by Indians, but was then befriended and protected by an Indian woman, with whom he then lived. He promised her wealth and a glorious life style when he took her back to England. En route though, his business instincts took over and he sold her to a merchant from Barbados! She pleaded with him on behalf of their unborn child but heartlessly, 'He only made use of that information to rise in his demands upon the purchaser.' Mary Wollstonecraft also included a short piece from Mrs Anna Laetitia Barbauld:

> *Negro woman who sittest in captivity and weepest over thy sick child; tho' no-one seeth thee, God seeth thee; tho' no-one pitieth thee, God pitieth thee: raise thy voice forlorn and abandoned one. Call upon Him from amidst thy bonds, for assuredly He will hear thee.*
> *(The Female Reader, 1788)*

It is not difficult to guess where her sympathies lay, and her intentions with regard to her young readers...

Feeling justified in their taking up the cause for religious, moral, and humanitarian reasons, and probably making the most of the excuse to be doing something a little more purposeful with their lives, many women were to take on the issue of slavery as a cause dear to their own hearts. They took up door-to-door canvassing, handing out propaganda in the form of poems and leaflets, they helped raise money for the new Abolition Societies that were forming, and in time they began to develop their organisational skills, formed their own societies and took their petitions to parliament. Their efforts may not have always been well received by some men – parliament is said to have laughed at their efforts, and it was very easy to ignore their work or discount their contributions – because they were merely women! Yet the anti slavery associations continued their work long after the 1807 Act in England had been passed. Anne Knight, an abolitionist campaigner and later important feminist from Chelmsford, Essex – where I used to live – received an important letter from the national activist George Thompson, in 1834. Referring to all the women's associations set up in support of antislavery he openly acknowledged, 'Where they existed they did everything ...In a word they formed the cement of the whole Antislavery building – without their aid we should never have been united.'

This comment was very much in accordance with one written earlier in a letter by Helen Maria Williams when she was in France:

> *For whatever the imperious lords of creation may fancy, the most important events which take place in this world depend a little upon our influence; and we often act in human affairs like those secret springs in mechanisms, by which, though invisible, great movements are regulated. (Letters written in France in the Summer of 1790)*

Possibly the most well known of their activities was the suggestion that women should take up the issue as individuals, as domestic heads of households, and strike out at the economic heart of the matter, in a sugar boycott. If enough women gave up the sugar that came from the slave labour in the West Indies, it was possible, some believed, that it would have a significant effect on the plantation owners in the long run. Elizabeth Heyrick described the exploitation in criminal terms, 'The West Indian planter and the people in this country, stand in the same moral relationship to each other as the thief and receiver of stolen goods.' (*Immediate not Gradual Abolition*, 1824) The Irish writer Mary Birkett had recommended the same action, while hopes were still high for an early Act of Abolition:

> *Yes sisters, to us the task belongs*
> *Tis we increase or mitigate their wrongs.*
> *If we the produce of their toils refuse,*
> *If we no more the blood stain'd lux'ry choose;*
>
> *In no small part their long-borne pangs will cease,*
> *And we to souls unborn may whisper peace.*
> (*A Poem on The African Slave Trade*, 1792)

From all these examples it is surely clear that slavery provided a very useful outlet for women who wished to become involved in political affairs – and I think you will agree that their written contributions were extremely powerful.

The final area I wish to consider, where women became politically involved, was in the matter of the French Revolution and all the arguments that surrounded it. I am not referring here to the French women themselves – although they had played a significant part during it. For the events of the Revolution, and the subsequent formation of a Republic, provided English women with many new opportunities for observation, journalism, political commentary and philosophical debate that few had experienced before. No matter how much Bluestockings and their associates may have tried to deny their political involvement at the time, their opinions and, at times, their actions, certainly contributed to the reactions in England. Other women, like Mary Wollstonecraft and Helen Maria Williams, wanted to travel to France and observe and report for themselves. Both had to face imprisonment in France, although Mary was able to avoid it, and both were forced to observe the extremely negative situations that unfolded, but it is the contribution of Helen Williams that was to be particularly important here.

Helen had been a frequent visitor to France before the Revolution, and was so impressed by the ideals of all the changes that she later decided to move there. She had been a respected writer before she left England so her comments were likely to be taken seriously, at least by some. She positively rejoiced in taking part in the festivities on the anniversary of the Storming of the Bastille, one year after the event, at La Fête de la Féderation. Helen then recorded her experiences in the detailed *Letters From France*, which were published over a six-year period. This was true political journalism, from a woman's personal point of view, and was to be one of the key texts to inform the period. It recorded her enthusiasm for the principles of liberty and human rights, the end to tyranny – as the French monarchy and ruling nobility had sanctioned it – and the joy with which the people celebrated the following year:

> *It was a triumph of human kind; it was man asserting the noblest privileges of his nature, and it required but the common feelings of humanity to become in that moment a citizen of the world.*
> *(Letters Written in France in the Summer of 1790)*

Also recorded were her reactions while paying a visit to England, when she found out that people there were being misled:

> *I hear of crimes, assassinations, torture and death. I am told that everyday witnesses a conspiracy; that every town is the scene of a massacre; that every street is blackened with a gallows, and every highway is deluged with blood. I hear these things and repeat to myself, Is this the picture of France? Are these the images of that universal joy, which called tears into my eyes, and made my heart throb with sympathy? (Ibid)*

From the onset she showed her awareness of the prejudice towards France and stated:

> *I wish that some of our political critics would speak with less contempt, than they are apt to do, of the new constitution in France, and no longer repeat after one another, the trite remark, that the French have gone too far, because they have gone further than ourselves… I cannot but suspect that some mean jealousy lurks beneath the ungenerous gesture…they wish to make a monopoly of liberty, and are angry that France should claim a share of that precious property. (Ibid)*

She honestly and openly admitted her own distress and disappointment when things were going badly wrong asking:

> *What is become of the transport which beat high in every bosom, when an assembled million of the human race vowed on the altar of their country, in the name of the represented nation, inviolable fraternity and union – an eternal federation! This was indeed the golden age of the revolution – But it is passed! – the enchanting spell is broken.*
> *(Letters from France, 1793)*

In spite of this she was always to maintain her own position, 'When I said that the French revolution began in wisdom, I admitted that it came afterwards into the hands of fools. But the *foundation was laid in wisdom*.' (*Letters from France*, 1793)

Regarding her own activity she became more involved in politics when it had began to touch her. She wrote:

> *Did you expect that I should ever dip my pen in politics, who used to take so small interest in public affairs, that I recollect a gentleman of my acquaintance surprised me not a little, by informing me of the war between the Turks and the Russians, at a time when all the people in Europe, except myself, had been two years in possession of the knowledge. (Letters Written in France in the Summer of 1790)*

I have come across several women who explained their lack of involvement in political affairs of the day – until they were affected particularly by it. Mary Hays was to write similarly:

> *I have paid very little attention to the venal politics of the day as conceiving they merited but little. But a benevolent mind cannot view with indifference its fellow creatures sinking into depravity and consequent misery. Plain general principles are obvious to everyone who stops to reflect. (Letters and Essays, Moral and Miscellaneous, 1793)*

The reason why Helen Maria Williams was so affected by events in France was because a male acquaintance there had suffered grievously through the actions of his tyrannical father; a notorious *lettre de cachet* had been obtained which legally authorised his arrest and imprisonment indefinitely, just because his unjust aristocratic father had managed to fix it. For her:

> *The old constitution is connected in my mind with the image of a friend confined in the gloomy recesses of a dungeon, and pining in hopeless captivity; while, with the new constitution, I unite the soothing idea of his return to prosperity, honours and happiness. (Letters from France, 1790)*

Not surprisingly she came in for personal criticism for her outspoken views, to which she responded:

> *Must I be told my mind is perverted, because I do not weep with those who have lost a part of their superfluities, rather than rejoice that the oppressed are protected, that the wronged are redressed, that the captive is set at liberty, and that the poor have bread. (Ibid)*

If you expected that such an outspoken female would be criticised for her sex you would not have been disappointed. When she took to reporting on the less savoury aspects of the Terror in 1795, the *Gentleman's Magazine* criticised her heavily: she had 'debased her sex, her heart, her feelings, her talents' because she had recorded such dreadful events. Unfortunately she too, like Mary Wollstonecraft and Catherine Macaulay, had broken with sexual conventions, in her case having decided to live with her sexual partner – rather than marry – and of course this too worked against her. However in the case of Helen Williams her work was still of major importance at the time because of it being an eyewitness history. Not all important works concerning the revolution were...

One such particularly significant work, which led to major debate on the political issues involved in the revolution, was that of Edmund Burke, called *Reflections on the Revolution in France*. His version of the Revolution was alarming and bloody – contrasting drastically with Helen Williams first volume of *Letters*, written in the summer of 1790 – but it was not based on personal experience or knowledge. It was based on hearsay and fear. He was a great supporter of the traditional patriarchal set up, with the landed aristocracy having a major role in government. His emphasis on riots, blood and gore terrified the English people – there were major fears of riots and revolt. It was he who suggested that the French king could be in danger for his life – and in later *Letters From France* it was pointed out that Edmund Burke's influence could have led others to consider the possibility – and thus he could even possibly be held partly responsible for the king's ultimate death! (*Letters from France*, 1793)

Within a few months of the *Reflections* being released, other publications followed. Mary Wollstonecraft's *Vindication of the Rights of Man* criticised Burke for his prejudice and determination to uphold what was basically a corrupt feudal system, and then Thomas Paine's *The Rights of Man* promoted elections and representative government, with emphasis on meritocracy rather than wealth and title. Political debate was everywhere – and, undoubtedly, women of the time played their part in it both in the major works cited above, as well as continued debate in fiction, non-fiction and poetry.

As Helen Maria Williams had done, Charlotte Smith was to comment on how politicians made use of untrue reports for their own ends:

That it has become an object with our government to employ such men; men whose business it is to stifle truths, which though unable to deny, they are unwilling to admit; it is a proof, that they believe the delusion of the people necessary to admit their own views; and have recourse to these miserable expedients, to impede a little the progress of that light which they see rising upon the world. (Desmond, 1792)

When I first read this quote I was shocked – after the events of 9/11 in 2001, the American President George Bush had begun a quest for weapons of mass destruction and persuaded our then Prime Minister, Tony Blair, to join in the Iraq War. The possession of these weapons of mass destruction had been the justification for the very unpopular war – and they had never existed. These were current affairs for me, but Charlotte Smith's sharp political comment seemed uncannily relevant at the time. In the same novel she also was to reveal why the English government and supporters like Burke were so worried by the French Revolution:

They fear for their own nation.. or know and dread that light of reason thus rapidly advancing, which has shown us how to overturn the massy and cumbrous edifice of despotism, will make too evident the faults of their own, which it is their particular interest to screen from research and information.

Like many politicians she was aware of the methods that could be used to subdue opposition, 'Where sound argument fails, abusive declamation is always substituted, and that it often silences where it cannot convince. I know too that where politics are obnoxious, recourse is always had to personal detraction.' (*Ibid*) Regarding Thomas Paine and The Rights of Man she warned, 'Those who feel the force of his abilities will vilify his private life, as if they were anything to the purpose.' (*Ibid*) She could easily have been talking about the reaction, by some, to women writers and thinkers!

In her preface to this work she admitted that she was prepared for criticism by those who would 'exclaim against the propriety of making a book of entertainment (i.e. a novel) the vehicle of political discussion.' Her answer was simple, 'Nothing appears more respectable than national pride; nothing so absurd as national prejudice.'

During the course of some novels occasional female characters were told, 'If she had been a man, she would have made a great figure in parliament.'(Charlotte Lennox, *The Female Quixote*, 1752) I think Charlotte Smith could have done well in Westminster!

Sometimes women were to show sympathy and understanding towards the revolutionaries. This was from Mary Hays:

> *It appears to me that all monarchical and aristocratical governments, carry within themselves the seeds of their dissolution, for when they become corrupt and oppressive to a certain degree, the effects must necessarily be murmurs, remonstrances and revolt.*
> *(Letters and Essays Moral and Miscellaneous, 1793)*

Charlotte Smith too wrote a poem that was particularly apt:

> *.................................rather here*
> *Study a lesson that concerns ye much;*
> *And trembling, learn, that if oppressed too long,*
> *The raising multitude to madness stung,*
> *Will turn on their oppressors.*
> (*Desmond*)

Perversely Mary Hays was also to raise a few eyebrows, I am sure, by showing sympathy towards the execution of the French royal family, blaming their upbringing at least in part for their attitudes towards their subjects, as well as the constant flattery they had received in youth which 'enervated their minds and destroyed their strength.' (*Letters and Essays, Moral and Miscellaneous*, 1793)

At the beginning, with the storming of the Bastille, even Hannah More, the Bluestocking, had felt that everyone in England should be delighted that it had been demolished and look forward to the time when 'one of the finest countries in the world' would be free. Initially her involvement was as a spectator – but later when fear of revolution gripped the English nation, and Edmund Burke's worst fears turned into a reality, she used some of her conservative *Tracts* (moral stories/writings for the lower classes) to stress her beliefs, and help reinforce the notion that the lower classes should not rebel against their governmental systems. Rather they should accept their station in life, serve God, work hard and uphold the status quo. This was from *Village Politics*, (1792), and took the form of a dialogue between Jack Anvil, the Blacksmith and Tom Hod the Mason:

> *Tom. What doest thou then take French* ***liberty*** *to be?*
> *Jack. To murder more men in one night, than ever their king did in his whole life.*
> *Tom. And what does thou take a* ***democrat*** *to be?*
> *Jack. One who likes to be governed by a thousand tyrants, and yet cant bear a king.*
> *Tom. What is equality?*
> *Jack. For every man to pull down every one that is above him, till they're all as low as the lowest.*
> *Tom. What is the* ***new Rights of Man?***
> *Jack. Battle, murder and sudden death.*
> *Tom. What is it like to be an* ***enlightened people?***
> *Jack. To put out the light of the gospel, confound right and wrong, and grope about in pitch darkness … Their mob parliament meets on a Sunday to do their wicked work, as naturally as we do go to church. They have renounced God's word, and God's day, and they don't even date in the year of our Lord.*
> *Tom. And dost thou think our rights of Man will lead to all this wickedness.*
> *Jack. As sure as eggs are eggs … We have a king so loving, that he would not hurt the people if he cou'd: and so kept in, that he cou'd not hurt the people if he wou'd. We have as much liberty as can make us happy, and more trade and riches than allows us to be good. We have the best laws in the world, if they were more strictly enforced; and the best religion in the world, if it was but better followed. While Old England is safe, I'll glory in her and pray for her, and when she is in danger, I'll fight for her and die for her.*
> *Tom. And so will I too, Jack, that's what I will.*

This was indoctrination; political propaganda, pure and simple, directed only to the lower working classes, by a woman who was purportedly a Bluestocking. The quotation above quite clearly shows that, even as a more conservative woman, she did acknowledge there were faults in the system – regarding both government and religion, and she clearly stated, ' I don't pretend to say they are a bit better than they should be ... I wish they would set us a better example.' (*Ibid*) She did not believe in radical change, rather favouring internal reform – but 'no' they were not involved in politics! Nor of course was her friend Elizabeth Montagu, who was so worried about the threat to social stability in England, that she too starting sending out copies of Hannah's work!

What all this evidence shows is that, women or not, all these exemplary individuals, regardless of any customary restraints and beliefs on how women should behave, felt it was their incumbent religious, moral and social duty to stand up for what they believed was right. In the course of their literary work they were to take on direct confrontations with other women, and men, who held different moral, philosophical, political, and religious views. Women like Frances Burney, Mary Hays, Mary Wollstonecraft, Charlotte Smith, Mary Robinson, Eliza Haywood and even Jane Austen, would take on stalwarts of tradition like Hannah More, Elizabeth Helm, Elizabeth Griffith, Elizabeth Hamilton, or the less extreme Jane West. It did not seem to really matter then what political stance one held, or even whether one was a supporter of the patriarchal system at all. During the course of this work, I have tried to show that there were women who were prepared to challenge the assumptions regarding the nature and capabilities of women, who were prepared to challenge the stereotypical images, and were to use their writings not only to record their views, but also to spread them. They were to call for better education, happier marriages, fairer treatment, greater respect and a more purposeful life. In her *Letters to Literary Ladies* of 1795, Maria Edgeworth had noted the significance of print for women; one of her 'gentlemen' said, 'It is absolutely out of our power to drive the fair sex to their former state of darkness: the art of printing has totally changed their situation; their eyes are opened, – the classic page is unrolled, they will read...' One could also add 'and they will write!'

Although it was necessary periodically to put back the mask, or tone down the level of their activity, or find ways of suitable justification for their less than commonly acceptable behaviour in times of political and social turmoil, women were on the move, both as individuals and, by the end of the period, at times, as a group – with some form of common cause and identity. They were beginning to believe in themselves.

During my research I have been on the look out for a suitable quotation for my concluding paragraph. The one I have chosen may be a little sentimental, and even from a different era, but it is apt nonetheless. It concerns a fictional woman called Dagmar, who was a 'new woman' at the end of the nineteenth century; a woman dedicated to social reform. Her mission was to rescue girls who had been badly treated by society and lead them on to better, purposeful, successful lives. Her obituary was written thus:

> *There are very few Dagmars in the world.*
>
> *Thus her brief life, and all the good she might have done came to an abrupt end. But all the same, Dagmar's life was not in vain, for she was one of those who leaves footprints on the sands of Time, she was one of the pioneers of a great movement; and although her life ceased when her work was hardly begun, there are still some women in London who remember her and can never forget her. There are weary and despairing women, and brave women whom her example has encouraged, and noble and courageous women who got their first impetus from her, who but for her would not have dared to break through the thraldom of the narrow walls of old prejudice, and those women still in memory hear her voice, and touch her hand. (L. T. Meade, The Cleverest Woman In The World, 1898)*

This obituary could have been describing several of the key female writers included in my work, but somehow the tide had washed over the sands of Time and I had known virtually nothing about all of them, or the contributions they were making at the time to our history. I may never have known these women, or held their hands, but during the course of my journey through the long eighteenth century I have certainly heard their voices.

A Final Word

During my introduction I made reference to the Atticus principle – the need to experience events from someone else's point of view in order to understand them. My journey has been an attempt to do just that. At the outset I thought I was writing a book, as a feminist, about feminism in women's literature but during the course of my research my position changed.

When I was a postgraduate student at University in the late 1970's I became interested in sexism in children's literature, and discovered a disturbing 'alternative book' for children produced by a feminist group. This was for young children; a story about elephants. However, in it the group of pink elephants took over and became just as domineering and despotic as the previously leading blue elephants had been. I should have been warned. The danger of feminism is that it can become just as biased and prejudiced as the male assumption of being the superior sex, and this is not where I wish to stand. Regarding the history of women in the long eighteenth century the situation was not as clear-cut as I had imagined it to be. For, in general, I do not think the term feminism really applied to the period. While it is true that women were the lesser citizens, for laws and customs did favour the opposite sex, my journey brought other issues to light. There was little or no sense of group solidarity amongst women, not all women wanted change or even the same changes, not all men were oppressive, women themselves could act as an effective break – operating very much against other women's interests, and some men were extremely supportive in promoting women's talents. Rather than being a black and white situation there were indeed many shades of grey. Also from being a feminist I have altered my own position to being more one of a humanist – or at least so my elder daughter tells me!

Following what has been an apparent tradition in women's writing

I suppose I ought to include an apologia. Although I have read a great many women's novels as well as more serious works of the period, I have not read every one, written by every author. I have been guided by instinct to a large extent and have not followed a particularly academic formula. It has been a journey guided by personal interest and spontaneous whim; a genuine voyage of discovery. As I expect other readers may be interested in reading some of the texts I have referred to, I have included a simple bibliography, and a short biography of key women. For readers more interested in the details of historical events, the personalities and so on, there are so many books available it becomes a matter of personal choice which I leave to the reader.

I had originally intended to look at Victorian women's literature, but had to go back into the eighteenth century in order to gain a better perception of what had gone on before, and to see how it was to affect the future. In so doing I have gained a clearer understanding of some of the patterns that affected women's lives then, how women felt, and what they were doing about it. After reading this work try the works of Jane Austen again or a Victorian, like Mrs Gaskell for example, and you will see what I mean. I hope you find it useful.

Appendix One

Key Texts

I have chosen to present this simplified bibliography in a slightly unorthodox way, as I think it may be helpful to be able to identify which primary sources were used for each section. This is followed by a short list of secondary sources.

Chapter One – An introduction

Mary Astell. *Some Reflections Upon Marriage*, 1700.
Jane Austen. *Northanger Abbey*, 1818.
Frances Burney. *The Woman Hater*, 1800-2.
Harper Lee. *To Kill a Mockingbird*, 1960.
Lucy Jago. *Regency House Party*; Little, Brown Book Group, 1984.

Chapter Two – Women as writers

Rosina Bulwer Lytton. *Cheveley*, 1834.
Frances Burney. *Evelina*, 1778; *Cecilia*, 1782; *The Wanderer*, 1814.
Eliza Fenwick. *Secresy, or Ruin on the Rock,* 1795.
Sarah Fielding. *The Adventures of David Simple*, 1744.
James Fordyce. *Sermons to Young Women*, 1767.
Mary Ann Radcliffe. *The Female Advocate, or An Attempt to Recover the Rights of Women from Male Usurpation* ,1799.
Mary Robinson. *Walsingham*, 1797; *A Letter to the Women of England on the Injustice of Mental Insubordination*, 1799.
Mrs Skinn. *The Old Maid*, 1771.
Charlotte Smith. *Desmond*, 1792; *Marchmont*, 1796.
Jane West. *A Tale of the Times*, 1799.

Chapter Three – A question of education

Frances Burney. *Cecilia or Memories of an Heiress*, 1782; *Camilla*, 1796; *The Wanderer*, 1814.
Maria and Richard Edgeworth. *Practical Education*, 1798.
Eliza Fenwick. *Secresy, or Ruin on the Rock,* 1795.
Susan Ferrier. *Marriage*, 1818.
Madame Genlis. *Adelaide and Theodore*, 1783.
Sarah Fielding. *The Adventures of David Simple*, 1744.
Elizabeth Hamilton. *Memoirs of Modern Philosophers*, 1800; *Letters on Education*, 1801.
Mary Ann Hanway. *Ellinor, or The World as It Is*, 1798.
Mary Hays. *The Victim of Prejudice*, 1789.
Eliza Haywood. *The Female Spectator*, 1775 vol 3.
Julia Kavanagh. *English Women of Letters: Biographical Sketches*, 1863.
Catherine Macaulay. *Letters on Education*, 1790.
Hannah More. *Strictures on the Modern System of Female Education*, 1799.
Amelia Opie. *Adeline Mowbray*, 1805.
Mrs Parsons. *Women as they are*, 1796.
Clara Reeve. *Plans of Education*, 1792.
Mary Robinson. *Walsingham*, 1797; *A letter to the Women of England on the Injustice of Mental Insubordination*, 1799.
Jean Jacques Rousseau. *Emile*, 1762.
George Savile, Marquis of Halifax. *The Lady's New-Year Gift; or Advice to a Daughter*, 1688.
Olive Schreiner. *The Story of an African Farm*, 1883.
Sophia. *Women not Inferior to Man*, 1739.
Mary Wollstonecraft. *A Vindication of the Rights of Woman*, 1792.

Chapter Four – A marriageable commodity

Jane Austen. *The Watsons*, 1805; *Pride and Prejudice*, 1813.
Robert Bage. *Hermsprong*, 1796.
Charlotte Bronte. *Shirley*, 1848.
Frances Burney. *Early Diary* 1768-78, vol 1; *Cecilia,* 1782; *The Wanderer*, 1814.
Susan Ferrier. *Marriage*, 1818.

Sarah Fielding. *The Adventures of David Simple*, 1744.
Elizabeth Hamilton. *Memoirs of Modern Philosophers*, 1800.
Mary Ann Hanway. *Ellinor, or The World as It Is*, 1798.
Eliza Haywood. *The History of Betsy Thoughtless*, 1751; *The History of Jemmy and Jenny Jessamy*, 1753.
Charlotte Lennox. *The History of Harriet Stuart, Written By Herself*, 1751; *The Female Quixote*, 1752; *Euphemia*, 1790.
Regina Maria Roche. *Children of the Abbey*, 1796.
Mrs Skinn. *The Old Maid*, 1771.
Sarah Scott. *Millenium Hall*, 1762.
Charlotte Smith. *Emmeline*, 1788; *Montalbert*, 1795; *The Young Philosopher*, 1798.
Jane West. *A Tale of the Times*, 1798.

Chapter Five – Marriage for better or worse

Anonymous. *The Hardships of the English Laws in Relation to Wives with an Explanation of the Original Curse of Subjection passed on Women in an Humble Address to the Legislature*, 1735.
Mary Astell. *Some Reflections upon Marriage*, 1700.
Jane Austen. *Pride and Prejudice*, 1813; *Northanger Abbey*, 1818.
Robert Bage. *Hermsprong*, 1796.
Rhoda Broughton. *Cometh up as a Flower*, 1867.
Frances Burney. *Camilla*, 1796; *The Wanderer*, 1814.
Jane Collier. *An Essay on the Art of Ingeniously Tormenting*, 1753.
Judith Drake. *An Essay in Defence of the Female Sex*, 1696.
Maria Edgeworth. *Patronage*, 1814.
Sarah Fielding. *The Adventures of David Simple*, 1744.
Hannah Foster. *The Coquette*, 1797.
Elizabeth Griffith. *The Delicate Distress*, 1769.
Mary Ann Hanway. *Ellinor, or the World as It Is*, 1793.
Mary Hays. *Memoirs of Emma Courtney*, 1796; *An Appeal to the Men of Great Britain in behalf of Women*, 1798, *A Victim of Prejudice*, 1799.
Eliza Haywood. *The History of Miss Betsy Thoughtless*, 1751; *The History of Jemmy and Jenny Jessamy*, 1753.
Charlotte Lennox. *Euphemia*, 1790.
Amelia Opie. *Adeline Mowbray*, 1805.
Clara Reeve. *The School for Widows*, 1791.

Mary Robinson. *Walsingham*, 1797; *The False Friend*, 1799, *A Letter to the Women of England on the Injustice of Mental Insubordination*, 1799.
Sophia. *Woman not Inferior to Man*, 1739.
Charlotte Smith. *Desmond*, 1792; *Montalbert*, 1795; *Marchmont*,1796; *The Young Philosopher*,1798.
Mrs Skinn. *The Old Maid*, 1771.
George Sand. *Indiana*, 1831.
William Thompson and Anna Wheeler. *Appeal of One Half of the Human Race, Women, against the Pretensions of the Other Half, Men, to retain them in Political and thence Civil and Domestic slavery,* 1825.
Jane West. *A Tale of the Times*, 1799.
Mary Wollstonecraft. *A Vindication of the Rights of Woman*, 1792, *The Wrongs of Woman or Maria*, 1798.

Chapter Six – Fallen from grace

Anonymous. *The Histories of Some of the Penitants in the Magdalen House*, 1759.
Jane Austen. *Pride and Prejudice*, 1813; *Mansfield Park*, 1814.
Mary Brunton. *Self Control*, 1810.
Charlotte Dacre. *Zofloya*, 1806.
Mary Davys. *The Accomplish'd Rake*, 1727; *The Reform'd Coquet* 1724.
Maria Edgeworth. *Patronage*, 1814.
Sarah Fielding. *The Adventures of David Simple*, 1744.
Hannah Foster. *The Coquette*, 1797.
Elizabeth Hamilton. *Memoirs of Modern Philosophers*, 1800.
Mary Ann Hanway. *Ellinor, or the World as It Is*, 1793.
Mary Hays. *Memoirs of Emma Courtney*, 1796; *On Novel Writing*, 1797; *Appeal to The Men of Great Britain in behalf of Women*, 1798; *The Victim of Prejudice*, 1799.
Eliza Haywood. *Love in Excess*, 1719/20; *Lasselia or The Self Abandon'd*, 1724; *The Adventures of Betsy Thoughtless*, 1751; *The History of Jemmy and Jenny Jessamy*, 1753.
Elizabeth Helm. *The Farmer of Inglewood Forest*, 1796.
Elizabeth Inchbald. *Nature and Art*, 1796.
Harriet Lee. *The Errors of Innocence*, 1786.
Charlotte Lennox. *The Life of Harriet Stuart, Written By Herself*, 1751.
Rosina Bulwer Lytton. *Cheveley*, 1837.

Rosa Matilda. *The Passions*, 1811.
Hannah More. *Strictures on the Modern System of Education*, 1799.
Amelia Opie. *The Father and Daughter*, 1801.
Ann Plumptre. *Something New*, 1803.
Mary Ann Radcliffe. *The Female Advocate, or An Attempt to Recover the Rights of Women from Male Usurpation* 1799.
Susanna Rawson. *Charlotte Temple*, 1794.
Mary Robinson. *The False Friend*, 1799; *Walsingham*, 1797; *The Natural Daughter*, 1799.
George Sand. *Indiana*, 1831.
Sarah Scott. *Millenium Hall*, 1762.
Felicia Skene. *Hidden Depths*, 1866.
Mrs Skinn. *The Old Maid*, 1771.
Charlotte Smith. *Emmeline*, 1788, *Montalbert*, 1795.
William Thompson and Anna Wheeler. *Appeal of One Half of the Human Race, Women, against the Pretensions of the Other Half, Men, to retain them in Political and thence Civil and Domestic Slavery*, 1825.
Mary Wollstonecraft. *A Vindication of the Rights of Woman,* 1792; *The Wrongs of Woman, or Maria,* 1798.
Virginia Woolf. *Professions for Women*, 1931.

Chapter Seven – A woman alone

A Modern Antique *The Spinsters Journal*, 1816.
Mary Astell. *A Serious Proposal to the Ladies*, 1694.
Jane Austen. *The Watsons*, 1805; *Sense and Sensibility*, 1811; *Pride and Prejudice*, 1813; *Mansfield Park*, 1814; *Emma*, 1816.
Mary Brunton. *Discipline*, 1814.
Jane Collier. *An Essay on the Art of Ingeniously Tormenting*, 1753.
Frances Burney. *Evelina*, 1778; *The Wanderer*, 1814.
Maria Edgeworth. *Letters to Literary Ladies*, 1795; *Patronage*, 1814; *Helen*, 1834.
Maria and Richard Edgeworth. *Practical Education*, 1798.
Sarah Fielding. *The Adventures of David Simple*, 1744.
Mary Ann Hanway. *Ellinor, or the World as It Is*, 1798.
Mary Hays. *Memoirs of Emma Courtenay,* 1796.
Elizabeth Helm. *The Farmer of Inglewood Forest*, 1796.
Charlotte Lennox. *Henrietta*, 1758; *Euphemia*, 1790.

Amelia Opie. *Adeline Mowbray,* 1805.
Mary Ann Radcliffe. *The Female Advocate, or An Attempt to Recover the Rights of Women from Male Usurpation* 1799.
Clara Reeve. *The School for Widows*, 1791.
Mary Robinson. *The False Friend*, 1799; *The Natural Daughter*, 1799.
Sarah Scott. *Millennium Hall*, 1762.
Mrs Skinn. *The Old Maid*, 1771.
Charlotte Smith. *Marchmont*, 1796; *The Young Philosopher*, 1798.
Mary Wollstonecraft. *A Vindication of the Rights of Woman,* 1792; *The Wrongs of Woman, or Maria,* 1798.

Chapter Eight – Woman on the move

Jane Austen. *Persuasion*, 1817; *Northanger Abbey*, 1818.
Frances Burney. *Cecilia*, 1782, *Camilla* 1796, *The Wanderer*, 1814.
Judith Drake. *Essay in Defence of the Female Sex*, 1692.
Maria Edgeworth. *Letters to Literary Ladies*,1795; *Helen*, 1834.
Elizabeth Hamilton. *Memoirs of Modern Philosophers*, 1800.
Mary Ann Hanway. *Ellinor, or the World as It Is*, 1798.
Mary Hays. *Letters and Essays, Moral and Miscellaneous*, 1793; *Memoirs Of Emma Courtenay*, 1796; *An Appeal to the Men of Great Britain in Behalf of the Other Sex* ,1799; *A Victim of Prejudice*, 1799.
Eliza Haywood. *The Adventures of Betsy Thoughtless*, 1751.
Elizabeth Inchbald. *Nature and Art*, 1794.
Dorothy Kilner. *The Rotchfords*, mid 1780's.
Charlotte Lennox. *The Female Quixote*, 1752, *Euphemia*, 1790.
Hannah More. *Village Politics. Addressed to all the mechanics, journeymen and day labourers in Great Britain, by Will Chip, a country carpenter*, 1792.
L.T.Meade. *The Cleverest Woman in the World*, 1898.
Amelia Opie. *Adeline Mowbray*, 1805; *Detraction Displayed*, 1828.
Lucy Peacock. *The Creole*, 1787.
Ann Plumptre. *Something New*, 1801.
Mary Ann Radcliffe. *The Female Advocate, or An Attempt to Recover the Rights of Women from Male Usurpation* 1799.
Clara Reeve. *The School for Widows*, 1791.
Mary Robinson. *The False Friend*, 1799; *A Letter to the Women of England on the Injustice of Mental Insubordination*, 1799.

Sarah Scott. *Millennium Hall*, 1762; *The History of Sir George Ellison*, 1766 *The Man of Real Sensibility*, 1774.

Mrs Skinn. *The Old Maid*, 1771.

Sophia. *Woman not Inferior to Man*, 1739.

Charlotte Smith. *Desmond*, 1792, *The Young Philosopher*, 1798.

Jane West. *A Tale of the Times*, 1799.

Helen Maria Williams. *Letters from France in the Summer of 1790*; *Letters from France*, 1793.

Mary Wollstonecraft. *The Female Reader*, 1788; *A Vindication of The Rights of Woman*, 1792.

Secondary Sources

Susan Tyler Hitchcock, *Mad Mary Lamb*, W.W.Norton & Company, Inc. New York, 2005

Dale Spender. *Mothers of the Novel*, Pandora Press, 1986

For those with more of an academic interest
I would recommend the following:

Eve Tavor Bannet, *The Domestic Revolution*, The Johns Hopkins University Press, London, 2000

Audrey Bilger. *Laughing Feminism,* Wayne State University Press, Detroit, 2002

Elizabeth Bergen Brophy. *Women's Lives and the Eighteenth-Century English Novel*, University of South Florida Press, Tampa, 1991

Moira Ferguson. *First Feminists, British Women Writers 1578-1799*, Indiana University Press, Bloomington, 1985

Moira Ferguson. *Subject to Others: British Women Writers and Colonial Slavery, 1670-1834*, Routledge, London, 1992

Vivien Jones (ed). *Women in the Eighteenth Century*, Routledge, London, 1990

Katherine Rogers. *Feminism in Eighteenth Century England,* University of Illinois Press, London, 1982

Dale Spender (ed). *Living by the Pen, Early British Women Authors*, Teachers College Press, New York, 1992

Appendix Two

Key Women Writers

Mary Astell 1666-1731

She was born into a middle class family. When she was 20 she moved to London and became friends with the aristocracy and gained support for her work from them, particularly Lady Mary Wortley Montague. Much of her writing was controversial, ranging from scholarly, religious and philosophical works to her *A Serious Proposal to the Ladies* and *Reflections Upon Marriage*, which went to several editions. Her *Serious Proposal* was so well received that a man claimed credit at the time for writing it. She also ran a charity school.

Jane Austen 1775- 1817

She was the daughter of a country clergyman and lived with members of her family all her life. She went to a boarding school for a few years with her sister Cassandra. She was an avid reader – including the works of women novelists, Mary Brunton, Frances Burney, Maria Edgeworth, Elizabeth Hamilton and Jane West. Jane started writing at a young age to amuse her family, reading her work aloud to them. Her father encouraged her. Her writing was mainly completed in the 1790's but all her works were published later, some posthumously. Her novels are well known and are regularly screened on television and in the cinema. (*Sense and Sensibility*, *Pride and Prejudice*, *Mansfield Park*, *Emma*, *Northanger Abbey* and *Persuasion*) All were published anonymously. She did receive one marriage proposal but changed her mind within 24 hours and never married.

Mary Brunton (née Balfour) 1778-1818

She was mainly educated by her mother, who taught her French, Italian and music. She married Alexander Brunton, a minister of the

Church of Scotland who later became Professor of Oriental Languages at Edinburgh. Initially she wrote for her own amusement, and when she did have her work published she chose to remain anonymous, as she was concerned that any failure could affect her husband's position. Her first novel *Self Control* had a heroine who was very virtuous, capable and resourceful – even escaping from an Indian encampment and heading down river in a boat by herself. It was a huge success. Jane Austen was very interested in her work, and felt her own forthcoming work *Sense and Sensibility* would be overawed by it. Jane Austen read the work several times, after having complained of some difficulty in getting hold of it, and even thought of writing an improved version with her heroine being able to cross the Atlantic single handed! *Self Control* sold 240 copies within the first week, and second and third reprints were swiftly called for. Other books were *Discipline* and her third novel *Emmeline* that was unfinished when she died, in childbirth.

Frances Burney 1752- 1840

She had little formal education but father's position as an important and fashionable musician was very important for her, as it gave her entry into intellectual circles and high society. Frances was a prolific writer creating journals, diaries and even a novel, *Caroline Evelyn,* at a very young age – although this she later destroyed. Her first published work *Evelina* led her to gain celebrity status. Two other novels, *Cecilia* and *Camilla*, followed this initial success. All of her novels illustrate how women were vulnerable under the patriarchal structure of society. Her last novel *The Wanderer* was published some years after it was written and was not so well received, as its contents were pro-women and appealed less to overt public opinion at that time. She was a part of the circle round Johnson and included amongst the Bluestockings. She became Second Keeper of the Robes to Queen Charlotte and was a witness to the madness of King George III at Kew. Later she married a French émigré – Monsieur d'Arblay, and had one son. She is also known for having to endure a mastectomy without anaesthetic; the full gory details are recorded in her diary.

Jane Collier 1710-1754/5

She was the daughter of a parson, learning Latin and Greek from him. His scholarly ambitions and her mother's extravagence meant that the family suffered from severe debt. After her father died she spent time living with different friends and family. Jane wrote *An Essay on The Art of Ingeniously Tormenting*; writing as a sufferer she used satire for humour. In it she showed that she was very aware of how women sap other women's confidence. She was a friend of the Fielding family, proof reading Sarah's work *The Governess* and writing a joint novel with her called *The Cry*.

Charlotte Dacre (née King) 1771/2- 1825

She was the daughter of a well known Jewish, self-made banker and writer, John King, who was known to be a supporter of radical causes. He abandoned her mother for a countess. Charlotte wrote novels and poetry. Her work *Zofloya* was published under her own name but *The Confessions of the Nun of St Omer, The Passions* and *The Libertine* were written under her pseudonym Rosa Matilda. It is believed she married twice.

Mary Davys (née ?)

She was born in Ireland. She married Rev. Peter Davys but when she became a widow she moved to England and lived by the proceeds of her writing. She was a successful novelist and playwright, and was able to open a coffeehouse in Cambridge with her profits. Her novels include *The Reform'd Coquet, Familiar Letters Betwixt a Gentleman and a Lady* and *The Accomplished Rake.*

Judith Drake

She wrote *Essay in the Defence of the Female Sex* and may have written other works before its publication. She was a medical practitioner but had to go before the Royal College of Physicians, as they were unhappy with her activities.

Maria Edgeworth 1767-1849

She was the oldest child in a family of Anglo-Irish gentry. Her mother died when she was five, and her father remarried three times. He was a well-known author and educator, and although Maria was sent to school, he was responsible for much of her education. He encouraged her in her writing and supervised some of her work. In turn she also helped him with the management of the family estate, acting as his agent and accountant. Her first novel *Castle Rackrent* was very successful and when she visited London she was a hit with the best society there. Writing mainly novels and works for children, some of her many works are *Letters for Literary Ladies, Moral Tales for Young People, Belinda, Tales of Fashionable Life, Leonora, Patronage* and *Helen*. Her works were so successful that publishers used to say works by other people had actually been written by her – in order to increase their sales! During her life Maria visited Paris, Brussels, London and Edinburgh. She corresponded with several other women writers like Elizabeth Hamilton and Elizabeth Inchbald. She never married.

Eliza Fenwick (née Jago), 1766-1840

She married John Fenwick, who was a political idealist. She had one daughter and nine years later then had a son. Her husband had a reputation for drink and is likely to have reduced her to poverty because of it. She separated from him and then struggled to support herself and her children by her writing. Eliza wrote several books for children as well as her novel *Secresy, or Ruin on the Rock,* which was published anonymously – 'By a Woman'. She was also a bit of a radical herself, and wanted to gain literary fame. She was a friend of Mary Hays, William Godwin and Mary Wollstonecraft, whom she nursed on her deathbed. For a time she worked as a governess, and later she moved to America to be with her daughter after her marriage broke up too. Here they tried to run schools together – somewhat unsuccessfully.

Susan Ferrier, 1782-1854

As she was the only unmarried daughter she had to take on the responsibility for caring for her father after her mother died. Susan wrote three novels: *Marriage*, *The Inheritance*, and *Destiny*. *Marriage* was written with the help of a close female friend and was particularly popular, even being praised by Sir Walter Scott.

Sarah Fielding 1710-68

When her mother died and her father remarried she was brought up by her Grandmother. She was a friend of Jane Collier. She was sent to a non academic school but later acquired French, Greek and Latin, learning the later two from her friend's father. Her first novel,

The Adventures of David Simple, was followed by *Familiar Letters Between the Characters in David Simple and Others*, and *Volume the Last* – the conclusion of the David Simple adventures. Sarah was concerned with the way women were stifled intellectually and the factors that inhibited women from earning their own living. She wrote several other novels and one book for children, *The Governess*. Like other women she did some works of translation, notably *Xenophon's Memoirs of Socrates*. She never married and lived on the proceeds of her writings, as well as contributions from her brothers and her friends.

Elizabeth Griffith (née Griffith) 1727-93

Her father was an actor. She had been an actress and married actor Thomas Griffith. Their letters of courtship were published as Letters between Henry and Frances, and were extremely popular. She continued to write in order to support her family. Elizabeth was a playwright, as well as a novelist, and some of her plays did well. Her novels were *The Delicate Distress*, *Lady Barton*, and *Lady Juliana Harley*. She also translated some French works, wrote a commentary on Shakespeare and conduct advice for ladies. Her husband left her for another woman.

Elizabeth Hamilton 1758-1816

Her family broke up after her father died and she was raised by her aunt. She learned the accomplishments at a boarding school but then was responsible for her own education. Her brother, who was an official in India, was very supportive of her writing and she completed some translation work with him. Elizabeth wrote several novels: *Letters of a Hindoo Rajah* was strongly influenced by his ideas and was well received, *Memoirs of Modern Philosophers* was a satire on William Godwin's radical circle and *The Cottagers of Glenburnie,* which was very popular. She also wrote several books on education. She was a keen journalist and published a local magazine.

Mary Ann Hanway 1756/70- 1823/5

Very little is known about her life, but she lived in London and wrote several novels including, *Ellinor, or the World as it Is*, *Andrew Stuart, or the Northern Wanderer*, and *Falconbridge Abbey; A Devonshire Story*.

Mary Hays 1760-1843

She was the daughter of radical dissenters but had little formal education, so was keen to learn from John Eccles, her fiancé. Her family had disapproved of the relationship but two years later they changed their minds. Tragically he died before the wedding took place. Love played an important part in her life and her unrequited love for William Frend influenced her work too. She never married. Mary did not feel that the way women behaved and were treated in society was natural, and felt it was absurd that men should expect women to accept it. Public pressure of the early 19th century forced her to tone down her writings. She taught, wrote the novels *Memoirs of Emma Courtenay* and *The Victim of Prejudice* as well as other religious and fictional works, and the anonymous *Appeal to The Men of Great Britain in behalf of Women*. She was a friend of Mary Wollstonecraft, as well as being greatly influenced by her ideas.

Eliza Haywood (née Fowler) 1693-1756

She was the daughter of a shopkeeper. She did marry but it is thought her husband abandoned her. She had a keen interest in the theatre, having worked as an actress. Eliza completed nearly seventy works during her life, which included novellas, novels, poems and historical works, and she even set herself up as a publisher of a periodical for a short while. The novels mentioned in this work include *Love in Excess*, *The Adventures of Miss Betsy Thoughtless* and *The History of Jenny and Jemmy Jessamy* but she wrote many more. Her earlier works indulged in passionate emotions but later ones showed a more morally upright position. One contemporary, Clara Reeve, said at this time Eliza was 'expiating the offences of the former', although it is more likely that as an astute commercial writer she was merely responding to the moral climate of the time.

Elizabeth Helm – died 1810

She had five children. She wrote several novels including *Louisa, or the Cottage on the Moor*, which was very popular and *The Farmer of Inglewood Forest*. She wrote moral and educational works and completed many translations of travel/exploration works.

Elizabeth Inchbald (née Simpson) 1753-1821

She came from a Catholic farming family, and was self-educated. She ran away from home as she was set on becoming an actress. She married Joseph Inchbald who was in a touring company and they travelled together, with her taking leading roles in the productions. When he died she chose not to remarry although she was not short of offers. She was a friend of William Godwin and Mary Wollstonecraft, although she broke off the friendship with Mary when she found out about her earlier illicit sexual relationship with Gilbert Imlay. Elizabeth was a successful playwright, completing at least twenty. Her novels include *A Simple Story* and *Nature and Art* and she also made a significant contribution to the 25-volume work *The British Theatre*.

Harriet Lee 1757-1851

She was the daughter of an actor/theatre manager. She became a novelist and playwright, and her works included *The Errors of Innocence* and *Canterbury Tales for the Year 1797*. Her sister Sophia was also a novelist. Her sisters ran a girls' school and she used to help out there. She received a proposal of marriage from William Godwin when his wife Mary (Wollstonecraft) died.

Charlotte Lennox (née Ramsey) 1729-1804

She was the daughter of an army officer, stationed in America, and her early experiences were used in her work. She came to England in her teens, and was helped by Samuel Johnson and Samuel Richardson. Her book *The Female Quixote* was published anonymously. Her other works were novels including *Henrietta, The Life of Harriet Stuart Written by Herself*, plays, translations and a periodical called the *Lady's Museum*. Charlotte was unhappy in her marriage to Alexander Lennox and it ended in a separation. She had one son and one daughter. In spite of her literary success she was always poor.

Catherine Macaulay, (née Sawbridge) 1731-91

She was the daughter of a landowner. Her mother died when she was young. She relied on educating herself from her father's extensive library. She married George Macaulay who was very supportive of her working and they had one child, but her husband died after only six years of marriage. Catherine had a passion for history and wrote an 8-volume *History of England*. She also wrote *Letters on Education*, pamphlets about the French Revolution and also on the monarchy. She held salons and encouraged political discussion. Her ideas were much praised by Mary Wollstonecraft. Later in life she married a much younger man in spite of much criticism at the time.

Hannah More 1745-83

She was the daughter of a charity school master, who taught her Latin and mathematics. However, when he decided it was unfeminine to be good at such subjects he discontinued his lessons. She helped her sisters run a very successful school for girls in Bristol. She became a friend of key intellectuals and Bluestockings of the time. She was a dramatist and a poet. As she grew older Hannah became more evangelical, establishing Sunday schools for the poor, and writing many *Cheap Repository Tracts* for the education of poor, working class adults. She was involved in the editing distribution and financing of the tracts too. She wrote one novel *Coelebs in Search of a Wife* and was very much in favour of the abolition of slavery, using her poetry in support of the movement. She was very successful and admitted to having 'made over £30,000 by my books.' She never married although she did receive a proposal and even gained a pension from her suitor.

Amelia Opie (née Alderson) 1769-1853

She was the daughter of a medical doctor, who was a radical. Her mother died when she was 15. She had little formal education, but learned French and music. In London she joined radical intellectual circles. She admired Mary Wollstonecraft, and was proposed to by William Godwin, but married a painter John Opie who created the most famous portrait of Mary. Amelia's novels include *The Dangers of Coquetry, The Father and Daughter* and *Adeline Mowbray*, which were well received and openly acknowledged in her name; she also wrote poetry and some more serious didactic works including some for children. She was one of the most popular and celebrated writers of the early nineteenth century. She also spent some time travelling with Anne Plumptre. In 1825 she converted to Quakerism then took up philanthropic work- particularly in prisons and hospitals. She was much involved with anti slavery.

Anne Plumptre 1760-1818

She was the daughter of the President of Queens College Cambridge, and Prebendary of Norwich. She and her sister Annabella were both writers, and translaters of German works. They moved to London and were friends of Eliza Fenwick and Helen Maria Williams. Anne travelled to France with Amelia Opie and stayed a few years there. Amongst her novels were *Antionette*, originally published anonymously, and *Something New*, she also did travel works including a narrative of her three years residence in France, which offered practical advice for the English abroad.

Mary Ann Radcliffe 1746-1810?

Her parents died young so she was sent to a convent. She was secretly married at 14 and bore eight children, two of whom died. Her husband liked to drink and was not good with money; he left her when she was 26. She tried taking in lodgers, sewing, and being a governess amongst other jobs in order to support her family. She wrote *The Female Advocate, or An Attempt to Recover the Rights of Women from Male Usurpation*, and respected the ideas of Mary Wollstonecraft.

Susanna Rawson (née Haswell) 1762-1824

Her father was a British naval officer, and she lived alternately in America and England throughout her youth. She was an author, actress and educator. Georgiana, Duchess of Devonshire was her patron. Susanna went to America again with her husband and started a school in Boston for young women running it for 25 years. She wrote eight novels of which *Charlotte Temple* was the first. It was first published in England but became a major best seller in America. She also wrote poetry and text books for children.

Clara Reeve 1729-1807

She was the eldest daughter of a clergyman and was well educated by him. After her father's death there were financial difficulties for the family, and she like her sisters had to find ways to earn their living. She wrote novels, poetry, and literary criticism. Her fiction includes T*he Old English Baron* (a Gothic novel) and *The School for Widows.*

Mary Robinson (née Darby) 1758-1800

Mary attended several schools including the boarding school run by Hannah More's sisters. Her father had a mistress and left her mother. Mary decided to become an actress and received patronage from David

Garrick of Drury Lane Theatre. She married Thomas Robinson, an articled clerk, but he had misled her and her family about his financial status, was into gambling and already had a mistress. He was jailed for debt and she went with him to the Fleet prison. She wrote and sold poems to support both them and their daughter, and also gained the patronage of Georgiana, Duchess of Devonshire. Later Mary returned to acting and was noticed by the Prince of Wales, becoming his Perdita. She kept his love letters and when the relationship was over was able to make use of them to gain an annuity for her and her daughter. She also had relationships with other famous men, including the politician Charles James Fox, and a British commander Lieutenant Colonel Tarleton with whom she went to France. After a serious illness she became partially paralysed and so took up writing as a more serious career. She wrote seven novels, which included *Walsingham*, The *False Friend*, and *The Natural Daughter*. In addition to poems, plays, and scandalous memoirs she also wrote under her pseudonym, Anne Frances Randall, *A Letter to the Women of England* in 1799. She died the following year.

Regina Maria Roche (née Dalton) 1764-1845

She was the daughter of a Captain Dalton, and took to writing from a very early age. She wrote sixteen novels, including *The Vicar of Lansdowne* and *The Children of the Abbey*, which proved to be a best seller, as well as the Gothic novel *Clermont* that was mentioned in Jane Austen's *Northanger Abbey*.

'George Sand' – Amandine-Aurore Lucille Dupin 1804-76

She was a French novelist who lived a very independent life and provided an important model for English women writers to follow. Her works began after the end of the long eighteenth century but the novels *Indiana*, *Lelia* and *Jacques* were all published in the early 1830's. She was to become called the 'Anti Matrimonial Novelist' and male literary critics were predictably harsh. The Bronte sisters and George Eliot were to think very highly of her.

Sarah Scott (née Robinson) 1723-95

She came from a clever and respected gentry family. Her father made sure the girls were educated in the accomplishments, ready for the marriage market, but they were encouraged in more intellectual pursuits and learning of French by their mother and maternal grandmother. Her sister Elizabeth Montagu became a Bluestocking although Sarah herself did not, but she was associated with them. She married George Lewis Scott but left him after only two years, with her father and brothers coming to forcibly remove her! Later she joined forces with Lady Barbara Montague and set up a female community at Bath Easton. Her work, which was published anonymously, includes the novels, *The History of Cornelia*, *A Description of Millenium Hall*, and *The History of Sir George Ellison* as well as some historical and biographical works.

Mrs Ann Skinn (née Masterman) 1747-89

She was the granddaughter and heiress of Henry Masterman of Settrington, Yorks. Her marriage to William lasted only sixteen months – she left him and took a lover. She claimed that the characters in her novel The Old Maid were drawn from real life. Reviewers disliked the book. When the divorce proceedings took place her husband accused her of adultery and she complained of his cruelty. He was granted the divorce. Apart from writing she is said to have tried to earn her living by doing needlework and running a day school, but died in poverty.

Charlotte Smith (née Turner) 1749-1806

Charlotte learned traditional accomplishments at her boarding schools, but benefited from free access to the classical library of her father. When he chose to remarry she did not get on with her prospective stepmother, so a husband was found for her at the age of fifteen. Although she was loyal to her husband for many years she was very unhappy in her marriage. Her husband wasted money – through fraud and gambling, at one point ending up in debtors prison and she accompanied him there. Knowing what his son was like her father-in-law tried to bequeath money for the children, but the will was so complicated it took many years to sort out. Eventually after more than 20 years she left her husband and relied on her writings to support herself and her family. She had twelve children, but had to cope with the pain and distress of losing five. She was constantly trying to provide for and help her surviving family, even after they reached adulthood, as well as having to give her husband money when he turned up. Her works illustrate many of the difficulties women faced, including problems with the legal profession, although within romantic frameworks. They include *Emmeline*, *Desmond*, *The Old Manor House*, *Montalbert* and *Marchmont*. She was criticised for using too much realism and personal experience in her work. In addition to her ten novels, her poetry was well received by contemporaries.

'Sophia'

Very little is known about 'Sophia' as her identity has not been uncovered. Her works *Woman Not Inferior to Man* and *Woman's Superior Excellence Over Man* did make use of the previously untranslated *De L'Égalité des deux Sexes* by Francois Poulain de la Barre (1673) so she must have been highly educated. Both her works were reprinted at intervals through the mid–late eighteenth century.

Jane West (née Iliffe) 1758-1852

She was self taught, and believed in education for women in order to regenerate society, particularly through the role of the mother. Her work was admired by Jane Austen and Mary Wollstonecraft, and '*A Tale of the Times'* was considered to be a major anti-Jacobin work by contemporaries. She also wrote the novels, *The Advantages of Education* and *A Gossip's Story*. Jane married a local farmer and had several children but was still able to combine her busy domestic role with writing poems, plays, novels and educational tracts. Politically she appeared to be conservative in her views and stressed this at times – however the actual contents of her novels, and the messages they conveyed were frequently somewhat mixed.

Anna Wheeler (née Doyle) 1785-1848

Her father was an archbishop. She married aged 15, but her husband was an alcoholic and she left him in 1812, taking their two daughters with her – one of whom was Rosina (later Bulwer Lytton) whose work *Cheveley* is mentioned in Chapter 6. She read philosophical works and admired Mary Wollstonecraft. After living in France for a few years she moved to London and became a friend of Jeremy Brentham and William Thompson. Her ideas were recorded openly in Thompson's *Appeal of One Half the Human Race, Women, against the pretensions of the other half, Men, to retain the in political, and thence in civil and domestic, slavery*, 1825, and he accredited her with joint authorship.

Helen Maria Williams 1762-1827

She was the daughter of an army officer, and received a poor education from her mother. However she became a poet and well-respected London literary hostess and was a friend of William Godwin (husband of Mary Wollstonecraft) and Charlotte Smith. She moved to Paris and established a salon there, continuing to write poetry and her famous *Letters from France*. She was a great supporter of the ideals of the French Revolution, and emphasised the important role women played in it. She was imprisoned during the Terror that followed the revolution. She also wrote *Julia, a Novel.* She had a liaison with a married man, John Hurford Stone, and lived with him for the rest of his life – but never married.

Mary Wollstonecraft 1759-97

She was the daughter of a violent and brutal tradesman and was a witness to his behaviour towards her weak mother, and tried to protect her from it. She was very concerned about family and friends, helping her sister escape from an unhappy marriage, assisting her mother during her last illness and her friends when they were ill. She had little formal education. She tried to support herself by working as a companion, and a governess, and set up a school with her friend Fanny Blood, and then later became a professional writer. She was supported by the publisher Joseph Johnson and through him met radical thinkers like Tom Paine and William Godwin. Responding to William Burke's *Reflections on the Revolution in France* she wrote first *A Vindication of the Rights of Man* and then *A Vindication of the Rights of Woman.* Interested in the revolutionary events in France she went to Paris and met Gilbert Imlay there with whom she had a daughter, Fanny. After he deserted her she fell in love with William Godwin. After a few months together they decided to marry, as Mary was pregnant again. She died only eleven days after her daughter Mary – who was to write *Frankenstein* – was born. Her friend Eliza Fenwick, mentioned earlier, nursed her on her deathbed. Mary Wollstonecraft also wrote two short novels, *Mary* and *The Wrongs of Woman, or Maria*, which were partly autobiographical and so reflect her radical ideas. She compiled a series of extracts for young women, called *The Female Reader*, and also wrote a children's book and did some translation and review work. During her life she had made two suicide attempts.